ROUTLEDGE LIBRARY EDITIONS: IMMIGRATION AND MIGRATION

Volume 1

A LAND OF DREAMS

A LAND OF DREAMS

A Study of Jewish and Caribbean Migrant Communities in England

SIMON TAYLOR

LONDON AND NEW YORK

First published in 1993 by Routledge

This edition first published in 2023
by Routledge
4 Park Square, Milton Park, Abingdon, Oxon OX14 4RN

and by Routledge
605 Third Avenue, New York, NY 10158

Routledge is an imprint of the Taylor & Francis Group, an informa business

British Library Cataloguing in Publication Data
A catalogue record for this book is available from the British Library

ISBN: 978-1-032-31713-7 (Set)
ISBN: 978-1-032-31715-1 (Volume 1) (hbk)
ISBN: 978-1-032-31720-5 (Volume 1) (pbk)
ISBN: 978-1-003-31097-6 (Volume 1) (ebk)

DOI: 10.4324/9781003310976

Publisher's Note
The publisher has gone to great lengths to ensure the quality of this reprint but
points out that some imperfections in the original copies may be apparent.

Disclaimer
The publisher has made every effort to trace copyright holders and would
welcome correspondence from those they have been unable to trace.

A LAND OF DREAMS

A study of Jewish and Caribbean migrant communities in England

Simon Taylor

London and New York

First published in 1993
by Routledge
11 New Fetter Lane, London EC4P 4EE

Simultaneously published in the USA and Canada
by Routledge
a division of Routledge, Chapman and Hall, Inc.
29 West 35th Street, New York, NY 10001

© 1993   Simon Taylor

Typeset in Baskerville
by NWL Editorial Services, Langport, Somerset

Printed and bound in Great Britain

British Library Cataloguing in Publication Data
A catalogue record for this book is available from the British Library

Library of Congress Cataloging in Publication Data
Taylor, Simon, 1953–
A land of dreams: a study of Jewish and Caribbean migrant
communities in England / by Simon Taylor.
p.   cm.
Includes bibliographical references (p.   ) and index.
1. England – Ethnic relations.   2. Immigrants – England – Social
conditions.   3. Jews – England – London – Social conditions.
4. West Indians – England – Birmingham – Social conditions.
5. Blacks – England – Birmingham – Social conditions.
6. England – Race relations.   I. Title.
DA125.A1T38   1993   92–19292
305.8′00942496 – dc20   CIP

ISBN 0–415–08447–4

Father, O father! what do we here
In this land of unbelief and fear?
The Land of Dreams is better far,
Above the light of the morning star.
(William Blake, 'The Land of Dreams')

To Freddie and Tuli,
'Ovamati noukadona va Africa'.

CONTENTS

CONTENTS

CASE STUDIES

PREFACE

This book explores two events in recent English history: the settlement of East European Jews in the East End of London, and the growth of an African-Caribbean community in Birmingham. Part I, the study of Jewish settlement in the East End, takes as its starting point the exodus from Eastern Europe in the early 1880s, encompasses the passing of the Aliens Act in 1905, and ends with the outbreak of war in Europe in 1914. Part II, the study of Caribbean migration and settlement in Birmingham, begins at the outbreak of the Second World War, and extends to the early 1960s and the passing of the Commonwealth Immigration Act.

However, this book does not address itself to the 'debate' about immigration; still less is it concerned with the question of 'race relations', although the issues of immigration and race are certainly engaged. On the contrary, it is an ethnographic study of two first-generation migrant communities. The book is built upon the experiences of the migrants themselves; it focuses upon the stories of their migration and their early days in England, and in particular, upon the stories of their working lives and their everyday struggles in the new land. As such it is a celebration of ethnic diversity and cultural pluralism.

But in placing these two studies side by side here, I want to do more than offer two social histories for the price of one! For an ethnographic study of Jewish and Caribbean immigrant communities in England exposes not only the diverse historical and cultural roots of the two migrant communities; it also exposes the quite different social and economic conditions which confronted the two groups of migrants upon arrival in England. Thus the

final chapters of Part I and Part II are given over to an examin-
ation of these social and economic conditions, and to an analysis
of the different 'settlement strategies' which the two migrant
communities adopted (or were forced to adopt) in the new land.

Part III has a quite different focus, for an historical study of
Jewish and African-Caribbean communities in England tells us as
much about the 'English' as it does about the immigrants
themselves. Hence Part III explores the way in which the
indigenous population of London and Birmingham reacted to
the Jewish and Caribbean migrant communities which
developed in their midst. It also traces the political and cultural
pathways which link the London-based British Brothers' League,
at the turn of the century, to the Birmingham-based anti-
immigration movement of the early 1960s.

This book has been many years in the making, and it owes a debt
to a great many people. Some of those who have contributed to
it are, unfortunately, no longer alive. Others, whose work has
helped to make it possible, may never be aware of its existence.

For Part I of this book, I owe an immense debt to Joe Bronsky
and his younger brother Stanislav, to his wife Emma, and to her
family and friends. Joe and Stanislav were 84 years old and 82
years old respectively when I worked with them in a cabinet shop
in Liverpool. They taught me a great deal about cabinet-making.
But their stories of life in the Jewish East End at the beginning of
the century caught my imagination, and were the seeds of this book.

Further ethnographic material on the Jewish East End was
gathered from the Museum of the Jewish East End, and from
Tower Hamlets Library, and I would like to thank the staff for
their help and consideration. I would also like to thank Maxine
Elvey for permission to reproduce her memoirs.

For Part II of the book, I have many individuals to thank. I
would like to record my appreciation of the work done by the
Race Relations Group at Fircroft College of Adult Education in
Birmingham, whose study of 'Colonial Migrants in Birmingham'
in the mid-1950s deserves recognition and appreciation. I would
also like to thank the librarian at Fircroft College for bringing the
Fircroft Survey to my attention, and the staff at Birmingham
Local Studies Library for being unfailingly patient in answering
my many requests for information and material.

A special thanks goes to YG for her invaluable help at the outset of this project. Thanks also to Michael Green, Director of the Centre for Contemporary Cultural Studies at Birmingham University for commenting on an early draft of this book, and to Carl Chinn in the History Department of Birmingham University for putting his encyclopaedic knowledge of Birmingham at my disposal.

Finally, so many members of the African-Caribbean community in Birmingham have given me their help with this project that I feel the end result is a woefully inadequate record of what they have told me. But I wish to record my appreciation for the trust that they have placed in me; and for the enthusiasm which they showed for this project. At the very least, I hope that this study will encourage the work of many groups who are now striving to recover the history of the black presence in Birmingham.

Part I

JEWISH SETTLEMENT IN THE EAST END OF LONDON, 1880–1914

I have been a Stranger in a Strange Land.
(Exodus 2.22)

1

LET MY PEOPLE GO

A JEWISH KINGDOM

'Poland should in all justice be called a Jewish kingdom', wrote the Muscovite officer V. Bronevsky on a journey through Eastern Europe in 1810.

> Rarely will you find a village without Jews. Jewish taverns mark out all the main roads. . .They possess enormous capital and no-one can get along without their help. Only some very rich lords are not plunged up to the neck in debt to the Jews.[1]

Bronevsky's description of Poland depicts an almost mythical age of Jewish influence in Eastern Europe. Acting as intermediaries between serfs and lords, the Jews leased or 'farmed' the taverns, the mills and the liquor stills from the aristocracy, and pressed payment in cash and kind from the peasantry. They controlled much of the early banking system, had their own postal service, and could quote prices on the stock market across Europe.

But, even in 1810, the 'Jewish kingdom' that Bronevsky described was in decline. The natural economy of Eastern Europe was crumbling. The great fairs and market towns that serviced the old feudal order were contracting. And as the age-old trade routes between east and west were disrupted by war and the frontiers of new nation states, the livelihood of the Jewish inn-keepers, the small merchants and the country peddlers became increasingly precarious. With the thrust of trade and commerce passing to the cities, the traditional Jewish way of life began to disappear.

The initial Jewish response was to migrate to the cities, in the hope of following economic fortune to the new centres of

3

commerce. Migration flowed eastwards towards Russia, and westwards into Germany and Austria. Between 1830 and 1880 some 350,000 Jews left Eastern Europe for good; yet during this time the Jewish population more than doubled from three million to seven and three-quarter million – a rate of increase nearly double that of the non-Jewish population.

For a time, though, the decline of the old feudal order and the erosion of traditional Jewish occupations was counterbalanced by the opening of new opportunities in the expanding domestic market. A Jewish proletariat came into being, working not in the factories and mines, but in the backyard workshops of the new cities. Here the Jewish artisans produced the pots and pans, the boots and shoes, the overcoats, caps and jackets, which fed, shod and clothed the new urban working class. By the end of the century nearly a third of Russian Jews lived in the 'Jewish quarter' of towns and cities, whereas at the beginning of the century they had been thinly scattered among the small towns or villages.

But whilst Russian and Jew alike lamented the breakdown of the old ways and the 'modernisation' of East Europe's economy, for the Jews the decline of the old order uncovered new political dangers. For not only were the Jews chained to an economic system that was sinking, they were also under threat from an autocratic Czarist regime which regarded them as economic parasites and eyed them as a potential scapegoat for popular discontent.

In Russia, Czar Nicholas I (1825–55) was determined to exclude the Jews from their traditional positions of economic influence. He enforced a mass of petty restrictions and a code of discrimination against the Jews, enshrined in the 'Charter of Disabilities'. Jews were driven off the land, expelled from many of the large cities, and Jewish children were conscripted into military service that was effectively a death sentence.[2] As the Czarist state alternated between repression and malicious attempts at 'Russianisation', hundreds of thousands of Jews were driven into ghettos strung out along the Pale of Settlement in Poland and the border-lands of Western Russia.

Under this assault, the Jews could do little other than retreat into themselves. The village (*stetl*) became the backbone of Jewish life.

4

> Look into one of these hovels [commented a contemporary observer] which is about to collapse and bury as many as fifteen male and fifteen female souls, and you will be struck by the filth and stench. The swarm of half naked children can hardly find room in this dark hut, three quarters of which is taken up by the stove, bed and table.[3]

Within this community of crowded hovels and hungry children, religious ritual and rabbinical authority provided a semblance of security. For despite the entreaties of the 'enlightened' Haskalah, who wished to transform Jewish life to meet the challenge of modernity, the great mass of East European Jews preferred shelter in the spiritual kingdom of the past.

However, whilst most Jews drifted into increasing poverty, a Jewish elite rose to the very pinnacle of Czarist society. They were the descendants of 'court-Jews': powerful families of Jewish bankers, financiers and merchants who had underwritten royal power in Europe since the late Middle Ages. Families such as the Poliakovs, the Brodskis, the Epsteins and the Gunzburgs lorded over huge fortunes and commercial empires. The mass of increasingly impoverished Eastern European Jews they held in contempt. The Jewish banker Baron Erzel Gunzburg, too valuable to Czar Alexander II and his retinue to be discarded as a 'mere Zhyd', showered appreciation upon his protector by bitterly condemning the Jewish lumpen masses for their lazy, parasitical behaviour. But he pleaded for a widening of opportunities for the Jewish elite, so that they too could plunder a share of the new commercial opportunities that were opening up in Russia in the mid-nineteenth century.

With the death of Nicholas I there was a lull in anti-Semitic agitation. Indeed during the late 1850s and 1860s it seemed as if the burden of discrimination against the Jews might be lifting. But this proved to be little more than a seasonal change – a mild prelude to a bitter winter.

POGROM

On Palm Sunday 1871 the Jewish ghetto in the Black Sea port of Odessa was attacked and sacked. For three days the Czarist police stood aside as the mob looted and burned at will. The defenceless Jewish ghetto was a tempting target for the hatred and frustration of the masses, and the massacre at Odessa was the harbinger of a wave of pogroms, many of them systematically provoked by Czarist agents. Indeed, as the Czarist regime began to shudder under the hammer-blows of rebellion, revolt and eventually revolution, so the threat to the Jews of Eastern Europe became ever more menacing.

On 1 March 1881 Czar Alexander II was assassinated by a terrorist bomb. The new Czar, Alexander III, hesitated only momentarily before setting into motion a new wave of political repression. On 14 August 1881 he signed a decree which *de facto* made Russia a police state. Even A.A. Lopukhin, the Czar's Chief of Police, admitted that the decree made 'the people of Russia dependent on the personal opinions. . .of the political police'.[4] In matters of 'state security' guilt was determined by the police alone.

The assassination of Alexander II was carried out by the terrorist group Narodnaya Volya; one of the activists was a young Jewess, Jessie Helfmann. Eight weeks after the assassination the first pogrom hit the Jewish quarter of Elizavetgrad. Scattered outrages swelled into a wave of arson, looting and murder, either organised or sanctioned by the authorities. The police, who watched passively whilst the mob murdered and pillaged, intervened only to prevent total genocide. The terror of the mob was backed up by the terror of the state. Police raids, allegedly to uncover 'illegal' residents and to apprehend 'subversives' and 'revolutionaries', fell consistently upon the Jewish quarter. Those who could neither flee, hide, nor bribe their way past the police faced arbitrary arrest, fines and imprisonment.

ACROSS THE SEA

During the first eighteen months of Czar Alexander III's reign nearly a quarter of a million Jewish families fled Russia for safer shores. For many, their haven was the United States, where the immigrant ghettos along the eastern seaboard held the promise of escape from persecution and formed a gateway into the Land of Opportunity.[5]

Yet tens of thousands of Jews fleeing Eastern Europe first set sail for the shores of England. Although, for most migrants, this was a passing through, en route to America via Liverpool, the journey across England could take years rather than days. Some migrants were the victims of con-merchants, crooks and swindlers who stripped them of their goods and cash. Others simply fell victim to despondency as the misery of migration took its toll upon the fables of fame and fortune. But there were also those who thought of England as a land of settlement, impressed by the apparent affluence and integration of English Jews, and encouraged by the reports of *landsleute* who had already made the journey. For them England offered promise of the new Jerusalem.[6]

Yet, even as the first wave of Jewish migrants landed in England in the wake of Alexander II's assassination, the Jewish community in Britain began a determined campaign to stifle immigration from Russia. In 1888 Nathan Adler (Chief Rabbi of England until 1880) beseeched his colleagues in Eastern Europe to 'publicize the evil which is befalling our brethren here, and warn them not to come to the land of Britain', for:

> There are many who believe that all the cobblestones of London are precious stones, and that it is a place of gold. Woe and alas, it is not so.[7]

Inevitably his warnings sounded hollow against the reality of life in Eastern Europe. Irrespective of persecution and pogrom, the economic facts of life were brutal. 'No work, no commerce, the harvest is unpredictable, nothing for the workman to do, no-one to sell the merchandise to', reported the *Yudisher Emigrant*. 'Now you don't need as many reasons to emigrate'.[8]

In the *stetl*, letters from relatives and friends in England were seized upon and scrutinised, for the dream of fortune in a far country helped blot out the misery of the Pale. 'When a letter comes from abroad', reported one migrant, 'especially with money, in the evening everyone all over the place knows who sent the money, who received the money, and everything.'[9] Such solid proof of England's riches particularly excited the imagination of the young. 'A man left our place – an old man who had no trade at all', reported a young Jewish mechanic. After only a few months 'he sent over £30. I made up my mind [to go].'[10]

The hardships of migration were, nevertheless, well

understood. Many would-be emigrants returned to their native villages, broken and destitute.[11] Few doubted that the English would be hostile to the 'alien Jews' in their midst. Yet however 'bitter' was the 'spirit of the native workers against the aliens, especially. . .from Russia',[12] it could hardly be less bitter than the cup of woe in Eastern Europe. Besides, poverty in England was at least accompanied by recognition of Jewish civil and political rights. Whether the streets of London were paved with gold was uncertain; but at least they were not spattered with the blood of innocent Jews.

THE JOURNEY

By the beginning of the twentieth century the tide of Jewish emigration from Eastern Europe was in full flood.[13] English steamships had begun to challenge the 'Atlantic Shipping Ring' run by the German companies. In 1902 the so-called 'Atlantic Rate War' broke out. Migrant fares from England to America were slashed from £6.50 to £2.00. The fare from Germany to America remained static at 120 marks. There was a new and overwhelming reason to reach England, whatever the final destination.

However, the German shipping agents possessed a crucial advantage in the 'Atlantic' war. For despite the cheapness of the English fares, Jews from Eastern Europe usually had to pass through Germany to reach their destination. At the Russo-German frontier towns, the German authorities established control stations. Here migrants were forced to register and undergo a rigorous process of disinfection and cleaning, which extended to their luggage and belongings. For this 'cleaning' they were heavily charged, and forced to pay up before being permitted to proceed through Germany to their next destination. At the same time, however, agents of the German shipping lines searched the migrants for money. Those who had ample funds or who happened to possess the address of an American friend or relative were deemed to be *en voyage* to the United States. They were 'expected' to book a passage to America with a German shipping line, whatever their destination may have been. Those refusing, or protesting at this treatment, would be informed that their papers were not in order, or that they had committed some offence under German law. Yiddish protests went unheard or unheeded, even when they were understood. Only when the helpless emigrants submitted to their fate, and booked a passage, were they allowed to proceed to the North German ports under the protection of the German shipping company.

For those gaining ship to England, the three-day voyage across the North Sea from Bremen to London held horrors enough, especially in winter when the weather could be foul. The ships themselves were little more than cattle-boats. Major Evans-Gordon, the anti-alien agitator not known to spare his sympathy for Jewish immigrants, described conditions on board the boats in 1904:

> The hold in which the emigrants were to travel was pitch dark and devoid of any ventilation that I could discover, except such as was provided by the hatchway. The head room between decks was about seven feet, and this space was divided by two long bunks or shelves. Upon these, straw mattresses were thrown, and the people lay alongside one another like sardines in a tin. For their meals they had to shift as best they could – in fine weather on deck, in rough weather below in their bunks.[14]

At Tilbury, the emigrants were decanted on to a quayside bristling with porters, beggars, thieves, con-men, and shipping agents seeking their money, and with Christian missionaries seeking their souls. 'It was no wonder', remarked Abraham Mundy, the Secretary of the Jews' Temporary Shelter in London, 'that emigrants, thinking that further torture was in store for them, displayed fear and nervousness.'[15]

NOTES

1 Quoted by Abram Leon, *The Jewish Question* (New York, 1970), p. 196.
2 See, for instance, the testimony of Maxine Elvey, whose grandfather's cousin died in an attempt to elude military service (p. 13).
3 Quoted by William Fishman, *East End Jewish Radicals 1875–1914* (London, 1975), p. 21.
4 Richard Pipes, *Russia Under the Old Regime* (Harmondsworth, 1977) p. 306.
5 The scale of Jewish emigration can be grasped from the fact that 46 per cent of the Jewish population left Eastern Europe between 1881

and 1914, whereas the next highest emigrant nation – Italy – lost about 15 per cent of its population. See Leon, op. cit., p. 217.

6 The previous experience of *landsleute* – close relatives or fellow villagers – frequently determined the actual pattern of migration. Thus extended families would migrate to London rather than Chicago as a result of a chain reaction that might be set off by the chance success of the eldest brother finding work in London's East End. Once one member of the family was 'set up' the rest would follow over a period of time.

7 In *Ha Maggid*, 3.1.1889, quoted by Lloyd Gartner, *The Jewish Immigrant in England: 1870–1914* (London, 1960) p. 24.

8 *Der Yudisher Emigrant*, 5.11.1907.

9 Royal Commission on Alien Immigration, 1903, minute 3363.

10 ibid., minute 3361.

11 See, for instance, the testimony of Mrs A, quoted by Jerry White in *Rothschild Buildings*. She remembers reaching London in 1905. But 'work for my father was difficult to get. He was a military tailor. . .but there wasn't that kind of work here [in England] for him. So he broke down and [we] went back after nearly a year'. Jerry White, *Rothschild Buildings* (London, 1980) p. 76.

12 *Ha Meliz* XXXIII (January 1892), quoted by Gartner, op. cit., p. 28.

13 The years 1904 and 1905 represented the peak of Jewish migration to England, fuelled by war, revolution and pogrom in Russia, and fear of restrictive immigration laws in England.

14 See 'Aliens in England: The Immigrant Problem' by Major Evans-Gordon MP, in *The Illustrated London News*, 30.4.1904.

15 See Memoirs of Abraham Mundy, Museum of the Jewish East End, London.

CASE STUDIES

The ghetto

Joseph Pennell observes 'The Jew at Home' for The Illustrated London News, *5 December 1891.*

Maramaros Sziget. . .is a typical Hungarian town, stretching in almost every direction from its large central square, its long streets inhabited mainly by Hungarians and Wallachs, who build their one-storeyed cottages and hide themselves behind their high wooden fences. When you get a glimpse into their yards, you see the usual farmyard litter of any other country town.

But unless the Jew has some business with these people he is never in their quarter. To find him you must come down to the centre of the town, where the great bulk of the eight or ten thousand Jews are herded together in one street, living no better than in Whitechapel. They have appropriated not only the old houses which lie at one end of the square, but half the large hotel and town buildings recently put up in the middle of it. And here they swarm, as if lodgings were as scarce and expensive as in the heart of a great city like London. They live in cellars and in garrets, in alleyways and up courts, in a state of filth and dirt. . .

With the exception of this filth – but this is horribly serious – there is little on the surface with which one can reproach them. They are always working, though rarely, if ever, with their hands; they are endlessly bargaining or haggling about something. If a peasant brings in a few water-melons, he turns them over to the Jew middle-man, who acts as a commission merchant. . .

One branch of trade which he has monopolised hereabouts is inn-keeping, almost all the inns, except the larger ones in the more important towns, being managed by Jews. Only by a stretch of the imagination, however, can the name 'inn' be given to the usually lonely house, with no bush or customary sign at the door. . .Inside [is], a big, bare room,. . .a few tables and the cage behind which the proprietor, as in all Hungarian inns, keeps his stock; or not infrequently nothing but a broken-down table, no less dilapidated chairs, and some framed Hebrew prints on the wall.

Pogrom!

From The Illustrated London News, *18 June 1881.*

We give another illustration of the distressing scenes lately witnessed at Kiev, in southern Russia. . .where the Jews have been cruelly attacked by a furious and rapacious mob. . .

The outbreak took the authorities by surprise. Commencing on May 4 (St. George's Day in Russia, and a holiday) with an attack on the bazaar, it lasted four days without intermission, and continued fitfully afterwards. The work of destruction was done by no single mob, but by bands of thirty to a hundred men, mostly under the age of thirty, and armed with choppers, hammers and bludgeons. Their proceedings were watched by large crowds of spectators, and it was difficult to distinguish the rioters from the well-disposed public. . .

These bands seemed to have been under the control of some organisation. Suddenly a whistle would be heard, and in a moment men would issue from the crowd and form themselves into a band, and an

11

attack would be made upon a house. When the work of destruction was over, another whistle would be heard, and the band would then disperse and mingle with the crowd again. Nearly all the largest and finest shops in Kiev and the principal storehouses in the bazaar belonged to the Jews. None were left unmolested. Warehouses were opened and sacks of flour poured out onto the streets; tea-shops were entered, and the chests of tea emptied into the gutter; jewellers' shops were broken open, and gold watches and all manner of jewellery thrown by handfuls among the crowd. . .

Everywhere cries and groans and shrieks were heard. The city looked as though it were given over to pillage; the streets were littered with broken furniture, goods of every description, and articles of clothing, among which carriages passed slowly, carrying away fugitive Jews and their property. . .

The authorities seemed paralysed. After allowing the riots to continue for three days, they made a display of vigour on the fourth, when they surrounded a house and captured fifteen Nihilist printers' proclamations. On the fifth day cannon were placed in the principal streets, and the military began to fire upon the crowds. The police also began to exert themselves, and 1,400 people were arrested. . .

The number of persons killed was six, three Jews and three Russians; 187 persons were injured. . .One man had his head split open by a sewing-machine, which his fellow rioters recklessly threw out of a top-storey window. Bloody headed as he was, he refused to go to the hospital, and continued wrecking the Jews' property till loss of blood compelled him from sheer exhaustion to desist. More than 20,000 Jews fled from Kiev to Berdicheff. . .Three thousand families remaining behind at Kiev were placed for shelter in the Arsenal, but it is not to the credit of the Russian authorities that for forty-eight hours they were without medical succour or food. In the end some compassionate Russians exerted themselves, and subscriptions were freely given by the educated classes to furnish them with the necessaries of life.

The eviction

Described by Joseph Pennell in The Illustrated London News, *26 December 1891.*

On the platform, right in front of me, I could just see a huddled-up group of people a few yards ahead. I walked towards them: there were two old Jews, a couple of younger men, two or three women, and some children.

They were accompanied by four soldiers in little black caps and huge overcoats, with immense swords, which they held drawn in their hands. There was a sergeant or corporal with them.

The engine and the luggage-van came slowly back, having picked up a car which, as there was a light inside, I could see had grated windows. It stopped; two of the Cossacks – one knows what a Cossack is a few hours after one has been in this part of Russia – seized one of the oldest Jews, who was literally doubled up under a great big bag, and shoved him towards the car. He stumbled, and a few miserable old rags, some tin pots and broken bread, rolled on the platform and on the track, but he was half thrown, half dragged, out of sight; the rest were pushed in after him as roughly as a man who had only one hand to use, while he held his sword in the other, could do it; a porter was called by the sergeant to pick up what he could find in a minute or two of the old Jew's possessions, and the train moved off.

A couple of the Cossacks were laughing on the platform, the porters said not a word. . .The putting of half-a-dozen people into a train by sufficient force to have moved ten times their number was the worst instance of childish brutality I have ever witnessed. Where the Jews went I do not know. When I awoke again in the morning, the van had disappeared. [Note that this description was by a man who showed utter contempt for the Jews in Eastern Europe.]

The journey

From the memoirs of Maxine Elvey.

In nineteenth-century Russia it was the law that one son from every family had to be conscripted into the army for five years. Army life was hard and cruel, involving long marches, little money, poor food and hard discipline. Because of this young men went to extremes to make themselves exempt. A common practice was for them to cut off their own fingers. However, this became so commonplace that the authorities ceased to be deceived by it.

A second cousin of my grandfather died in an attempt to elude army life. He asked someone to pierce one of his eardrums so that he could claim deafness as an excuse not to be conscripted. Unfortunately the ploy did not work and he was still obliged to join the army. His family received no news of him for a long time. They went to a clairvoyant lady in Nevel. She said he had died, and this later proved to be true. He had died of blood poisoning as a result of having his eardrum pierced.

When the Yigdalov family was told to send a son to the army, there was a lot of discussion as to which son should go. Nathan, the second son, was sickly with a bad hip. Eventually it was decided Max, the eldest, should go. As it worked out, army life was not quite so bad for Max as for many others. Because of his talent as a carpenter he was able to make wooden things for the officers. His handsome good looks helped too. He looked dashing in his army uniform – a tunic with epaulettes and pleated skirt.

However, in spite of his popularity with the officers, it was still a hard life. So when Max came home on leave, he vowed he would not return. At that time hundreds of young men were fleeing from army life, and escaping to the 'Golden Lands' of England and America. Max made a quick decision to go and set off with little money and few possessions, together with some friends.

They successfully crossed the border, the 'grenitz', and took a boat to London. This was in 1897. Max was 21. Once he had arrived, he contacted an acquaintance from Nevel who was already established in London. This was a furrier named Usiskin, who was fairly prosperous. He found Max some lodgings and helped him get established in his work.

Max found that England was not a Golden Land after all. Conditions were hard and he was homesick. He badly missed his 'lady love'. He wrote back frequently begging Maryasha to come and marry him. At this point Maryasha was working in her mother's grocery. The hours were long and she hated it. She was paid very little. She desperately wanted to get away. Basha was still very much against the marriage, and pleaded with Maryasha to remain in Russia. But at last, Maryasha got her way.

And so, in 1899, she set off on her long journey. Up to then she had never left her little stetl, or seen a railway. And now she was leaving Nevel for the first time in her life, to go to a strange country thousands of miles away. The prospect must have been frightening to both herself and her family. She left in the company of a 'Landsman' [someone from the same town] who was to look after her. His name was Zalman. They travelled hundreds of miles overland, then boarded a ship for London. It was full of Jewish emigrants and the conditions were terrible – worse than a cattle ship. The sea was rough and almost everybody was constantly seasick.

At last the port of London was reached. The passengers were all too eager to escape from the dreadful ship and pushed each other to disembark. In the confusion the young Maryasha lost the Landsman. Max had promised to meet the boat and she desperately looked for him, but he was nowhere to be seen. She began to cry. She was frightened, weary after many days' travel, and did not speak the language of the country.

14

A lady approached her, and through a Yiddish interpreter, asked what was wrong. 'My young man is not here!', wailed Maryasha. 'Never mind', said the lady, 'come with me to a house for the night. We will find your young man in the morning.' The lady was one of a group of missionary ladies who helped the immigrants when they arrived, providing temporary accommodation.

Maryasha did not trust the woman. She was full of suspicion and fear because she had heard tales of the white slave traffickers. . .So for a long time she refused to go.

However, in the end she had no choice, for there was no sign of either Max or the Landsman. She went, together with her luggage – a large wooden trunk called a 'Chimadan', that contained all her possessions, including a samovar. They arrived at the Leman Street area of East London. There were several houses used as temporary accommodation for the new immigrants. They came to a house in Burros Street. Every room was filled with bodies lying on the floor – other immigrants who had been brought there for a night's lodging.

The missionary lady made Maryasha some tea but she refused to drink it: she thought it would be poisoned. She sat up all night on the floor trembling. Early in the morning there was a knock on the door. It was opened and she heard someone call out: 'She's doo! [here].'

It was Max. He had recognised her Chimadan in the hall.

He had met the Landsman, and someone had advised them to go from house to house in the area where new immigrants were lodged, to find Maryahsa. Maryasha recognised Max's voice and rushed out into the hallway. They had a great reunion.

Maryasha went to live in Max's lodgings at Lower Chapman Street. They were married on Christmas Eve, 1899, in the East London Synagogue in Mile End Old Town. . .Max was 23 and Maryasha 21.

2

ARRIVAL AND DEPARTURE

Despite the desperate conditions which faced the Jews of Eastern Europe, and concern over their plight among British Jews, the ragged immigrants who disembarked at Tilbury found cold welcome from the Jewish community in Britain. Certainly, the refugees fleeing pogrom and persecution were afforded charity and aid by fellow Jews. But often it was the meagre charity of family and *landsleute*. Among the wealthy Jewish establishment, however, the ragged army of immigrants inspired as much contempt as pity. For the 'problem' of immigration split the Anglo-Jewish community long before it exploded in the form of anti-alienism on the streets of London's East End.

The Anglo-Jewish community faced a genuine dilemma over the issue of immigration. Many Jewish leaders, in Eastern Europe as well as in Britain and America, were convinced that flight was not *the* answer to the problem of political persecution and economic hardship in Eastern Europe. Massive emigration from Russia undermined the strategy of 'restructuring' in Eastern Europe, which was being pursued by the orthodox establishment. Orthodox leaders believed that vocational training and economic diversification would enable the Jewish minorities to integrate themselves into the national economies of Eastern Europe. Furthermore, they considered that educational reform and cultural tolerance would, in the long term, lead to the assimilation of the Jewish population into the nation state. After all, this policy of integration seemed to be succeeding in Germany. Conversely, mass emigration would lead to the loss of the youngest and the ablest from the East European Jewish communities. The educated and the well-qualified would make good their escape, so that only the aged, the sick, the poor and the very young would remain.

There was a further dimension to the problem of immigration which pressed hard upon the Anglo-Jewish community. If the tide of migration should become a flood, what effect would this have upon Anglo-Jewish relations? Might it not lead to a resurgence of anti-Semitism within Britain? And what demands would the immigrants make upon their co-religionists? The immigrants lacked work and homes and even the rudiments of the English language. Would the burden of charity not fall heavily upon the Jewish establishment?

THE ENGLISH JEWS

The Anglo-Jewish community was dominated by a clique of affluent families who were themselves descended from European Jews fleeing earlier persecutions. Many were descendants of Ashkenazi Jews, who began to arrive in force in England in the mid-eighteenth century, mainly from Holland and northern Germany. This immigration continued into the nineteenth century, spurred on by internal conflicts in Europe. Indeed a whole sector of the Jewish intelligentsia fled Germany for England in the nineteenth century, among them individuals as diverse as the political philosopher Karl Marx, the chemist Ludwig Mond, the financier Ernest Cassel.[1]

As in Russia, an oligarchy of wealthy Jewish families, led by the Montefiores, the Samuels, the Goldsmids and above all the Rothschilds, comprised the elite to whom most other English Jews aspired. Interconnected by business and marriage, this oligarchy had penetrated the bastions of British commerce and banking by the late nineteenth century, and could draw upon powerful political support.

However, in contrast to Russia, an affluent Jewish middle class had developed in England – not only a 'small class of prosperous businessmen, mainly engaged in textiles, banking and foreign trade', but also, especially in London, a stratum of shop-keepers, tradesmen and small entrepreneurs who had risen out of the ranks of earlier generations of Jewish artisans and peddlers. Joseph Jacobs estimated that there were over 600 London merchants with Jewish names in the early 1880s. They operated in a variety of trades, but were especially strongly represented in the food trade, the jewellery industry and the rag trade. In the food trade Jews were dominant in the wholesaling of citrus fruits and nuts, and they had established a major presence in cigar manufacture. In the jewellery trade Jacobs estimated that there were well over one hundred Jewish watch-makers, jewellers and silver-smiths in London whose businesses were sufficiently well-established to be included in Kelly's *Post Office Directory*.[2] Lastly there was the clothing trade, in which Jews were engaged in wholesaling, tailoring and second-hand garment dealing.

There was also a small, but growing, Jewish professional class in late nineteenth-century London as discriminatory religious barriers were abolished. In 1883 the first practising Jew was admitted to the Bar, and in the same year Joseph Jacobs counted 12 architects, 27 barristers, 47 solicitors, 19 dentists and 12 surgeons with Jewish names who were practising in London.

However, although individual Jews had reached positions of wealth and influence, or had created successful businesses as silver-smiths and jewellers, most Jews in England were poor. According to the *Jewish Chronicle* of 1881, 'a very large proportion of the Jewish poor are but little removed from the pauper classes ...many of them are petty traders or peddlers'.[3] Indeed, as the first wave of Eastern European Jews left their homelands for England and the New World, the archetypal English Jew still scraped a living from hawking and peddling, either on the streets of London or tramping the isolated villages of the Yorkshire moors.

Peddling had been a traditional way of life for many Jews during the early decades of the nineteenth century but by the end of the century, piety and frugality no longer sufficed to earn a living even in the countryside. 'As soon as they show their nose ...they are told "Not today!" Or others slam the door and leave [the peddler] standing in the street like a dummy',[4] wrote Nathan Berlin in 1888. In the cities, hawkers of fancy goods, the wandering glaziers and the bodgers humping their piles of chairs, both Jewish and Gentile, were gradually driven off the streets by economic competition and the attentions of the police. Forced out of their traditional way of life, many Jews were driven to find work either as piece-workers in the burgeoning back-street workshops or as porters in the wholesale markets. Where Jewish traders attempted to gain a foothold among the 'costers' who sold from street-barrows, they came into direct competition with English and Irish costermongers who reacted bitterly, and sometimes violently, against the Jewish traders, abusing them for 'undercutting prices', 'adulterating goods' and working 'unreasonably long hours'.

The great majority of English Jews lived in London. In the 1850s, there were perhaps 25,000 Jews living in the capital. Two separate studies of that decade came to roughly similar conclusions, namely that half of these Jews were in 'the lower orders barely making a living' and that among the lower orders the majority were 'scarcely able to obtain sufficient to support existence'.[5] In London the traditional Jewish dominance of certain trades did help to protect small traders against the winds of economic change. Jewish traders had secured a foothold in the London fruit trade during the eighteenth century, so that the Jewish 'lemon-man' was a familiar figure on the city's streets, and Jews were also dominant among street-sellers of oranges and cherries. Cherries, for example, were brought to London on a Sunday, fresh from Kent. Jewish street-sellers could thus hawk them around the city on the day that their Gentile competitors observed the Sabbath.[6] On a smaller scale, the dietary requirements of the Jewish religion guaranteed a livelihood for kosher meat-sellers and the traditional baker.

However, whilst some traders prospered because of their specialised market knowledge, and indeed their ability to move with the times, most Jewish street-sellers sank ever deeper into poverty. Like the Gentile paupers, they eked out a precarious existance in the poorest quarters of the metropolis. Many sank into the criminal underworld as receivers of stolen goods, coin-clippers and vagabonds.

Whether this ragged Jewish proletariat had a welcome for their persecuted East European brethren mattered not – their voice was not heard. For whilst the very poorest Jews frequently shared what little they had with fleeing relatives from Russia and Poland, the politics of Jewish immigration was debated and fought out among the Jewish bourgeoisie.

THE STRUCTURING OF JEWISH MIGRATION

The divisions within the Anglo-Jewish community over the issue of Jewish immigration into Britain can be traced to the beginning of the eighteenth century. As early as 1732, wealthy British Jews had invested in Oglethorpe's settlement in Georgia, achieving double value for their money by 'exporting' some of their unwanted poor to Georgia on the outward voyage. 'Exporting' poverty soon became a consistent policy, whereby the Jewish community encouraged migration to the colonies to reduce the burden that the poor placed upon the charity of the wealthy.[7] In the latter half of the eighteenth century the Elders of the Great Synagogue in London encouraged government restrictions upon the offloading of European (and hence Jewish) paupers in England.[8]

Immigrant Jews were able to qualify for poor relief from the Jewish community, but only when they had been resident in England for six months. This was intended to encourage an ethic of self-reliance and thrift – it also helped discourage poor Jews from landing on English shores in the first place. But the first wave of migration from Eastern Europe in the 1880s clearly created a deeper alarm among the leaders of the Anglo-Jewish community. In 1885 the *Jewish Chronicle*, mouthpiece of the Jewish establishment in London, warned:

> Able-bodied foreign Jews who have no prospect of doing useful work must not be supported. . .but for the sake of themselves and their relatives abroad, as well as their own, they must *either earn their own living without charity or return to the land whence they came* [my emphasis].[9]

Yet the dividing line between the policies of 'control', 'exclusion' or even 'expulsion' was a thin one. If 'foreign Jews' were excluded or expelled from Britain, could this not justify demands to exclude *all* Jews from Britain? The suggestion that British Jews might encourage legislation to exclude East European Jews provoked a furious reaction in the pages of the *Jewish Chronicle*:

> It is a new and astounding thing for the Board of Guardians to hint that a multiplication of the foreign poor may one day become a public evil of which the intervention of the state may be demanded. *It must not be demanded by Jews at least. . .such a*

proposal is full of danger [my emphasis]. The letters which spell exclusion are not very different from those which compose expulsion.[10]

By the end of the 1880s the Jewish establishment was hesitating between the option of preventing further wide-scale immigration, and offering help to thousands of immigrants who had already found their way to the Jewish quarter in London's East End. In 1890 the Jewish Board of Guardians warned:

> every right-thinking person among our brethren in Germany, Russia and Austria [must]. . .persuade these [migrants] not to come to a land they do not know. *It is better that they live a life of sorrow in their native place than bear the shame of famine and disgrace of the missionaries and perish in destitution in a strange land.*[11] [my emphasis]

But by 1890 at least 25,000 East European Jews were living in the East End.[12] Fearing dire consequences if these immigrant Jews did not quickly 'assimilate' to English ways, the *Jewish Chronicle*'s leader writer pleaded:

> We must not, we dare not longer allow our foreign brethren to remain in their isolation, to form a commmunity within a community, with us yet not of us, materially living in London yet spiritually and morally still living in Poland. To attach those of our brethren to the main body of the community is a holy task in which no Jew should hesitate to help personally and pecuniarily.[13]

And indeed, the *Jewish Chronicle*, ever on the look-out for forms of separatism (or radicalism) 'likely to embitter the relationships of Jews and their neighbours', constantly lectured the immigrants on the need to throw off their religious orthodoxy and become 'true Englishmen'.[14]

But as the nineteenth century drew to a close, it was apparent that appeals to the East European Jews to 'live a life of sorrow in their native place' were falling upon deaf ears. More drastic action to curtail immigration was considered. Benjamin L. Cohen, Conservative MP for Islington, informed *The Times* that he and other Jewish MPs were:

disposed to assist in the establishment of such regulations as would discourage the immigration of undesirable persons provided that precautions were taken to preserve inviolate the right of asylum.[15]

For Cohen, as for many after him, restrictive legislation was intended to discourage the immigration into Britain of 'undesirable persons', whilst simultaneously the 'right of asylum' remained *'inviolate'*. In effect only the rich (with the exception of political radicals) would be able to claim sanctuary in Britain from discrimination and poverty.

The spirit of Benjamin Cohen has stalked British immigration policy ever since.[16]

NOTES

1 For further details of the role of German Jews in the development of English manufacture and commerce in the nineteenth century, see Harold Pollins, *Economic History of the Jews in England* (London, 1982) pp. 96f.
2 ibid., p. 105.
3 *Jewish Chronicle*, 28.1.1881.
4 Nathan Berlin, *Die Tsukunft*, June 1888.
5 Pollins, op. cit., p. 119.
6 On the other hand, peas, beans and potatoes arrived on Saturdays (Jewish Sabbath), so that the vegetable trade tended to be dominated by Gentiles.
7 Of course this was simply a reflection of contemporary British policies of exporting the poor to the colonies.
8 See Lloyd Gartner, *The Jewish Immigrant in England: 1870–1914* (London, 1960) p. 49.
9 *Jewish Chronicle*, 15.5.1885.
10 *Jewish Chronicle*, 26.2.1880.
11 See *Ha Meliz*, XXII, November 1886, quoted by Gartner, op. cit., p. 25.
12 Llewellyn Smith estimated that between 1880 and 1886 Jewish immigration into London's East End totalled some 20,000. See Charles Booth, *Life and Labour of the People of London* (London, 1902), Vol. 3, p. 102.
13 *Jewish Chronicle*, 12.7.1893.
14 See article entitled 'The Foreign Poor', in the *Jewish Chronicle*, 15.5.1885.
15 *The Times*, 21.3.1894.
16 In 1905 Cohen voted for the Aliens Act – the first substantial piece of legislation to restrict immigration into Britain in the modern era. Not long after he became Baron Benjamin L. Cohen. See Gartner, op. cit., p. 55.

CASE STUDY

Policing Jewish immigration

From the Memoirs of Abraham Mundy, Secretary of the Poor Jews'
Temporary Shelter, Chapter 17. (Museum of the Jewish East End.)

INFLUX OF JEWS FROM ROMANIA

*On June 9th 1900 the Shelter was suddenly beseiged by a party of 170
Romanian Jews, who had arrived at Milwall Docks from Galatz,
Roumania, by the steamer* **Vaglianus**. *The Shelter was not informed, as
usual, of its arrival, as it was not a passenger ship, and as they were not
met by anybody, the party marched from Milwall to the Shelter
accompanied by police. Only four of them had addresses of friends in
London, who, however, could not receive them, with the result that the
whole party had to be provided for by the Institution.*

*They stated that, although all the male adults of military age had
served their full term in the Romanian army, their country would not
recognise them as citizens, though they were born there, owing to their
being Jews. They were thus considered outlaws, and as in consequence
their lives had been made intolerable in their native land, they decided to
leave the country that treated them so cruelly and find a place in the sun
where they would at least enjoy human rights. The most pathetic figures
were the 43 children who belonged to the party, their innocent souls and
young minds could not comprehend what it all meant. . .*

*On the 30th June, another party of 91 arrived, and were followed by
a further batch of 146, and with smaller groups that continued to arrive
daily, the total number of Romanian Jews to whom the Shelter afforded
protection and care during the month of June and July came to 650.
There can be no doubt that had it not been for the prompt measures taken
by the Shelter, these 650 wanderers would have been parading the streets
of London, homeless and hopeless, with dangerous results to themselves
and to the whole Jewish community.*

*Quietly and without attracting undue attention, the poor people were
taken charge of by the Institution, and as a result the strain upon the
slender resources of the Shelter, both physical and financial, became very
great. Advice was promptly sought of the leaders of the Jewish community,
and Lord Rothschild, and Messers F.D. Mocatta, Ellis A. Franklin,
Claude G. Montefiore, Alfred L. Cohen [President of the Jewish Board*

23

of Guardians] and others, were most prompt in rendering the Shelter both personal and pecuniary assistance, so that the Institution was enabled to cope with this great influx and forward the people to the various parts of the world. . .

The batch of 91 who arrived on June 30th and consisted of young men, were the first to be decided upon for Canada, by reasons of their having had handicrafts and looked very promising emigrants, and they duly sailed for Quebec by the steamer Lake Superior. *They were followed by another party of 183, two of whom were destined for New York, and the rest for Winnipeg, Canada, all of whom sailed on July 10th. . .whilst a third party of 144, of whom 42 were sent to various places in Canada, and 102 to the United States, sailed on July 17th. . .*

A small party of 8 went to Paris, so that altogether 426, out of a total of 650, definitely left the United Kingdom, through the medium of the Shelter, within five weeks of the arrival of the first party.

It should not be assumed that the remaining 224, who went to stay with friends, settled in the country, because only one or two of them are known to have remained here, namely one who became a Reader in the Romanian Synagogue,. . .and another who became a vendor of Yiddish Newspapers. All others gradually dwindled out of sight. . .

3

THE EAST END
LABOUR MARKET

The East End appears as an ugly carbuncle upon the economic and social map of nineteenth-century London. It was a place of morbid fascination for journalists and writers of popular fiction, not least for being the abode of pimps, prostitutes and criminals, but, most sensationally, for being the haunt of Jack the Ripper. It was also 'home' for many thousands of London's outcasts; not merely the despised East European Jew or the immigrant Irish, but, even more so, for the human flotsam who scratched a living on the streets and among the slums of the great metropolis. And, precisely because the area simultaneously scandalised and repelled, fascinated and threatened Victorian high society, the East End became the testing ground and human laboratory of social scientists and moral improvers, from Mayhew in the 1840s through to Booth, Webb and Smith at the dawn of the twentieth century.

THE ECONOMIC DECLINE OF THE EAST END

'The development of the East End in the Victorian period', writes Stedman Jones in *Outcast London*, 'presents a general picture of the decline or collapse of old staple industries, and the growth of new industries parasitic upon that decline: industries characterised by low wage rates, irregular employment, and the subdivision of skilled processes into unskilled ones.'[1] However, these new industries (or more strictly trades) such as clothing, footwear and furniture production, were not only parasitic upon the decaying remnants of the East End's traditional industries, they also fed upon London's seemingly instatiable demand for consumer goods. Indeed the East End was unique. Its character was shaped by its relationship to a great capital city that was both a 'national emporium' and the heart of a world-wide political and financial empire.

It was London's unrivalled position as the capital of Britain's growing political and commercial empire in the nineteenth century that sounded the death-knell of the East End's traditional industries, especially silk-weaving and shipbuilding. The scarcity of land and the increase in rents and property values within central London stripped away any industry that failed to yield high profits from minimal land use. Silk-weaving was decimated by foreign competition and advances in technology. Shipbuilding moved down-stream from the East End, or to new centres of heavy engineering in northern England and Scotland.

Overall, the main effect of the industrial revolution upon London was to return the city to a 'pre-industrial' state. Artisan production maintained a hold whilst heavy industry was forced to migrate to the provinces. London's central zone retained many of its small workshops side by side with retail shops, wholesale warehouses and offices. But interspersed among the commercial premises, especially in eastern London, were squalid alleyways and tenement blocks where the very poor clung like limpets to the place of their birth and to the traditional patches that they 'worked', whether as beggars, thieves, prostitutes or sweated labourers and homeworkers. Within this mix of squalor and affluence:

> Caste distinctions were particularly intense. . .[London's] craftsmen catered to the exacting demands of the wealthy, its artisans tended to be recruited from the cream of the provinces; its skilled wage rates were in these trades decidely higher than those of the provinces. Yet on the other hand London thrived on its surplus of unskilled labour; although its unskilled rates seem to have been higher than those in other towns, pressure upon house room and irregularity of employment meant that its living conditions were often inferior.[2]

The decline of the East End's traditional industries and the rise of the new trades can be traced to the 1840s, although Mayhew dated the birth of the Bethnal Green and Spitalfields 'slaughterhouse system' of furniture-making to the 1820s. The slaughterhouse system embodied the main features of what

26

became known as the 'sweated trades', whereby 'masters' working from garret-room workshops bought materials on credit, employed low-paid semi-skilled labour, and mass-produced for immediate cash sales to local wholesalers.[3] Mayhew estimated in mid-century that only 10 per cent of the workers in the clothing, footwear and furniture trades were 'honourable' men, i.e. members of trade societies, properly apprenticed and collectively controlling the conditions of work, pay and production. Indeed, it is indicative of the state of the sweated tailoring trade that Charles Kingsley wrote about it in 1850 under the pseudonym Parson Lot, entitling his book *Cheap Clothes and Nasty*.

The trend towards the vertical *disintegration* of production (the division of manufacture into separate parts and processes) in the tailoring, footwear and furniture trades was encouraged by the invention of the sewing-machine, the band-saw and steam-powered saw-mill. Such machines made it possible to mass-produce from the home or the small workshop. In practice, it was possible to reproduce the economies of scale and the division of labour found in the factory by breaking down production into separate processes and sub-contracting each of these stages of production to the cheapest bidder. This in turn led to a generalised 'de-skilling' of the work, as each task was simplified to the level where elementary repetition could be mastered by even the slowest learner, and only a few skilled crafstmen (since women rarely filled this role) were necessary to assemble the finished garments and products.

Of course, the major incentive for factory organisation, namely the application of ever more sophisticated technology to the process of mass production, could not be applied to sub-contracting and outwork. Hence the sweated trades concentrated upon products which were either fashion-led, as in the clothing trade (where the volumes were too small to make mass production viable), or for which machinery lacked the sophistication and speed of the hand-worker, as with many aspects of furniture production. So, for example, although boot-making was one of the most notorious sweated trades, most sweaters produced fashion boots; the production of traditional industrial boots was concentrated in factory premises in the provinces.

Certainly the London masters may have envied the northern

27

capitalists' sophisticated machinery and specialised factories. Yet they had one overriding advantage over factory competition; labour costs were significantly lower. This followed not only from the appallingly low wages paid to the sweated worker, but also from the complete 'flexibility' of production which perpetual sub-contracting permitted. Hence in the tailoring trade the cost of switching from one fashion garment to another was borne not by the entrepreneur, in costly changes of machinery and production processes, but by 'small masters' who competed against *each other* for the new sub-contracts. When styles changed, there was a constant reservoir of workers and workshops willing to take on new orders at a moment's notice. 'Here all the conditions of the economist [are] satisfied', wrote Llewellyn Smith: 'mobility perfect; competition unremitting; modifying conditions almost absent; pursuit of gain an all powerful motive; combination practically inoperative.'[4]

Therefore the key to 'sweating' was not, as the Trades Union Congress was told in 1894, that the Jewish worker was *willing* to 'work fifteen hours a day. . .on cold coffee and bread and cheese',[5] although many did so. It was the fact that most immigrant Jews (and certain other groups of workers) *had no alternative* to trades that operated by 'sweated labour'. Even Beatrix Potter could mistakenly attribute the prevalence of Jewish workers in the sweated trades to a mythical 'Jewish' propensity for unremitting toil, asserting that '*the Jew* [my emphasis]. . .is unique in possessing neither a minimum nor a maximum'. Yet she simultaneously observed that 'Polish Jews and English*women* [my emphasis] will do any work, at any price, under any conditions'.[6] So the immigrant Jew was *not* unique. English women were also at the mercy of the East End labour market. And as we shall see, even the native artisan was not immune, for at times of seasonal slack, the family was thrown upon the vagaries of 'women's work' to keep hearth and home together until the next busy period.

THE EAST END LABOUR MARKET

The sweated trades were not unique to the East End. However, they were concentrated in the East End for specific historical reasons.

First, as the traditional industries of the East End declined and died, the labour force could not be absorbed into expanding industries. Shipwrights displaced from shipbuilding drifted into the furniture trades where their wood-working skills were put to new uses. But desperate for work, the shipwrights undercut the wage rates of the artisan cabinet-makers. Displaced cabinet-makers frequently set up as 'small masters' themselves, employing yet cheaper labour to produce at lowest price, and thereby giving a further twist to the spiral of sub-contracting and cut-throat competition. Secondly, although tailoring, boot-making and furniture-making had long been located in the East End, a string of wholesale merchants along the eastern edge of the City provided a cash market for small masters producing on credit. Thus the Curtain Road furniture wholesalers were within barrow-pushing distance of the mass of small cabinet shops that sprung up in the East End, for in the late nineteenth century 'it was the wholesalers who dominated these trades rather than the retailers or manufacturers'.[7] Thirdly, and of critical importance to understanding the growth of the Jewish-dominated trades, there was a super-abundance of unskilled, cheap labour within the East End. Among the East End poor, mobility was virtually nil. For even artisans found it essential to live within walking distance of their work, a factor that only changed with the 'democratisation' of the railway system at the beginning of the twentieth century.

Such were the technical limitations and conditions which fashioned the East End labour market. But what did this mean in practice for the tens of thousands who were reliant upon this market for their daily bread?

Elsewhere in Britain, the growth of factory production had begun to level out the seasonal variations of production and employment that had been a fact of life until the nineteenth century. But in London, and especially in the East End, the virtual absence of factories and the seasonal rhythm of London High Society meant that the worker, especially the casual labourer and the homeworker, remained hostage to the fashions of the rich and the terrors of the winter until well into the twentieth century.

29

The London season began in early April, and reached its zenith in June and early July. By midsummer the round of sumptuous parties and balls was over, and most of the wealthy retired to their out-of-town houses. However, for workers who supplied the fashion trades, as well as the great army of London's casual poor, the end of the season meant the start of hard times. Demand for fashionable clothing and furniture dropped until its revival at Christmas. Opportunities for casual work, from portering to message running, also declined as high society emigrated. Above all, women's work – laundering, needlework, fresh and artificial flower-selling and charring – dropped off dramatically. When the end of the season coincided with a slump year, and there were many at the end of the nineteenth century, the effects upon the poor were catastrophic.

Hard winters were particularly cruel to the poor. Not only did they have to keep themselves alive in the vicious winters of the early 1880s and 1891 and 1895, but seasonal unemployment caused by the harsh weather had a knock-on effect throughout the East End. When the river traffic of the Thames was brought to a halt by ice floes, as in 1895, thousands of hourly-paid lightermen, dock workers and warehouse men were thrown upon the labour market. This in turn destroyed the deadly equilibrium of outcast London, as the 'deserving poor' swarmed on to the streets, ousting the casual poor – the old, the disabled, the diseased and the insane – from their traditional pitches as match-sellers, sandwich-board-carriers, firewood-choppers and charity-milkers. And they in turn were knocked off the bottom rung of the labour ladder into the underworld of crime, despair and institutionalised destitution.

Women's work

The stranglehold of seasonal work, both for the artisan and the casual labourer, created a market for 'women's work', especially in the slack season. Indeed, as one employer who relied upon women's labour remarked, 'it is the men going idle that keeps our factory going'.[8]

The women's labour market was stratified by marriage (or widowhood) as well as class. Unless the family was relatively well-off, unmarried daughters usually sought work in the jam

30

and confectionery industries or in the local match, hemp and jute factories.[9] Such work was usually unskilled, and wages in the 1890s averaged about 10s. for a full week's work – equivalent to the wage of 'a greener' in the cabinet shops, or one quarter of a highly skilled cabinet-maker's wage. Moreover, since the fruit season coincided with a slack period in match-making, competition for work in the factories was ferocious. Women would literally fight at the gates for employment that could last for a month, or merely a few hours.[10]

Most married women were forced to find work in their homes. Not only was there a stigma attached to them going out to work, but they were already enslaved to a regime of domestic chores which made homework the only viable method of obtaining a cash wage. In the East End, the sewing of sacks, trousers, vests and boots, as well as matchbox-making, were among the commonest forms of women's work carried on in the home. Moreover, because of the vast pool of labour, women seeking work were reliant upon 'keeping in with their employer', just as they had to 'keep in' with the local shop-keeper or publican if they needed credit to tide them over the worst times.[11] In practice the poor were rooted into their neighbourhood by their poverty, and rooted into their poverty by the neighbourhood.

NOTES

1 Gareth Stedman Jones, *Outcast London* (Oxford, 1971), p. 100.
2 ibid., pp. 30–1.
3 Henry Mayhew, *London Labour and the London Poor*, (London, 1861), Vol. 3, pp. 221–30.
4 *Jewish Chronicle*, 13.11.1891.
5 *Trades Union Congress, Report*, 1984, p. 59.
6 See Sidney and Beatrice Webb, *Industrial Democracy* (London, 1897), Vol. I, pp. 687–8.
7 Stedman Jones, op. cit., p. 108.
8 Royal Commission on Poor Laws, 1909, Vol. XVII, Appendix, p. 9.
9 Domestic service was an outside possibility, but most 'reputable' households preferred 'country girls' in this role. See Chapter 4, n. 2.
10 Stedman Jones, op. cit., pp. 85–6.
11 Artisan families tended to purchase furniture and fancy goods in the high season, which could be pawned during the slack season.

4

EARNING A LIVING

The mass migration of Jews from Eastern Europe took place at a time of prolonged and severe recession within the British economy. The cyclical slump of 1884–7 seriously affected even modern industries in London, such as engineering, printing, chemicals and textiles, and devastated much of the traditional industry still clinging to the capital's inner perimeters. Industrial slump in the 1880s also coincided with an agricultural depression, which had a severe knock-on effect in the capital and throughout the rest of the economy.

The harsh reality of mass unemployment and chronic seasonal under-employment in London at the end of the nineteenth century was reason enough for the exclusion of immigrant Jews from many traditional sectors of the labour market in eastern London. The 1891 census indicates that almost 50,000 men (nearly 20 per cent of the male population of eastern London) were employed in the transport and storage industries that were associated with the docklands. Virtually no Jews found work in this sector; indeed the coal-whippers and stevedores were virtually caste-aristocrats among the East End workforce, whilst the great mass of casual dock workers, most of Irish origin, brooked no interference from 'interlopers' in their trades.

Much the same was true of other trades and industries in eastern London. In sectors such as retail and distribution (employing 22,875), the building industry (employing 13,685), metal and engineering (employing 11,918), and printing and paper (employing 8,244), which together provided employment for nearly a quarter of the workforce of eastern London, virtually no Jews found work. In fact, the major industries into which immigrant Jews crowded – tailoring, cabinet-making, boot and shoe manufacture and the tobacco trade – account for only one sixth of the total labour market in eastern London in 1891.

Only in the census returns for women's work in eastern London is there some matching of the employment patterns of Jewish and native workers.[1] The clothing trade, accounting for over 10 per cent of the female workforce, was a dominant employer for native and Jewish women alike (27,466 women were recorded in this sector). However, personal and domestic service accounted for an even greater number of women's jobs (28,347), and this sector was almost totally dominated by English women, especially those from the provinces.[2] Other important sectors of women's employment, especially manufacturing industries, were more or less closed to Jewish women, with the exception of the furniture industry, where some Jewish women found work as gilders, upholsterers and leather-dressers.

THE CHARACTERISTICS OF JEWISH LABOUR

Although it is impossible accurately to assess the distribution of Jewish employment in the East End, Professor Gartner has pointed to the irony that 'in a new and liberal land the Jewish immigrant worker earned his livelihood in a narrower range of trades than he had under the conditions of the Russian Pale of Settlement'.[3] In Britain, Gartner suggests, 'the great majority of [East European] immigrants sought their livelihoods in a complex of interrelated vocations which were intimately associated with immigrant life and even its folklore. . .These were the "immigrant trades" '.[4] However, before looking in detail at these so-called 'immigrant trades', it is necessary to ask whether the apparent exclusion of Jews from so many sectors of the East End labour market came about as a direct result of native discrimination and hostility.

A definitive answer, supported by a battery of statistical evidence, eludes us. But there is ample evidence that immigrant Jews faced considerable hostility and discrimination *if* they attempted to find work outside the 'Jewish trades', whether in the East End or elsewhere in Britain.[5] Certainly most immigrant Jews *believed* that it was virtually impossible to find employment with Gentile employers, and as a result, only a minority ever tried. For in the conditions that characterised the East End labour market, immigrant Jews were disadvantaged in every way in attempting to find work in the 'goy' world.

Most obviously, there was the problem of language. Very few East European Jews could converse in any language save their own dialects or Yiddish. Even for skilled workers, who might have found work in the expanding building, engineering, printing and transport industries, ignorance of English was a major barrier to finding work. But actually speaking English did not give the Jewish immigrant *entrée* into the local labour market. This was especially true of the East End, where street-level, informal networks of contact between bosses and casual workers (frequently centring upon the local pub) effectively banished any 'outsider' from contact with potential employers.

However, most immigrant Jews were simply unqualified for work in England. A glance at the survey carried out by the Poor Jews' Temporary Shelter in London to assess immigrants' previous 'vocations' confirms what should be obvious from our brief study of the conditions of life for East European Jews at the end of the nineteenth century (see Chapter 1). First, hardly any Jewish immigrant had experience of factory life, or of employment in the mining, ship-building or steel-making industries. Secondly, although migrants claimed a vast range of skills, from circus acrobats to coopers, there was a predominance of trades and skills which were artisan based, with a concentration of garment-makers (29 per cent), boot- and shoe-makers (11 per cent) and carpenters (7 per cent). Equally predictable was the fact that nearly one quarter described themselves as being involved in trade and selling.[6]

But in a modern capitalist economy, few of these trades or skills had any value. Wide-scale factory production rendered traditional skills in metal-working, coopering and shoe-making redundant. Experience of building or horticulture in Russia was irrelevant in England. And the exclusion of Jews from the universities and new technological industries in Eastern Europe meant that most East European immigrants had little chance of finding work as technicians or managers. There were Jews who found such work, but their number was very small. Thus in Rothschild Buildings, which housed the 'better sorts' of Jewish workers in the East End, there were 63 tailors, 23 cigar- and cigarette-makers, 22 cabinet-makers, 18 boot-makers, etc., but only one 1 engineer.[7]

But whatever the attitude of potential employers or native workers towards the immigrants, East European Jews were themselves reluctant to seek work outside the Jewish community. Many of the barriers which prevented them from gaining work with Gentile employers were cultural bonds that bound them to the Jewish community. Yiddish-speaking was a case in point. Few Jewish immigrants would have willingly chosen isolation in an English-speaking firm. Equally, for the ultra-orthodox Jews of Poland and Russia, whose 'attempts to transplant ghetto life into a free country'[8] were the bane of the Anglo-Jewish establishment, the keeping of the Sabbath conflicted directly with non-Jewish work practices, which demanded a full day's work on Saturday. In effect, any Jew wishing to observe the Sabbath either had to work for an orthodox Jewish employer, or else be self-employed. So for the first generation of settlers, the cultural barriers against working for a goy (Gentile) employer whose working week included the Jewish Sabbath were at least as strong as the prejudices which discouraged native employers from hiring Jewish labour.

So given the constraints of the English labour market at the end of the nineteenth century, and the cultural preferences of immigrant Jews to work for and among fellow Jews, the 'immigrant trades' were virtually the *only* viable way for Jewish immigrants to scratch a living in the new land. Yet it must be borne in mind that it was not only Jewish immigrants who plied the so-called 'immigrant trades'; such trades (notably the making of garments, boots, cigars and furniture) long predated East European immigration, and constituted the only viable employment for many native East Enders. Certainly the influx of Jewish labour gave a new impetus to these trades, and in the process pushed the system of sub-contracting to new extremes in the East End. But the claims of contemporary observers that the Jews were the *cause* of labour market overcrowding and the *perpetuators* of sweating[9] were but popular myth.

Looked at another way, however, the very existence of the sweated trades within the East End provided a window of opportunity for immigrant Jews to establish a toehold on the economic ladder. For the sweated trades were controlled only by

35

the 'laws' of cut-throat competition, in which low production costs and high entrepreneurial skills were crucial. Precisely because the Jewish immigrant had virtually no choice but to work for a Jewish employer, and had little opportunity to find alternative work in the slack season, the Jewish worker was *anything but 'mobile'*.[10] Average wage rates per hour were therefore even lower than those endured by native workers in similar trades.[11] As a result, Jewish entrepreneurs were given a competitive edge in the grim business of bidding for sub-contracts.

Additionally, Jewish entrepreneurs possessed certain 'cultural' advantages over their native rivals. The experience of artisan production in Eastern Europe meant that Jewish immigrants were quick to perfect the techniques of mass production in the tailoring and furniture trades. Unable to penetrate the traditional English cabinet shops and tailoring establishments, the talents of the Jewish artisans had, of necessity, to be harnessed to an entrepreneurial spirit. Even the notoriously easy passage from work-hand to 'master' worked to the advantage of the Jewish entrepreneurs. One or two pounds was all that was needed to set up as an independent tailor or cabinet-maker in the East End – an unusual situation in an advanced industrial economy where manufacturing normally required large-scale capital investment. Hence immigrant workers with the necessary drive, ambition and luck *could* succeed in the 'immigrant trades'. In turn, the possibility of success further reinforced the ethic of self-advancement and 'hard work' which the Anglo-Jewish establishment continually strove to implant among the East European Jews.

For many Jewish immigrants, England, and in particular the East End of London, became the Promised Land that they were seeking; even if the promise was sometimes greater than the achievement. For others, crushed by the burden of overwork, ill-health and poverty, the dream became a nightmare. And it must be remembered that those who 'failed' rarely remained in the East End to record their tale of woe; they were 'moved on' to the Americas, or, worse still, 'sent back' to their miserable *stetl* in Russia or Poland.

Yet it was the establishment of a strong Jewish presence in the so-called sweated trades in the latter years of the nineteenth century that provided a springboard for later economic advancement, as the sweated trades evolved into the new consumer goods industries of the early twentieth century.

THE JEWISH TRADES

Cabinet-making

Cabinet-making was just one of a number of wood-working trades that flourished throughout the East End during the period of Jewish immigration. There is evidence that Jews entered a number of the wood-working trades, finding employment as sawyers, turners, coopers, shipwrights and carriage-builders, as well as colonising the furniture trade, with its sub-divisions of cabinet-makers, chair-makers, table-makers, upholsterers and French-polishers. However, it was the traditional cabinet-making trade which attracted by far the greatest concentration of Jewish immigrant workers. In 1901, for instance, cabinet-making was the third largest employer of Jewish immigrant labour. By 1911, with the demise of the boot-making trade, cabinet-makers were second only to tailors in the employment league.

Charles Booth estimated, on the advice of local tradespeople, that some 700 Jews were employed in the East End furniture trade in the late 1880s. This estimate probably encompasses only the 'formal' furniture sector, where Jews worked in shops which could be recognised by their Jewish names and were known through their commercial relationships with the large wholesalers. Almost certainly Booth's estimate did not include an unknown number of 'garret' makers, employing only one or two workers, whose wares were 'hawked' in the streets rather than sold through the wholesale trade. Such garret-room shops were to become synonymous with sweating within the furniture trade, and undoubtedly a number of immigrant Jews did set up in this manner. In general, however, furniture-making was a distinct cut above the tailoring trade for both Jewish immigrants and English workers, whilst the better class of cabinet-maker was a veritable labour aristocrat among the working class of both communities.

Jews generally worked in Jewish shops. Joseph Benjamin

began his apprenticeship as a cabinet-maker with 'a local Jewish firm which were also frumm [orthodox]. That's why I went into them, because I was orthodox and I never worked Shabbos [Sabbath] or Yontif [i.e. Yontov, Jewish festivals].'[12] But although the Jewish shops observed the Saturday rather than the English Sabbath, in most other respects the Jewish furniture trade was entirely characteristic of the local scene. And in order to have an understanding of the Jewish cabinet trade, it is necessary to form a picture of the furniture trade within the East End as a whole.

Unlike coopering and shipwrighting, which declined with changes in technology at the end of the nineteenth century, cabinet-making expanded as a result of the rising demand for domestic furniture for lower middle-class and working-class households. And as the production of fine furniture for the upper classes became less of a dominant factor in the market, so the methods of production began to change.

The traditional West End cabinet shop employing a wide range of skilled labour gave way to the specialised firm making just one type of furniture, such as occasional tables or wardrobes. Indeed some shops produced only one part of a larger piece of funiture; perhaps the carved frame of a mirror-backed dresser, or the doors of an inlaid showcase. In turn working practices changed. The traditional apprenticeship, followed by a period as a journeyman and finally a master cabinet-maker which encouraged the acquisition of all-round wood-working skills, became irrelevant to the demands of highly specialised production, in which the necessary skills could be learned though familiarity with a specific task. Moreover, the growth of a mass market for furniture encouraged the creation of mass production techniques. Craftsmanship was no longer the essence – the essential was speed.

Thus by the beginning of the twentieth century the East End furniture-making business was a peculiar mixture of the archaic and the modern. At one end of the market were the remnants of the old-style guild shops, where master craftsmen and apprentices produced work fit for the nobility, as well as for the new bourgeoisie who aspired to become nobility. Such shops employed perhaps fifty workmen, and most items were made to order, necessitating makers who could see a piece of furniture through from design to final polishing. Their inlaid cabinets could fetch £100. At the opposite extreme were 'garret makers', where one man, perhaps with a boy to assist him, knocked out gipsy tables to hawk on the streets of London for 1s. each. The middle ground was occupied by a vast array of small and medium-sized workshops which flowed out of attics, living rooms and basements, and straggled across backyards, pavements and alleyways, in a grim struggle to 'beat the market'.

Along Curtain Road

Nearly half of the London wood-working trade was concentrated in the East End, which in turn centred upon the districts of Bethnal Green and Shoreditch. 'Bethnal Green does hardly anything but make', noted Ernest Aves. 'Shoreditch also makes, but it is there that the Curtain Road – the chief market of the trade – is located.'

Curtain Road was the heart of the East London trade:

> The whole neighbourhood pulsates with its movements. In every adjacent street are seen signs of the dominant industry of the district, and the shops of cabinet-makers, french-polishers, upholsterers, turners and chair-makers (with here and there a timber-yard) are found at every turn. . .
>
> 'The Road' itself is almost entirely made up of warehouses, and these establishments are also numerous in Great Eastern Street, the main thoroughfare that crosses the Curtain Road, and in three or four of the principal adjacent streets. Many of these warehouses are simply showrooms, some of great size; a few have workshops of different kinds on the upper floors, but for the most part the buildings flanking 'The Road' are places of sale.[13]

Conversely, in Bethnal Green where the making took place, Gossett Street was the centre of activity:

> there are no warehouses; even large workshops are few and far between, and the most conspicuous signs of the chief crafts of the district are the timber-yards and the saw-mills. But in many of the houses, and in nearly every workshop, furniture is being made: there are fewer polishers and upholsterers than there are further west, but chair-makers, cabinet-makers, turners and carvers abound. It is the region

of small makers, whose presence in the trade in such large numbers gives at once the most striking characteristic of the East End furniture trade.[14]

Until well into the twentieth century, the Bethnal Green makers were almost entirely reliant upon Curtain Road for their market. It was the nearness of Curtain Road, allied to the presence of the saw-mills, which accounts for the importance of furniture-making both to the East End and to the immigrant Jews. On Saturdays (although this was the Jewish Sabbath) Curtain Road was alive with barrows and carts hauling furniture 'in the white' to the French-polishers and finished articles to the wholesale dealers. A sale provided the week's wages, not to mention the cash to buy a new stock of timber. And for most small makers, it was this access to cash and credit which ensured their survival.

The Jewish trade

Although there were Jewish journeymen and apprentice cabinet-makers who worked at the high-quality end of the trade, they were exceptional.[15] A small number of foreign-born Jews, generally Poles and Germans, were employed on highly skilled cabinet work, bringing their 'continental skills' to a market that was undergoing rapid changes of style and fashion. The popularity of card-playing at the end of the nineteenth century created a demand for finely inlaid card-tables, which German-born Jews, already experienced in such work, were able to meet.

However, the great mass of Jewish cabinet-makers occupied a middle ground, producing bedroom suites, pedestal tables and duchesse tables that usually found their place in the homes of the suburban middle classes. Indeed it is possible to recreate the 'typical' Jewish cabinet shop at the turn of the century in the memories of the makers, who transformed the raw timber from the saw-mills into the furniture that graced the showrooms of Curtain Road.

Although there were a number of well-known medium-sized Jewish firms in the East End, most Jewish furniture-makers worked in shops employing half a dozen to a dozen men. (Women worked in the industry, but mainly as upholsterers and gilders – the traditional shop was a fiercely male preserve.) Joseph Benjamin, for instance, began work at the beginning of the century in a shop employing fifteen workers making bureaux, 'after that. . .I went into a place making bedding furniture'.[16]

If bedroom furniture was being made, the workshop was generally in a cellar, where there was space to store and joint the large planks required for the construction of wardrobes. For the manufacture of smaller pieces of furniture, the attic could be pressed into use as a workshop. In one place:

> half the floor was missing, and you could see right through into the corridor below. So we put down the long boards of mahogany to cover it, and it was safe – at least until the end of the week when we had used all the boards for the furniture – and then you really had to watch out![17]

But wherever the workshop was situated, the air was fouled by the stench of animal glue warming in the glue-pot, and by the haze of wood-dust that never lifted, however frequently the 'boy' swept up.

Timber was generally bought every Monday morning from the local saw-mill. This was either mahogany, for the facing parts, or deal, for the inner carcase and for veneering work. If the previous week's suite had not been sold, but was 'in stock', it was possible to buy new timber on credit. Only sufficient timber was bought to cover the week's needs, and it was transported by hand cart from the local mill to the shop to be 'marked-up' from templates. After marking-up, the timber was returned to the saw-mill for sawing.

The sawyer, a self-employed man, who rented bench room and steam-power at the mill,[18] cut the marked timber to pattern, for which he was paid cash. The shaped timber was then returned to the workshop. In the meantime, the large planks of mahogany were planed by hand and then rub jointed to make the doors of the wardrobe and the sides of the chests of drawers. Monday was regarded as an 'easy day' in the Jewish workshop:

> Monday was considered a lazy day, see, after Sunday. And they didn't do much. Knocked off early and had this party. . .They used to get a couple of bottles of beer, or someone would bring in a bottle of whisky. . .Yes and the boss would join in.[19]

But during the rest of the week the pace of work picked up gradually, reaching a crescendo on the Friday morning. The working day stretched from eight in the morning to eight in the evening. Each man had a particular job, whether rebating, chamfering, gluing up or cleaning out, and the work changed according to the stages of construction. In some shops, the men worked in pairs (the 'hand in hand system'), one pair on wardrobes, the other on dressers and chests of drawers. All the while the 'greener' was at the beck and call of all – sweeping up, refilling the glue-pot, running out for pickled herrings or taking messages:

> In my first year, all apprentices had to get the tea for the men in the shop. We went out, and we had a long stick with nails – stopped the can from slipping off the stick – and they were beer cans at that time. We used to go into a local caff nearby. There we used to order kippers and rolls, buttered rolls and so on, and cans of tea, you see. So you was a teaboy! Sweep out the shop, burn all the shavings, and so on, and tidy up, set the wood up, help in that.[20]

Only gradually did the apprentice learn anything of the wood-working trade, and more often than not this was as a result of the loss of a work-hand for a few hours.

Finally, after all hands were put to work on the sand-papering and cleaning up, the suite would be ready on Friday afternoon. The furniture still needed to be French-polished; but it was sold 'in the white' to a dealer on Curtain Road, on the Friday. Unlike dealers elsewhere in London, Curtain Road operated on a cash basis. This meant that wages could usually be paid before the end of the week, and in good times there might even be a small profit. Just as often, though, times were not so good. Wages were usually paid, but often it meant that there would be no work for a week or two after that.

In fact Curtain Road, although providing an essential market for the East End furniture trade, also exerted a crushing pressure upon the hundreds of businesses which grew up around it. No firm, large or small, could afford to tie up capital and labour in long-term production, since profit margins were shaved to the bone by the cut-throat competition among makers. Furniture was made in anticipation of the demand from Curtain Road wholesalers, so that flexibility to copy the very latest styles and sheer speed in production governed the viability of any company. And the ease with which any maker, having learned the rudiments of a particular branch of the trade, could set himself up as a 'master' meant that there were always downward pressures upon market prices. Even the most unskilled worker could purchase the shaped pieces of a gypsy table from a sawyer at the local mill, and with the aid of a hammer and nails, rather than mortice and tennon, he could bash together a table that could be hawked in the streets and pubs. By the time the table collapsed a month later, the 'maker' had disappeared!

Wages and conditions

Writing at the end of the nineteenth century, Ernest Aves estimated that the better class of Jewish cabinet-maker was unable to command the wage rates of his Gentile counterpart, who would probably work in a West End firm. Yet, averaged out over the year, the Jewish cabinet-maker was able to make up for slightly lower rates by working longer hours (a twelve or thirteen hour day compared to an eleven hour day). By the turn of the century, a top-rate Jewish maker could earn perhaps £2.00 a week, compared to 50s. in Gentile West End workshops. At the bottom end of the scale, Jewish 'greeners' worked for much less than the 7s. a week which an English learner (formal apprentice-ships became increasingly rare) could expect to get even in his first year.

As in the tailoring trades, seasonal unemployment, and with it the spectre of dire poverty, was always a threat in the furniture trade. However, seasonal fluctuations were less violent in cabinet-making, and even in the worst times it was possible to 'hawk' furniture for a price. Thus in 1887 the Jewish Board of Guardians relieved only 27 cabinet-makers, in contrast to nearly seven hundred workers in the tailoring trade.[21]

Profit margins are more difficult to assess, especially for Jewish concerns where retailing and wholesaling was rare until the first decade of the twentieth century. Larger concerns might extract sufficient profit, perhaps 5 to 10 per cent, to be able to capitalise the business properly and pay a bonus to the boss. More often, though, profits were just sufficient to enable the company to survive and for the boss to take home a skilled worker's wages. Being a successful entrepreneur meant greater protection from seasonal unemployment rather than a bourgeois life style; at least until the boom conditions that accompanied the First World War.

Yet for all the difficulties which faced the Jewish cabinet-maker, one basic fact should be borne in mind. Although virtually no Jew was employed in the top West End cabinet shops – a reflection both of discrimination and the immobility of London labour – the existence of a Jewish furniture trade was guaranteed by two economic 'facts of life' in London. First, at a time when transportation was still difficult and costly, the metropolis had a virtually unlimited appetite for furniture, which *could not be met by factory production techniques* until the mid-twentieth century. Secondly, the existence of a cut-throat free market, based upon an almost archaic form of production and exchange, allowed the Jewish furniture trade to wedge itself into the East End with little capital, few formal skills and a great deal of personal sacrifice.

Shop-keeping

The survey carried out by the Poor Jews' Temporary Shelter indicates that the development of the Jewish trades such as cabinet-making and tailoring, in the East End was in part a result of the immigrants' previous vocations in Eastern Europe.[22]

However, nearly one quarter of the immigrants reported that their previous experience was in trade and commerce. Clearly being in 'trade and commerce' was a catch-all that included some shop-keepers, market traders and commercial travellers, but because of conditions in Russia and the Pale, it must have included a huge number of hawkers, peddlers and hustlers, whose livelihood was as insecure as that of London's casual poor. None the less, faced with the realities of the East End labour market, an immigrant who lacked any technical or manual skill might still be tempted to try his luck (and risk the remnants of his savings) as an East End trader. Come what may, the alternatives, working as a 'greener' in a sweated workshop, or seeking casual labouring work, were hardly attractive.

Hawking or, one step higher on the ladder of commerce, costermongering were possible openings for Jewish immigrants

44

– especially those immune to the snubs, insults and occasional assaults of other petty traders, who bitterly resented the intrusion of 'alien Jews' upon 'their patch'. For those with greater aspirations, or, more likely, savings brought from home, shop-keeping was an attractive option.

Few shop-keepers in the East End could pose grandly outside double-fronted premises where mysterious barrels, sacks and boxes spread out across the pavement. Shops in the Jewish East End were mostly house fronts, ground-floor flats or single rooms, roughly converted and pressed into service as retail outlets. As a result, in 1910, Flower and Dean Street could boast 'seven grocers' shops. . .[with] thirteen more in Brick Lane, up to the railway, and a further thirteen in the [Petticoat] Lane'.[23] All that was needed was a counter, some shelves and a pair of scales, and the willingness to open from six o'clock in the morning until midnight. In return, the shop-keeper gained 'independence', the freedom to close on the Jewish Sabbath and the gratitude or approbation of the neighbourhood, depending upon how readily credit was given.

The Cohen family arrived in England:

having no special skills, and went into [shop-keeping]. . .as it offered the best opportunity of making a living, without pressure to break the observance of Shabath and Holydays. . .

The opening hours were between 6.30 a.m. and 12.30 after midnight. . .most purchases were for small quantities, just for the next meal, except on Thursday and Friday mornings, when preparations were being made for the Sabbath. . .all this meant that the customers shopped, or sent their children to the shop, several times per day. . .

Most goods were delivered to the shops in bulk and either had to be pre-weighed or otherwise made ready for sale on the premises or in most cases at the request of the customer. . .Among other foodstuffs sold were herrings, smoked, cured, pickled or preserved in brine, smoked salmon and haddocks, and milk, which. . .even when delivered to the house, was measured from a large churn or other container and poured into the customer's own receptacle.[24]

For some, shop-keeping could seem like a respite from the iron

45

discipline of the workshop. Thus Abraham Isenberg gave up carpentry work after getting married, to open a newsagent's and tobacconist's shop in Dorset Square, in the West End. However, religious orthodoxy prevented him from opening his shop on Saturdays, with the result that his mostly Gentile customers deserted him and his business failed. He then opened a news-agent's shop in Commercial Road, in the heart of the East End:

> Here he again encountered problems as a result of being closed on the Sabbath because many of his customers who lived in the streets adjoining Commercial Road were dock labourers. Unable to make his business a profitable concern, he approached Rabbi Aba Werner. . .and asked what he should do. . .The rabbi advised that the shop should remain open on the Sabbath, provided that its control was entrusted to a Gentile on that day and that he did not later ask for explanations as to what had happened in his absence.
>
> He found a trust-worthy Gentile lady who ran the shop on the Sabbath and, to help pay her wages, Abraham Isenberg made cigarettes which he supplied to other traders. After some years she demanded a rise in wages which he could not afford. She left and the shop remained closed on the Sabbath.[25]

The experience of Abraham Isenberg tells us that the distance from the East End to the West End cannot always be measured in miles. Even for a man of some capital, 'being Jewish' could prove a serious handicap outside the Jewish ghetto.

NOTES

1 Of course, the divergent experiences of men and women within the immigrant population need to be recognised. An understanding of women's labour cannot be gained simply by looking at census returns. Such statistics ignore women's labour power when it is unwaged, and many areas of women's wage labour, such as prostitution, are unrecorded.

2 For a discussion of domestic service in London during this era see Leonore Davidoff, 'Class and Gender in Victorian England' in *Sex and Class in Women's History* (London, 1983). London employers also preferred to take on men from the provinces, believing them to be 'better bred' – stronger and more resilient – than the 'race' of inner-city dwellers. See Gareth Stedman Jones, *Outcast London* (Oxford, 1971), pp. 127 ff.

3 See Lloyd Gartner, *The Jewish Immigrant in England: 1870–1914* (London, 1960), p. 57.

4 Gartner adds 'so called not only because Jewish immigrants worked at them, but in recognition of other common characteristics'. ibid., p. 63.

5 In Leeds, Jews did attempt to find work in the mines, on the railways and in the brewing industry, but, according to Rosalind O'Brien, they were effectively barred from these areas. See R. O'Brien, 'The Establishment of the Jewish Minority in Leeds', Ph.D., University of Bristol, 1975. In London, the testimony of Jack Brahms, who found work in a large West End provision dealers, is instructive. Even in 1913 he was the only Jewish worker in the firm, and he recalled 'Oh they were very anti-Semitic – Yes, oh yes.' See Jerry White, *Rothschild Buildings* (London, 1980), p. 244.

6 For more detailed figures see Gartner, op. cit., pp. 57–8, although he incorrectly gives the figure of boot- and shoe-makers as 9 per cent.

7 See White, op. cit., p. 196.

8 *Jewish Chronicle*, 24.1.1896, p. 13.

9 See, for instance, the evidence of Frank Brien to the Royal Commission on Labour, 1892, Vol. XXIV, p. 61.

10 See Llewellyn Smith's statement, 'mobility perfect. . .' p. 28 above.

11 See p. 43–4 for details.

12 From 'Joseph Benjamin Remembers'. Tape 70, the Museum of the Jewish East End. Begun at 83 years, taped 1977.

13 Charles Booth, *Life and Labour of the People of London* (London, 1902), Vol. 4, p. 160.

14 ibid., p. 161.

15 Some immigrant Jews gained their apprenticeships in England under the auspices of the Jewish Board of Guardians. Between 1884 and 1888 24 Jewish lads were apprenticed as cabinet-makers, with a smaller number apprenticed in other sections of the furniture trade, such as carving, chair-making and marquetry inlaying (an average of 19 per year). ibid., p. 210.

16 'Joseph Benjamin Remembers', op. cit.

17 Interview with Joe Bronsky, July 1979.

18 Sawyers worked in a partitioned section and shared floor space with other sawyers and turners, who, according to Aves, were invariably English. Booth, op. cit., p. 170.

19 'Joseph Benjamin Remembers', op. cit.

20 ibid.

21 See Booth, op. cit., p. 210.

22 See p. 34 for details, although the survey makes no distinction between skilled craftsmen/women and unskilled homeworkers.

23 White, op. cit., pp. 239–40.

24 See Norman A. Cohen, 'Dr Thomas and the Milkroom', in Aubrey Newman (ed.) *The Jewish East End, 1840–1939* (London, 1981), pp. 53–4.

25 See John Cooper, 'The Bloomstein and Isenberg Families', in ibid., pp. 62–3.

CASE STUDY

Getting on in the East End

Interview with Morris Serlin. Cabinet-making and early life. Tape 71, Museum of the Jewish East End.

[My father came] from Poland originally. . .I think about 1910. They were big families then. There were five brothers and two sisters. . .they were all joiners or window-makers in Poland and of course. . .there was no life there – apart from the pogroms and everything else you just couldn't make a living. So they, all of them. . .with one or two exceptions. . .came over and they started up cabinet-making and small joinery and that's how they grew.

[My father's name] was Gershen. He was the youngest one. But funnily enough he was one of the few that could write properly. I mean they could all write Hebrew but he could write in Russian and English and he spoke Russian; so he did most of the correspondence. He also wrote love letters for my aunts. . .

[When he came over he was] about 17 or 18. They went [to the Jewish Shelter] first – they were helped and sent somewhere, and then the first ones, the uncles who came early, you know, they didn't all come at the same time, so they would put up the other brothers.

[My father was] one of the middle arrivals. There were two here before him, and they lived in Brick Lane, Lesley House. . .and I think they had two bedrooms and a living room and a kitchen. The whole lot would go in. And there they brought up families. I think my father also stayed there until he found somewhere. . .

My father got married here and then in 1914 the war broke out, and he was sent to build huts on Salisbury Plain as a joiner.

[My two elder uncles] started working for someone else, not on their own. . .There was a very well-known firm. . .called B. Cohen in Curtain Road. I think one of them started there.

My grandfather didn't come over. Just the brothers. The eldest one was Lazar, and my father Gershen, and Rufki and Joe. . .They decided just before the First World War that they ought to get together instead of working here and there, so they formed Serlin Brothers. There were four brothers and the two or three sons. They were all in the business and it was quite a respectable sized business for that sort of thing.

And then of course there was the war. First World War. Yes. Mixed

48

things up a bit. One of them went away early on and the others carried on working because there was still a demand for furniture. . .And that's how it started to grow. I think it grew for about four or five years after the war. Then in the nature of things it got too big. . .to get five brothers and sons working together – it's an impossibility.

My father thought that he would. . .continue making as a cabinet-maker. . .He was working on his own and bought a grocery shop in Balls Pond Road with a basement. So he did the cabinet-making in the basement and my mother was in the shop. They put me on a sack of corn during the day.

So he carried on. And in Balls Pond Road there was a company opposite called Times Furnishing Company. . .The Times Furnishing had a director called Jacobs. . .Well my father was opposite in the basement·making very good furniture. . .and so a rapport developed between the Jacobs and my father. So when they opened the Ridley Road market he could see that a small independent grocery wouldn't get anywhere against the market. So he sold the grocery and started out making furniture as a full-time occupation with the support of Jacobs who was the Times Furnishing.

Now the Times Furniture started to grow. I think they had ten, twenty, thirty shops. And we still had a very good rapport – you know – from a young Jacobs expanding into retail. And my father – a young man making furniture.

49

5

THE DAILY RHYME

THE EAST END

Jews had lived in areas of east London ever since the Resettlement. In the early nineteenth century, wealthy Jewish families intermingled with poor Jews along Mansell Street, Great Prescott Street and Leman Street, in the manner of a medieval ghetto. And although the settlement was small, its character was unmistakably Jewish. On the Feast of the Tabernacles and at Pentecost, it was reported that every private house was decorated with greenery, whilst the Feast of Purim was the occasion for a huge outdoor carnival in St James's Place or Goulston Street. 'Those were happy days for the London Jewry', claimed Lucien Wolf at the end of the nineteenth century. 'Rich and poor lived within a stone's throw of each other, and the poor were not very poor, and the rich were not proud.'[1]

By the end of the era of the Napoleonic Wars, however, the rich were indeed becoming prouder. They moved away westwards, although this dispersal was relatively slow. But by the latter half of the nineteenth century, the less wealthy middle classes also began to leave the East End. They migrated to the new London suburbs, notably Hackney, Clapton, Kennington and Walthamstow. Then 'for a long time nothing distinctive was left to the East End Jewry but a certain number of peculiar industries',[2] such as the 'Old Clo(thes)' trade, and boot-making.

The East End once again became the focal point of the Jewish community in London with the beginning of East European immigration. Almost inevitably, it was the first point of arrival for immigrant Jews, and as immigration swelled to its peak in the early years of the twentieth century, so the East End increasingly

50

took on the character of an 'immigrant ghetto'. According to Jerry White:

> For a Jewish family, needing to live within walking distance of a synagogue, a kosher butcher and the ritual baths, there was no alternative to living in the ghetto. . .freedom of choice was further restricted by blatant discrimination.[3]

The ghetto therefore had two boundaries. The most obvious to the visitor was the physical boundary formed by the 'Jewish streets'. On the western side, the ghetto backed against the commercial heart of the City of London. Moreover, as the era of Jewish immigration coincided with a major expansion of the City, the western margins of the Jewish quarter were constantly eaten away by commercial redevelopment. This in turn pushed the ghetto ever eastwards, so that the Jewish East End reached its zenith shortly before the First World War with Aldgate Pump proclaiming the western boundary, the Great Eastern line the northern boundary and Cable Street the southern boundary. To the east the border was fluid, running into Stepney Green, Jamaica Street and Jubilee Street, with ribbons of settlement in Soho, Notting Hill and Hackney.

But there was also a psychological boundary to the ghetto. To most immigrant Jews, the boundary of the ghetto was marked by the edge of the familiar 'Jewish world' and the beginning of the 'unknown', and presumably hostile, Gentile world. The precise line of this boundary varied from individual to individual. Some never dared venture beyond a few familiar streets. Others, especially the young, wandered more widely, albeit some streets were to be avoided at all costs!

HOUSING

As the City of London was transformed in the nineteenth century into a vast encampment of warehouses, offices and railway terminals, the price of land and its rentable value increased dramatically. In the twenty years from 1861 to 1881, the population of the City more than halved from 113,387 to 51,439. During the same twenty years the rateable value of the City leapt almost threefold, from one and a third million pounds to almost three and a half million pounds. By the end of the century the figure had nearly reached five million pounds. Yet:

> while the residential population of the City was drastically reduced, the volume of manual work located there proportionately increased. . .The result was first of all to intensify overcrowding in the City itself, and then in the areas immediately adjacent to it.[4]

The inexorable process of development, and subsequent overcrowding, in eastern London was observed by George Godwin as early as 1859. In Holborn, Clerkenwell and Spitalfields people were:

> huddled into any hole and corner they could put their head into – not from poverty, but from sheer want of any dwelling within reach of their work: respectable artisans. . .have been forced into the same dwellings with some of the worst class who have been driven from Field Lane and the slums near Sharp Alley.[5]

Most demolition was carried out for commercial redevelopment, but even when the old slums were torn down to make way for new housing, the consequences for the very poor were just as severe. In 1885:

> some old places were pulled down [in the East End], and a large block of good buildings was put up instead, and we fondly imagined that many of our over-crowded, ill-lodged families would remove into them. Our hopes were however in vain.
>
> The rooms, though cheap for their real value, were still necessarily dearer than the filthy dens in which so many of the people live, and for which they pay but little, one room generally serving for a whole family. . .Owing also to the interval which elapsed between pulling down the old building and building up the new houses, the people who had been turned out got scattered; the few who could afford to pay had gone elsewhere, and the many who could not, had crowded into any old place they could find. For these reasons, no applications for the new rooms were made by the [old] inhabitants, but a thousand new people, chiefly from the country, and seeking for work, came into them;

consequently. . .we thereby helped to cause more want and misery in those places into which our scattered hundreds crowded.[6]

As large-scale Jewish immigration began, a local charity committee reported that: 'In Whitechapel, in large parts of Swan Street, Rosemary Lane [etc.]. . .warehouses have been continually displacing dwellings and tenement houses. The houses in Prescott Street and Leman Street were formally occupied by one family; they are now tenanted by several.'[7]

Yet despite considerable Jewish immigration, the East End experienced a net loss of over 130,000 people between the years 1871 and 1891, although this did little to alleviate the chronic overcrowding. In Whitechapel in 1841 there were on average less than 8.5 persons per dwelling house. By 1881 this has risen to 11.28 persons per house. In Bethnal Green further to the east the rise was less spectacular but still alarming, from 6.1 to nearly 8 per dwelling.[8]

Between 1880 and 1886, Llewellyn Smith estimated that some 20,000 immigrant Jews crowded into the East End. Fewer houses simply absorbed more tenants, since Jewish immigrants, unlike native-born East Enders, did not leave the area. In Whitechapel, in the heart of the Jewish East End, the population rose from 75,552 to 78,768 between 1871 and 1901 despite a drop of some 30 per cent in the housing stock. By 1901 each house in Whitechapel contained about 14 residents.[9] In effect, landowners and landlords discovered that chronic overcrowding could be as lucrative as commercial redevelopment, as two square miles of faded grandeur became home for tens of thousands of Jewish migrants.

Within the Jewish ghetto, overcrowding reached a peak around the turn of the century, when it was reported that no house could be rented without the payment of 'key money'. Key money could constitute six months' rent in advance – two months' wages even for a skilled worker. Of course discrimination in the housing market added another notch on the ratchet of overcrowding and rack-renting, so that the financial impact of a street 'turning Jewish' could be spectacular. Gartner estimates that 'rents rose fifty per cent or sixty per cent when a street turned Jewish',[10] although the Royal Commission estimated the increase at 70 per cent. Jerry White notes that in the ten years after the Rothschild Buildings were first occupied it was said that rents in the Jewish quarter had nearly doubled – at a time when the wage rates were rising only slowly.[11]

But as in other parts of the East End, overcrowding was not simply an index of poverty; even well-off families could not find adequate housing within the East End. Emma Bronstein remembered that although 'we were not too badly off at the time, 'cos both [my uncle and my father] was earning good money then, we was all crowded together into the same tiny place – we couldn't get nothing better for love nor money!'[12] Nor were Jewish families small, despite the distorting effects of migration. One case study estimated that Jewish families averaged more than 5 children per family unit, compared to the English family of similar status, with, on average, 3.6 children.

LANDLORDS, LANDLADIES AND TENANTS

Despite a general trend towards institutional investment in London property towards the end of the nineteenth century, a class of small landlords still existed in poorer districts, such as the East End. They were, according to the Medical Officer for Limehouse, 'not a nice class of people as a whole'.[13] There was also a class of landladies. For the most part the landlady was:

> struggling, cheated, much worried, long-suffering; soured by constant dealing with untrustworthy people; embittered by loss; a prey to the worst lodgers, whom she allows to fall into debt, and is afraid to turn out lest she should lose the money they owe her.

Conversely, there were those who were 'bullying, violent, passionate, revengeful and cowardly'.[14]

In Whitechapel small tradesmen who owned property in the district were considered to be shoddy landlords and tenacious opponents of sanitary reform and renovation. However, small landlords were far from the only culprits. The notorious Booth Street Buildings were a case in point. Owned by the unscrupulous Jewish landlord Gershon Harris, the buildings have passed into East End folklore.

The 600 tenants of this tenement block were mostly Polish Jews. Their rents were no less than those in incomparably better 'model dwellings', such as the Rothschild Buildings. But whereas in the Rothschild Buildings there was a WC for every five people, the 600 Booth Street tenants shared just 30 WCs between them. Not that this statistic impressed the Medical Officer of Health for Whitechapel. He blamed the disgusting state of the WCs and the fact that the drains were consistently blocked with filth on the Polish Jews themselves. The tenants, he claimed, were unused to modern water-closets and consequently they put their refuse down them.[15] In fact, when the drains were eventually dug up they were found to be falling the wrong way, and were infested with rats.

However, as overcrowding became endemic in the East End, it was the middlemen who could make the greatest profits in the rack-rented market. 'House-knackers' could take a house on a lease from the landlord and 'knacker' it into single rooms at a considerable profit. A house rented at 15s. a week could easily yield £1.00 a week if sub-divided. In turn, families were forced to sub-let their own crowded space, so that 'the lodger', sometimes an entire family, became a fixture in most homes:

Lodgers! What Jewish ghetto doesn't know what a lodger is, and what ghetto doesn't board a few lodgers.[16]

THE JEWISH QUARTER

In the early 1880s the East End still contained a very high proportion of Irish-born families, who were the descendants of immigrants who had fled the terrible famines of the 1840s and 1850s. Their reaction to the Jewish 'newcomers' was occasionally hostile and aggressive. But it would be a mistake to think that the immigrant Jews simply 'took over' the very worst of the local housing and thereby pushed the Irish poor one step up the ladder of respectability. In fact pockets of chronic poverty – where Irish- and London-born paupers scratched out an existence in the notorious rookeries – punctuated the 'Jewish' streets of the East End ghetto. Along streets such as Flower and Dean Street in the heart of the East End, crowded with the lodging houses of Irish- and London-born prostitutes, no respectable Jewish child would dare to go!

In fact the Jewish East End was as ridden by distinctions of class and ethnic origin as any community in central London.

There were clear status and cultural differences between the new East European immigrants and the descendants of earlier Jewish migrations, especially those from Holland. Each ethnic group had its own synagogues and community organisations. Dutch Jews and Polish Jews would not inter-marry, and maintained a distrustful hostility towards each other.[17] Even the new Jewish immigrants, coming as they did from a host of different countries, were often as strange to each other as they were to the indigenous East Ender. Romanian Jews knew that Polish Jews were God's lowest creation, although Polish Jews believed the reverse. Lithuanians were seen as intellectual; Austrians as bad-tempered; and the Romanians as selfish.[18]

But despite these distinctions, the shared cultural and religious experience of being Jewish, and the common language of Yiddish, held the community together, especially in the first generation. 'Yiddish was used in shops, at work, at union meetings, among neighbours and friends and in families. . .Anglo-Jewish families and Sephardic Jews from Holland, the Chuts, who did not speak Yiddish tended to be a disadvantaged minority', comments Jerry White in his study of the Rothschild Buildings.[19]

As with the rest of London society, class divisions among the Jewish immigrants could also take on caste-like qualities. Indeed, as the cultural divide between Jewish settlers of different nationality narrowed, dissolving into myth and humour especially in the second generation, the cleavage of class tended to widen. This was evident even to the children:

> I remember making friends with a young boy from down the road. I don't know that he had a father. But I remember his mother – she seemed very young.
>
> Anyway, I don't think that they could manage the rent. I went down one day to play, and they was sweeping up the room they lived in. 'I'm going away', he said, and I never saw him again. But my mother; I remember her saying, after they had gone, that it was a good thing that I didn't play with him no more. ' 'Cos they was not our class of people!'[20]

Status differences between 'rough' and 'respectable' working-class families, and between men and women, were strikingly apparent to the whole community, both Jewish and Gentile.

Families where the father was in regular work, even if this was disrupted by seasonal troughs, were sufficiently well-off to afford the services of a washerwoman and household help. In fact nowhere was the gulf between the 'working' families and the chronic poor, especially single women, better illustrated than in the existence of the casual domestic help. Laundering, whitening the stairs and washing the floors – a hard day's work – could be bought for 3d. or 4d. This back-breaking work was usually taken on by the poor women of the lodging houses, who combined charring and prostitution to eke out a meagre and usually miserable existence. Nora, an Irish woman who lived in a decrepit room in a nearby lodging house, was employed by the Bronsky family:

> She used to 'do' for us – every Thursday I think it was – do the cleaning, the stairs and clean out the grate. Poor woman, she was on her own, although she said she had a sister somewhere in Lancashire. And I remember going round to her room when I was older – ugh, it was terrible. . .paper peeling off the walls, rags instead of curtains. And all she seemed to eat was bread pudding, bread dipped in hot water with some milk when she could get it.[21]

STREET-LIFE

Even in London, East European immigrants lived much of their lives out-of-doors. Chronic overcrowding ensured that the daily round burst out on to the streets and into the communal alleyways. And some vestiges of the 'old life' still remained. Many of the tenement blocks sprouted flower boxes in a vain attempt to drive off the dirt and smog. A few families even found room for some animals:

> [We] had a rabbit, chickens. What about the chickens! We had chickens in the flat! I still remember the cockerel standing on the edge of the bed (and crowing). And a few pullets she had. When she thought it was time she used to get hold of one of the pullets and put it in the tin bath and cover it up with. . .the scrubbing board until it started clucking, when we knew it had laid.[22]

Donkeys were also a common sight in the East End. As the Jewish costermongers wedged themselves into the London street markets, the costermonger's donkey, tethered in the disused (or still used) privy at night, became an object of delight to the children and fury to the adults, who were woken by its early morning braying.

> Bloody donkey! There was a donkey in the courtyard and it would start up braying at five o'clock in the morning. . .so I never needed an alarm clock to wake up for work. Except I didn't need to get up until six [o'clock]![23]

Nor was the costermonger especially popular with other tenants. Not only did he monopolise the erratic water supply for washing and preparing his vegetables; he also tended to sling his vegetable wastes out of the window into the courtyard, where they were picked over by the street 'grubbers' and rats alike.

Another unwelcome form of animal life which drove many tenants to their wits' end were the bugs. The bugs were no respectors of class or status. The unwashed poor and the scrupulous artisan alike had to suffer the bugs' nighttime attacks. In many cases it was the landlord who was the real culprit. Cheap and shoddy building techniques offered havens for the bugs, whilst the temptation for landlords to move tenants as quickly as possible into an empty property often provided the bugs with a secure and tasty home in the walls of the flats:

> We were to move from Newbold Street due to the fact that some of the rooms in the house were infested with bugs, irrespective of all the efforts of my parents to keep the house free from the vermin. But it was all to no effect! Consequently we found it unbearable to live there.
>
> All this was due to the landlord saving himself the cost of stripping the walls of the existing wall-paper. He decided to paste one lot of paper on top of another![24]

Many families, when leaving accommodation infested with the bugs, would take only bare necessities such as tables and chairs, abandoning all else lest the bugs should travel with them. All too often, though, this proved a useless precaution. Most new homes already had a resident population of bugs and vermin.

Yet street-life had its compensations in the unchanging rhyme of the days and seasons:

There was the wheelbarrow-man with his fresh herring, and the round brush at the end of one of the rods, also the sack he collected the soot in. The muffin man with his clanging bell and tray of muffins. The street lamp-lighter and his long pole whereby with a few movements. . .the lamp was lit. The old clothes man, who shouted at the top of his voice: 'Old rags for toffee apples!', thus causing us youngsters to rush indoors and nag our mums for old rags and meat bones to exchange for that delicious apple on a stick covered with toffee. The knocker-up man and his long pole, knocking on the various people who needed to start work early in the morning, taking into account that alarm clocks were not so abundant. The one-man band with every conceivable musical instrument strapped to his back, arms and legs; add to that, the monkey on his shoulder holding a little bag to collect the few coppers offered him.[25]

There were, too, outbursts of violence and aggression, which were but street-theatre to local people, when they involved the 'local' characters. Detective Sergeant Leeson remembered 'Mog the Man', reputed to be the daughter of a north-country clergyman:

When she was drunk she was a 'he-man' and a terror. Stripped bare to the waist, I have seen her fight the worst Amazons of Spitalfields and Whitechapel, and despite their inborn knowledge, nearly beat the life out of them. After which she would resist the united efforts of several policemen to remove her to the station, which they were never able to do until they had strapped her to an ambulance.[26]

Stand-up fights between local heavyweights spurred on by a watching crowd were another part of the local scene:

Once a fight started, money would start changing hands – bets you see, on who would win. But then the police would arrive, tipped off by someone who reckoned they were about to lose their money. So that would start another punch-up, between the people watching and the police, and between the men who were betting on the fight itself.[27]

PROSTITUTION

Another established part of the East End scene was prostitution. Of course, prostitution was firmly rooted in the East End long before widespread Jewish immigration. But whereas for the indigenous working class, prostitution tended to be casual, Jewish immigrant women faced particular difficulties and hazards which could force them into long-term dependency upon prostitution. And the greatest hazard was to be Jewish, single and poor.[28]

Because immigrant Jewish women found employment desperately difficult to come by (and what work there was tended to be seasonal and unreliable) there was little opportunity for a single women to become financially independent. For a married woman this was bad enough, especially if her husband had unreliable, poorly paid work. But for older single women, especially those who were widowed, divorced or separated from husbands, the results could be catastrophic, since Jewish law specifically forbade divorce or remarriage without proof of widowhood or the husband's written permission. (This was referred to as a 'get'.) In a community torn apart by persecution and emigration, there were literally hundreds of women who fell into this trap.

Single Jewish women thus fell prey to two forms of prostitution. The first was the organised white slave trade, which could entrap the helpless woman emigrant at almost any point in her travels, or even before she set out from Eastern Europe.[29] Undoubtedly many Jewish men were involved in this trafficking, and an international network of gangs could literally 'disappear' young women into brothels as far away as New York and Buenos Aires.

Secondly, many Jewish women accepted prostitution in the East End as 'an alternative to starvation and worse degradation',[30] for Jewish women who had been 'deserted' risked the workhouse or deportation (and sometimes both) if they attempted to seek 'official charity'. According to one Jewish commentator in England, applying the full force of his male logic to the problem:

> To compel these women to enter the workhouse is at the same time the best test of their deserted and destitute

condition, the greatest deterrent to this course of conduct on the part of men, and the most practical way of compelling them to resume their proper responsibility for the support of their families.[31]

Effectively shut out of the mind of 'respectable' Jewish society, such women found some understanding from the poorer East End Jews whose own experiences of poverty and discrimination induced a sense of empathy for their sisters:

> There was one woman. . .three kids she had, whose husband left her and went off, to America I should think, But anyway, he never sent for her – she never heard from him again. . . Well I suppose she was lucky really, in that she was a good-looking girl – know what I mean – she simply had to sell what she had, didn't she, or she would have starved. Some people was a bit stuck up about her, wouldn't talk to her or cut her dead, but she kept those kids clean and decent.[32]

And there is evidence that Jewish prostitutes and pimps, cast out from orthodox Judaic life, formed separate religious institutions, including their own synagogues and burial grounds.[33]

LOOKING IN – LOOKING OUT: THE JEWISH COMMUNITY

For most first-generation immigrants, the outside world tended to be regarded with 'hostility and suspicion'. Yet the outside world did break in upon the Jewish community – in a minor way because of Jewish religious custom (the Shabbos Goy), and in a major way through the influences of schooling, education and work.

Thus Gartner's image of the East End as a self-contained community, true though this rings for many first-generation migrants, needs some qualification. Indeed, the relationship between the 'Jewish ghetto' and the wider East End was symbiotic. The Jewish East End was a society apart; but its character was moulded by *London's* East End, where the 'peculiar' economic structure and labour market of the great metropolis nurtured and protected it.

So the Jewish community 'looked in' upon itself, recreating its old East European image in the religious and cultural life of the ghetto. However, it also 'looked out' upon the Gentile world, sometimes with fear and trepidation, but also with the knowledge that England was now the homeland. Indeed, there was a constant struggle between the religiously orthodox who sought merely to recreate the spiritual Jewish homeland within the ghetto, and the Anglo-Jewish establishment which strained to 'attach. . .our brethren to the main body of the [English] community'; a mission which they propounded as 'a holy task'.[34] The two sides fought out this struggle on many fronts – religious, cultural and economic – but the tensions were especially apparent in the domain of schooling and education.

The heder

Most immigrant Jews had been educated in the '*heder*' of Eastern Europe. The heder (literally a 'room') was usually a shabby, decrepit schoolroom in the house of the local schoolmaster. Here the Melammed drilled the unwilling child in the rudiments of literacy and numeracy and taught the complexities of Judaic prayer, Biblical study and religious ritual. In the East End:

> the heder mushroomed. Abetted by the ancient tradition that every possible moment ought to be devoted to sacred study, and by the more immediate desire to keep children out of the house and somehow occupied, the heder was in nearly continuous session.[35]

The East End heder was almost invariably unhygienic and overcrowded, although few Jewish parents would have given this a thought, given the conditions in which their children lived for the rest of the time. One heder in Whitechapel, investigated by the local sanitary inspector in 1881, consisted of a room, nine feet long, eight feet wide and nine feet tall, where twenty-five children were being 'educated'.[36] As with one-room schools in the English system, no standards of education were requested, measured or imposed. None the less, for the Jewish family whose sweated day extended from dawn to dusk and well beyond, the heder had three great virtues – it was religiously orthodox, local and cheap (from 6d. – 1s. 6d. per week) and it swept the children out of the house, which was often a workshop first and a home second.

But the heder was the object of the Anglo-Jewish establishment's scorn and fury. The *Jewish Chronicle* constantly railed against their 'appalling' standards, their 'dirty' conditions and the fact that they undermined their own attempts to regulate the 'proper' education of Jewish children as British citizens. The Rev. A.L. Green, an Anglo-Jewish minister sent to converse with the ignorant immigrants in Yiddish, expressed the native Jewish establishment's viewpoint most clearly when he explained that 'Hebrew learning did not pay in this commercial country', and that 'it was incumbent upon them to do something more than to educate their children soley in Hebrew and Rabbinical teachings'.[37] The education that the Anglo-Jewish establishment had in mind for the immigrants' children was exemplified by the Jews' Free School in Spitalfields, a vast enterprise of modern educational practice and Judaic tradition, underwritten by the Rothschild family. Ironically, the Jews' Free School could trace its origins to the heder so detested by the Anglo-Jewish establishment. Yet at the turn of the century it enrolled 4,300 children in the largest elementary school in England.[38]

During the nineteenth century, the Jews' Free School was synonymous with Moses Angel, its Principal for fifty-one years. Angel had no doubt about the sort of pupils who came to his school: they were either 'very regular or very irregular' and he considered it a 'cruelty' to keep a boy at school past the age of 11 just 'to cram his head' rather than allow him to earn his daily bread at work. Added to this was his belief that 'Jewish children were. . .less amenable to the natural laws of discipline than English children. . . [so] he punished the bad and rewarded the good'. Regrettably his teachers could only 'tap' rather than 'flog' their pupils.[39] Just how heavy this 'tap' could be was remembered by one ex-pupil of the school:

> I carried on at the Jews' Free School for about two years in all. Masters there were very strict, and if you fell foul of any one of them, you were really for it.
>
> I particularly remember one master who, if you came out in front of him for some misdemeanour, he would stand you about a foot away facing him. After some admonition and whilst talking to you he would be stroking your face, perhaps with his left hand. Then he would bring his right hand up and you received a resounding wallop on the side of the face

he wasn't stroking. Or at times he'd wallop the side he was
so gently stroking.

Another master...was Mr Solomans. When his hand
came down with the cane...he certainly made your fingers
tingle. After a while I learned to keep some resin in my
pocket, which I rubbed into my hands preparatory to a
caning. It managed to ease the pain somewhat. I reckoned
it was up to us pupils to keep ahead of the masters![40]

Moses Angel, for one, had no doubts that the Jewish East
European immigrants were, in part, 'the refuse population of the
worst parts of Europe', whose 'first object in sending the children
to school was to get them out of the way'. Some of the children,
he asserted, 'were ignorant even of the elements of sound; until
they had been Anglicised or humanised, it was difficult to tell
what was their moral condition, and many of them scarcely knew
their own names'.[41] And although Angel's comments caused
something of a furore among the Jewish community, they were
hardly untypical of the Anglo-Jewish establishment's attitude to
the newcomers, which mixed paternalistic concern with a large
measure of contempt.

Although the Jews' Free School was by far the largest Jewish
education establishment in the East End, its pivotal role in the
education of the Jewish community declined after 1870 with the
establishment of the elementary schooling system. The Act of
1870 created a network of state-supported elementary schools
throughout the East End, which were first penetrated and later
'colonised' by Jewish children. Thus Mowlem Street Boys'
School, opening in 1887, had no Jewish children until the turn
of the century. Whereas Christian Street Girls', which opened in
1901, did so with 'great difficulty' due to the number of Jewish
children 'unable to speak English and to understand when
spoken to'. In the same year, some 90 per cent of the First
Standard could not speak English at St Jude's School.

Such problems with language persisted until the First World
War. In 1912 the Annual Report of Dempsey Street School noted
that it was necessary

to train a large number of foreign girls to use with fair facility
the language of the country in which they live...Until
comparatively recently the great majority of children who

attended were of English parentage. . .Now there is a large
foreign element in the school. . .Many children enter the
school ignorant of English.[42]

Of course, speaking English was connected in the minds of most
educationalists with 'being English'. In the case of the Jews' Free
School, 'being English' meant a rise in economic status for the
immigrant, and, irrespective of the issue of Jewish culture and
religion, it demanded submergence in the values of upper-class
England. Hence on Empire Day in 1904 the Jews' Free School
demonstrated its loyalty to country, King and Empire in no
uncertain fashion:

> At 3.40 the song 'Flag of Britain' was sung simultaneously
> throughout the school. Kipling's 'recessional Hymn' was
> then recited and lessons on patriotism followed – 'What the
> Empire does for us, and what we must do for the Empire'.
> Finally, at 4.15 the Cadet Corps marched to the Rothschild
> Hall, where they sang, to the accompaniment of the brass
> band, 'God Save the King', all the classes joining in. The
> Union Jack was saluted in proper military fashion, and the
> ceremony concluded with cheers for 'King and Country'.[43]

No doubt the connection between the Rothschilds, King and
Empire remained a mystery to most children, and not only those
who had 'no facility' with the English language.

However, other schools in the East End taught pointedly
different lessons about 'being English'. For many teachers, aware
of the political controversy surrounding immigration, Jewish
children were an alien wedge in the heart of Empire. Hostility to
the immigrants and their children could be overt and blatant,
although it also assumed subtler forms in the reports of
administrators and educators. The Head of Dempsey Street
Girls' School reported on 9 September 1904 that the nurse had
examined the children's heads for vermin. Unfortunately,
because of the 'Black Fast', it was necessary for the nurse to
return to the school on the next day to examine the Jewish girls,
who were 'the great offenders'.[44] Even academic success in Jewish
children could be attributed by a governmental inquiry to a
'Jewish 'smartness. . .in commercial things' which was not uncon-
nected with a 'perfect want of moral sense' in telling the truth.[45]

Hostility could also be explosive. At Commercial Street School chronic staff shortages often meant that teachers were drafted in with no experience of the Jewish pupils. One such teacher was Miss Jackson, who wore her patriotism upon her Union Jack apron. She arrived at the school just after the Kishnev pogroms:

> She took the class and she said, 'Now all you foreigners who come from Russia – you should get back to your country!'

Unfortunately for Miss Jackson, one pupil at least required no 'facility with the language' to reply:

> A girl sitting at the front – her name was Yetta Solomons – she was so incensed about that. . .she took out this inkwell and flung it at her.[46]

Breaking away

The transition from school to work usually took place at the age of 13 or 14. Freed from the tyrannies of capricious teachers and the tortures of rote learning, most children abandoned the classroom with joy. A paypacket, even when it contained only a few shillings, was a symbol of self-reliance and adulthood, which in the case of the poorest families actually made the difference between poverty and just scraping by.

Nevertheless, finding work was difficult. At the turn of the century, the world outside the East End 'ghetto' still seemed a hostile place to a young Jew – even to those who had been born in England:

> I remember walking out [of school] and thinking, 'Im goin' to get me mother some jewellery – 'cos she never had nothing nice see – just us kids hanging around her neck! Course, I had no money – nothing. Not even a job.
> An' I did too! Took me twelve years mind![47]

NOTES

1 Lucien Wolf, 'The Jews in London', *Graphic* (1889).
2 ibid.
3 Jerry White, *Rothschild Buildings* (London, 1980), p. 62.
4 Gareth Stedman Jones, *Outcast London* (Oxford, 1971), p. 161.
5 George Godwin, *Town Swamps and Social Bridges* (London, 1859), p. 20.

6 Katie Cowper, 'Some Experiences of Work in an East-End District' in *The Nineteenth Century*, Vol XVIII (Nov. 1885), p. 786.
7 Quoted by Stedman Jones, op. cit., p. 165.
8 ibid., p. 176.
9 Lloyd Gartner, *The Jewish Immigrant in England: 1870–1914* (London, 1960), p. 147.
10 ibid. p. 156.
11 Tenants 'are now paying 14s. per week, with a premium of £5.00 for the key for houses that, two years ago, they were paying 7s. for'. Quoted by White, op. cit., p. 61.
12 Emma Bronstein, interviewed July 1979.
13 They were, according to the Medical Officer for Limehouse, 'people who have saved a little money; people who have been in trade'. Quoted by Stedman Jones, op. cit., p. 210.
14 Octavia Hill, *Homes of the London Poor* (London, 1875), p. 38.
15 White, op. cit., pp. 63–4.
16 Gartner, op. cit., p. 172.
17 See Harold Pollins, 'East End Jewish Working Men's Clubs' in Aubrey Newman (ed.) *The Jewish East End, 1840–1939* (London, 1981), p. 173.
18 White, op. cit., p. 79.
19 ibid., p. 81.
20 Emma Bronsky, interview July 1979.
21 ibid.
22 White, op. cit., p. 39.
23 Joe Bronsky, interview July 1979.
24 From memoirs of J.J. Titton, Transcript, in the Museum of the Jewish East End.
25 ibid.
26 Sergeant B. Leeson, quoted by White, op. cit., p. 126.
27 Joe Bronsky, interview July 1979.
28 Lara Marks ('Jewish Women and Jewish Prostitution in the East End of London' in *The Jewish Quarterly*, Vol. 34, No. 2, 1987, p. 7) aptly sums up this when she writes 'the Jewish woman thus faced a double oppression – as a woman and as a Jew – whilst the Jewish prostitute faced a triple oppression – as a woman, as a Jew and as a member of the Jewish working class'.
29 According to the Report of the Jewish Association for the Protection of Girls and Women, 1908: 'In Russia, Romania and Galicia the conditions in which the Jews are largely forced to live is a direct incentive to the White Slave Traffic. Girls are only too glad to escape from the weariness and grinding poverty of homes where they are often not allowed to learn a trade. Their parents, seeing seemingly eligible young men come to their villages. . .entrust them to their care in order to have "excellent situations" found for them abroad.' ibid., p. 8. See also the testimony of Maxine Elvey, pp. 13–15.
30 ibid., p. 10.
31 *Jewish Chronicle*, 30.5.1902.

32 Emma Bronsky, op. cit.
33 According to E.J. Bristow, *Prostitution and Prejudice* (Oxford, 1982), p. 3.
34 *Jewish Chronicle* Leader 1890, cited by Ann Ebner, 'The East End as Seen Through the Pages of the *Jewish Chronicle*' in Newman, op. cit., p. 284.
35 Gartner, op. cit., p. 231.
36 *Jewish Chronicle*, 9.12.1881.
37 See *Jewish Chronicle*, 1.4.1881.
38 Gartner, op. cit., p. 222.
39 ibid., p. 223.
40 J.J. Titton, op. cit., p. 5.
41 Gartner, op. cit., p. 223.
42 For above see I. Osborne, 'Achievers of the Ghetto' in Newman, op. cit., p. 168.
43 *East London Observer*, 28.5.1904.
44 Osborne, op. cit., p. 170.
45 Gartner, op. cit., p. 230.
46 White, op. cit., p. 168.
47 Joe Bronsky, op. cit.

6

THE MAKING OF THE JEWISH EAST END

> The prototypical Jewish immigrant from Eastern Europe
> reproduced his familiar environment in the ghetto. . .
> spatially distinct and socially distant from other groups of
> people. The experience of persecution induced a fear of the
> non-Jewish world; the immigrants' strict religious
> upbringing imposed an insurmountable barrier between
> them and the Christians, and to prevent the crime of
> inter-marriage, social intercourse was frowned on and,
> where possible, prohibited.[1]

The exhausted immigrants who disembarked at Tilbury had left
a way of life in Eastern Europe which was almost medieval. Shut
out of the foundries and factories of Eastern Europe, penned into
the Jewish ghettos in the major cities, and crowded into an ethnic
enclave along the Pale of Settlement, few immigrant Jews had any
experience of industrial capitalism. Yet in England they were
thrown upon a labour market where capital reigned supreme.
Indeed, within days of arrival at Tilbury, the immigrants were to
be found hovering around the pig market in Whitechapel, 'with
eyes full of grief', in the vain hope of finding a 'master' to give
them work.[2] Such a scene, with the masters 'scurrying about like
poisoned mice among the dishevelled men' seemed eloquent
testimony to the proletarianisation of the great mass of Jewish
immigrants upon arrival in London.

However, those Jewish immigrant workers who settled in the
East End were hardly 'typical' proletarians. They were not
'typical' of the English rural labourers who flocked to the capital
in November and December seeking casual work, or food and
shelter from the London charities; for winter was 'the homeless
man's London season'.[3] Still less were the Jewish immigrants

'typical' of the lumpenproletariat, the great majority of whom were London-born, who scratched out an existence in London's East End.[4] In fact, the Jewish immigrants who settled in London's East End were not altogther 'typical' Jewish immigrants. For to understand the way in which an immigrant class structure formed within the Jewish community, it is necessary to explore how the historical and cultural distinctions which marked out the Jewish immigrant from the native proletariat also set in train the development of a specifically 'Jewish' labour market and even a 'Jewish' economy within the East End. It is necessary, too, to appraise the strategy of the Anglo-Jewish establishment in 'policing' Jewish immigration, and to assess its capacity to shape the social structure of the East End's Jewish community.

ARRIVAL (AND DEPARTURE)

Heavy with trepidation, but heady with hope and ambition, the Jewish migrants struggling on to the quayside at Tilbury must have thought that the worst of their ordeal was behind them. For the would-be Jewish migrant, however, arrival in England was just the first step in becoming an immigrant. For if the desperate Jewish masses who sought escape from Eastern Europe were sifted and sorted by the hardships of migration, the process of selection was completed by the wealthy Jewish oligarchy in England.

Ever fearful that a wave of poverty-stricken, Yiddish-speaking aliens, washed up on the shores of England, would raise the dreaded spectre of anti-Semitism against *each and every Jew* in the country, the Anglo-Jewish oligarchy sorted and sifted, ejected and assisted, until the Jewish migrants remaining in England matched *its* assessment of the migrant's potential to become an 'Englishman' (sic). (Hence Abraham Mundy's remark that without the prompt action of the Poor Jews' Temporary Shelter, the 650 Romanian Jews arriving at Tilbury in June and July 1900 'would have been parading the streets of London, homeless and hopeless, with dangerous results to themselves and to *the whole Jewish community*'.[5] [my emphasis] And although it would be an exaggeration to suggest that the suitably graded immigrant who 'made it' into the East End was infused with the virtues of thrift

70

and enterprise, those infected with contagious diseases, poverty or fecklessness, not to mention political or religious radicalism, discovered that the route from Tilbury to Commercial Road was every bit as tortuous as the route from Russia to England.

For the grandees of the Anglo-Jewish community, the protection of their existing economic and social privileges outweighed their vestigial identification with the suffering of the Jewish masses in Eastern Europe. The Poor Jews' Temporary Shelter was aptly named. Indeed it was initially shunned by all the Jewish grandees except for the Montagu family, for fear that 'it would attract immigrants to English shores who were incapable of supporting themselves'. In fact the Shelter provided 'a roof' and 'food that was little better than bread and water' to newly arrived migrants for a maximum of two weeks; and then only to immigrants 'who could prove that they had led respectable lives'.[6] In many cases the Shelter was simply a revolving door for Jewish migrants arriving at Tilbury, providing them with a respite from the miseries of the first voyage, before they were sent on to the New World with 'pecuniary assistance' from 'leaders of the Jewish community'.[7] Additionally, the Jewish Board of Guardians resolved to send back to their native lands immigrants who were still without work six months after arrival in England, unless they 'gave promise of becoming industrious members of the community. . .who raised their children as Englishmen [sic]'.[8]

This selection process, designed to weed out the 'uneconomic man' of Victorian liberalism, did more than regulate the numbers and 'quality' of Jewish immigrants settling in Britain. It played a part in the Jewish establishment's strategy of sustaining an entrepreneurial culture among the East European immigrant community. And it was also designed to undermine the appeals of political and religious radicals within the immigrant community, whom the Anglo-Jewish elite considered might 'inflame' relationships between Jews and 'native Englishmen' in the new land.

WORKERS OF THE GHETTO – WORKERS OF THE WORLD

Precisely because the Anglo-Jewish establishment had urgent reasons for ensuring the 'success' of its immigration policy, it could not ignore the consequences of the new Jewish settlement that did occur. For those who did make it to Commercial Road there was little respite from the hectoring and admonishment of their wealthy patrons. And as we have seen, the *Jewish Chronicle* constantly lectured the immigrants on the need to throw off their religious orthodoxy and become 'true Englishmen'.[9] Equally, the values of thrift and enterprise could not be permitted to wither on the vine, even when the grim reality of the new life caught up with the sweated immigrant work-hand. For the Anglo-Jewish establishment believed that a self-reliant immigrant community would help make it 'invisible' to outsiders. And that 'invisibility' was considered to be a good investment. Between 1900 and 1910 the Jewish Board of Guardians made a total of 26,479 loans to enable immigrant Jews to capitalise their infant businesses.[10]

Of course, the efforts of the Anglo-Jewish establishment to create a petite bourgeoisie in its own image never managed to blot out the conflicts which accompanied the emergence of new class structures within the Jewish immigrant community in the East End. The struggles of the bakery workers, the boot- and shoe-makers and the sweated labourers of the tailoring trades against poverty-line wages and appalling conditions of work are, even today, a part of Jewish folklore.

Initially these struggles were a distinctly Jewish affair. Thus the Great Tailors' Strike of 1889 pitted the 'Jewish Unemployed and Sweaters' Victims' against the Master Tailors' Protective and Improvement Association, headed by the powerful Jewish clothing contractor, Mark Moses. The struggle was bitter and, at times, violent. *The Times* explained to its readers that the strikers were 'protesting against the labour sweating indulged in by certain members of the Jewish community. . .[The strikers were] complaining of the indifference of the rich Jews, and calling upon the work people "not to depend upon the rich class but to organise in a strong body for the abolition of the capitalist ruling class" '.[11]

However, despite some local successes in the struggle for better wages, Jewish radicals such as Aron Lieberman and the German Rudolf Rocker faced an uphill struggle to span the divide between the Jewish working class and the rest of the British labour movement. The emergent socialist movement was particularly weak in London, where a more archaic, artisan radicalism still held sway at the end of the nineteenth century. Many trade union leaders were openly hostile to 'alien immigration', believing that the downward pressure on wage rates was exacerbated by 'Jewish sweating'. There was the difficulty, too, of organising any group of workers in the casual trades that dominated the East End.[12] So, virtually shut out from the English labour market, and often sharing the same overcrowded garret workshop and home, the Jewish worker was locked in an uneasy symbiosis with the Jewish entrepreneur. In a society where the social relations of production were becoming increasingly impersonal, the immigrant Jews were thrown into intensely personal social relations with their employers. Small wonder that one Jewish tailoress could remember an employer who paid her just 1s. a week as a 'learner', with some affection:

> They were very nice to me. She used to sew 2s. 6d. in my coat sleeve; I took my coat off and they sewed 2s. 6d. in it – they knew I was poor. And I always remember. I went to work one dinner time and when I came back it was pouring with rain. She took me to a shop, threw my shoes in the gutter and bought me a new pair of shoes.[13]

As a result, the Anglo-Jewish establishment did succeed in its primary aim. It largely 'contained' the consequences of Jewish immigration within its own sphere of influence, by exporting the problems of poverty to other lands and policing the Jewish immigrant quarter in such a way as to minimise the frictions of settlement and maximise the opportunities for the immigrants' economic advancement.

This patrician strategy was not without its setbacks, as we shall see when examining the rise of the anti-alien movement in Part III. But anti-alien sentiment even played its role in reinforcing the Jewish oligarchy's influence over the Jewish ghetto. For when the class antagonisms between the Jewish proletariat and the emerging immigrant bourgeoisie sparked into bitter strife, class consciousness was tempered by a fear (sustained by bitter experience in Russia and the Pale) that the English proletariat and the native bourgeoisie could make common cause against all Jews, irrespective of class.

So, ironically, however, much the wealthy Jewish establishment in England tried to distance itself from the poor immigrant rabble of Eastern Europe, or deny the significance of their common Jewish heritage, they were in fact tied to each other by the fear of anti-Semitism. The Jewish establishment's passionate involvement in the debate about immigration, and its attempts to control the influx and life style of immigrant Jews, stemmed from self-interest – from the fear that anti-alien sentiment might explode into popular forms of anti-Semitism which would have direct repercussions upon their own privileged position in British society. They believed that helping the immigrants to become prosperous, and influencing the immigrants to abandon the 'foreign habits' which set them apart from the native population, were essential measures in the struggle against English anti-Semitism.

Yet in attempting to 'remake' the *stetl* of Eastern Europe in the heart of London, Jewish immigrants were not simply trying to rekindle the cultural community of the Pale – as the Jewish establishment frequently asserted. More importantly, as Jerry White has suggested, they were also seeking to 're-establish the *economic independence and security* [my emphasis] which they and their parents had lost'.[14] For, as Nathan Glazer points out, 'what is really exceptional. . .is the degree to which [the Jews] had been forced out of their age-old pursuits and proletarianised' in Eastern Europe. Immigrant Jewish workers

> were the sons – or the grandsons – of merchants and scholars. . .business and education were, for Jews, not a remote and almost foreign possibility, but a near and familiar one. They, or their friends and relatives, had the necessary experience and knowledge.[15]

Certainly, there is no doubting the leaven of artisan experience and business acumen among the Jewish immigrant petite bourgeoisie in the East End. But of course, this potential could only be realised if the nascent consumer industries which the Jews had colonised continued to grow and expand.

So even though the East European Jews crowded into the same streets and crumbling tenements as the native poor and shared the poverty of their fellow East Enders, their restless ambition to regain a paradise lost, and their latent potential to succeed within an unfettered capitalist system, marks them off from the native working class. Above all, they had not become locked into a cycle of systematic under-employment, poverty and despair, which was the fate of the London residuum. On the contrary, the Jewish immigrant believed that Whitechapel was the first step on a journey which would, in time (and God willing) lead to the New Jerusalem. For many a native East Ender, Whitechapel was usually the last stage on a descent into hell.

THE JEWISH EAST END – AN ETHNIC ECONOMY?

Whilst the social relations of production which evolved within the ghetto were intensely personal and close, it was the *impersonality and anonymity* of the social relations of exchange outside the ghetto that made this possible. Metaphorically speaking, the Jewish East End, at least from the mid 1880s until the First World War, can be likened to a satellite community, with its own 'atmosphere' of religious values and Jewish culture and even its own social relations of production. Yet simultaneously, this 'satellite community' *revolved around the great mass of the host society, being subject to the gravitational pull of its economic system, its class relations and its ideological formations.*

The economic equilibrium of this satellite community was maintained by the showrooms along Curtain Road and the wholesale warehouses that flanked the East End. They linked the Jewish immigrant entrepreneurs to the national and international economy. Through the warehouses flowed the products of the Jewish community in exchange for the finance that capitalised the cabinet and slop shops, and which in turn paid the (minimal) wages of the Jewish workforce. So it was the readiness of the London wholesalers to purchase at lowest cost, regardless of whether surplus value was sweated from Jewish, English or Irish labour, which created the guarantee of equality of economic opportunity to the nascent immigrant Jewish bourgeoisie. In these circumstances, the door of opportunity was open for a Jewish working class to evolve within an ethnic economic enclave, heavily insulated from the social relations of production that generally characterised the metropolis.

However, the 'freedom' of the Jewish entrepreneur to compete within the domestic wholesale markets was a comparatively recent phenomenon. The modern Jewish community in Britain can be dated from the time of Cromwell. Even in 1700 there were less than one thousand Jews resident in England. At the peak of Jewish immigration in 1905, very few Jewish families could trace ten generations who had lived and died in Britain, and there were many 'Englishmen' who wanted that lineage to cease forthwith.

So the 'freedom' of the Jewish entrepreneur to compete within the domestic wholesale market was a *historical* freedom. It evolved, in large measure, out of the particular importance of venture and finance capital in the expansion of British capitalism. Yet even at the beginning of the twentieth century, the Jewish communities in Britain were vulnerable to attack. In August 1911, marauding youths looted and burned Jewish shops in towns throughout South Wales, causing damage estimated at over £16,000.[16] In the East End the system of exchange which linked the Jewish East End to the wider national economy could easily have been disrupted, either through populist boycott actions and physical assault, or through the intervention of the state. Indeed, in June 1903, the periodic harassment of Jews in an area known as 'Jews' Island' in the heart of Bethnal Green 'erupted into open violence, with stone throwing, looting and serious injury'[17] Moreover, the Jews of eastern London needed only to look across the Channel to find examples of both populist boycotts and forms of legalised discrimination that effectively crippled the economic potential of the Jewish community.[18]

The viability of this 'ethnic' economic strategy at a time of national economic stagnation, the support of the wealthy Anglo-Jewish establishment for Jewish businesses, and the weakness of the forces advocating political alliance with the native working class (and vice versa) meant that a Jewish proletariat came into being 'alongside' rather than inside the East End proletariat.

Hence it was the very *separateness* of this Jewish proletariat, developing within a community of labour and cultural values outside the direct influence of the native class system, that characterises the evolution of the Jewish immigrant community. That is in no sense to deny that the Jewish immigrant sweated at the same trades, under the same atrocious conditions, and often in the same street as the Gentile labourer. Nor is it to suggest that the Jewish East End developed in isolation from English society and its class system. But in general *the Jewish proletariat was not thrown into a direct and personalised form of contact or competition* with native East Enders and provincial immigrants. Instead the point of economic competition occurred at the point of exchange, principally in the wholesale markets, where an incipient Jewish bourgeoisie clawed each other, and their native competitors, for sales and contracts.[19]

The consolidation of this ethnic economic enclave, tenuously linked to a growing commodity market by an emergent class of Jewish entrepreneurs, had far-reaching consequences for the Eastern Europen immigrants. For, much as the native working classes, especially within the East End, railed against the presence of the Jewish immigrant who could 'work fifteen hours a day on cold coffee and bread and cheese',[20] and, however, systematically they attempted to exclude immigrant Jews from the local labour market (or colluded with employers to implement such strategies), the consolidation of the 'ethnic economy' prevented the emergent Jewish working class from becoming locked into a structural cycle of unskilled work, under-employment and economic and social marginalisation – the very cycle of deprivation which they were fleeing in Eastern Europe.

DIASPORA

The Jewish East End also needs to be placed in the context of the massive movement of peoples in the nineteenth and early twentieth centuries.[21] The Jews of Eastern Europe, like other ethnic, political and religious minorities, were fleeing westwards in search of social tolerance, economic prosperity and religious freedom. To this extent the Jewish community which coalesced in London's East End was an 'immigrant ghetto' which celebrated and cherished the heritage of the Jewish past, just as the Italian immigrants of the period created 'Little Italies' in London, in Holborn, Hatton Garden and Saffron Hill.

Yet precisely because there was no 'Little Israel' to celebrate in a foreign land, the Jewish ghetto was much more than a cluster of ethnic Jews. For Jewish emigration from Eastern Europe was of a quite different scale and magnitude than that of any other national grouping. By the outbreak of the First World War, nearly half of the Jewish population of Eastern Europe had forsaken their homes for the Americas, or for the great cities of Western Europe. The significance of this emigration can be understood when it is realised that the next highest emigrant nation, Italy, lost less than one sixth of its population.[22]

Even so, England remained a minor diversion in the vast exodus from Eastern Europe. Although, in 1914, London contained more Jewish settlers from Eastern Europe than any other city in the world, except for New York and Chicago, nearly as many Jewish immigrants entered the United States in 1904 as entered England in the entire period from 1880 to 1914.[23] Significant, too, is the fact that, unlike the Jewish immigrant ghettos that sprang up along America's Eastern Seaboard, the Jewish East End was an immigrant settlement in an 'old country', where the political structure was dominated by ancient elites, and where no great 'new opportunities' beckoned. As such, any 'immigrant ghetto' was an anomaly, especially in a society which preached the virtues of emigration as a response to poverty, and settlement in Canada, South Africa and Australia as a response to imperial 'duty'.

Yet whereas the massive movement of peoples across national boundaries in the nineteenth century was a new phenomenon in history, brought about in the birth pangs of industrial capitalism, the resettlement of Eastern European Jews was part of a strategy adopted over two millennia, as a means of survival in the face of persecution, pogrom and deportation which constitute the Jewish diaspora. And the particular history of the Jewish diaspora ensured that the migration of Jews to England or New England from Eastern Europe was a distinctly Jewish affair – a matter of passionate concern and interest to Jews throughout the world.

In point of fact, the attitude of the Jewish elite in England differed little from the Jewish establishment in America. But whereas in America, the mainly German-Jewish establishment also sought to turn back the tide of Jewish 'paupers', complaining that 'America is not a poorhouse', their efforts were generally in vain.[24] In England the strategy was more enforceable – not least because the 'paupers' could be moved on to America!

Hence the ability of the Anglo-Jewish establishment to control the sluice gates of immigration into England (albeit, at times the gates could not hold back the flood) makes the Jewish East End a quite unique community in the history of modern Jewish settlement. For, unlike the Jewish enclaves in other parts of the United Kingdom, the Jewish East End was large enough to form a coherent economic and social unit, that had all the trappings of the traditional Eastern European 'ghetto'. Yet precisely because this ghetto was in the heart of the most advanced capitalist economy in the world, its traditional characteristics dissolved within a generation. On the other hand, the East End was not an 'immigrant ghetto' like those in the United States, precisely because it stood mid-way between the Old World and the New. As such, the Jewish East End took on the characteristics of a balancing reservoir in the international flow of emigration and resettlement.

And yet for all its success in controlling Jewish immigration into Britain, the Anglo-Jewish establishment's strategy of 'making the immigrants invisible' did not fully succeed. The issue of Jewish immigration did provoke a reaction in Britain, which drew upon familiar anti-Semitic motifs. Equally the Anglo-Jewish oligarchy's attempt to ride the tiger of the anti-alien movement, by 'holding back' Jewish immigration and supporting a restrictionist policy, failed to prevent the issue of 'race' from being poked on to the wider political agenda. Indeed, the passing of the Aliens Act in 1905, far from merely closing a 'loophole' in immigration policy, was to open up a new chapter in the history of 'race' in Britain.

NOTES

1 Harold Pollins, *Economic History of the Jews in England* (London, 1982), p. 142.
2 Isaac Stone in *The Polish Yidel*, September 1884, quoted by Lloyd Gartner, *The Jewish Immigrant in England: 1870–1914* (London, 1960), p. 71.
3 See the Charity Organisation Society, *The Homeless Poor of London* (London, 1891), p. 18.
4 According to the 1881 census, 64 per cent of the population of Whitechapel were London-born. This rose to 71 per cent in Stepney

and to 84 per cent in Bethnal Green. The percentages living in poverty (according to Booth) were 39 per cent, 38 per cent and 45 per cent. See Gareth Stedman Jones, *Outcast London* (Oxford, 1971), p. 132.

5 See page 23.
6 Chaim Bermant, *Point of Arrival* (London, 1975), p. 140.
7 See p. 24. Hence, of 650 Jews who arrived from Romania in June 1900, 426 'definitely left the United Kingdom, through the medium of the Shelter, within five weeks of the arrival of the first party'. ibid. Generally, immigrants who intended travelling on to America took passage to the north-east of England, and travelled by rail to Liverpool.
8 See Stanley Kaplan, 'The Anglicisation of the East European Jewish Immigrant as Seen by the London *Jewish Chronicle* 1870–1897' in *YIVO Annual of Jewish Social Science*, 1955, p. 270.
9 See Chapter 2, p. 21 and n. 14.
10 The average loan was just over £7.00. Jerry White (*Rothschild Buildings*, London, 1980, p. 257) calculates these figures from V. D. Lipman, *A Century of Social Services 1859–1959*.
11 See William Fishman, *East End Jewish Radicals, 1875–1914* (London, 1975), p. 166.
12 For the Jewish socialist movement in the East End, see ibid. For labour and socialism in London at the turn of the century, see Paul Thompson, *Socialists, Liberals and Labour: The Struggle for London, 1885–1914* (London, 1967).
13 White, op. cit., p. 212.
14 ibid., p. 252.
15 Nathan Glazer, 'The American Jew and the Attainment of Middle-Class Rank: Some Trends and Explanations', in Marshal Sklare (ed.) *The Jews: Social Patterns of an American Group* (Glencoe, 1960), p. 144.
16 Details in Colin Holmes, *Anti-Semitism in British Society 1876–1939* (London, 1979), pp. 99–100.
17 ibid., p. 16.
18 Nathan Glazer, op. cit., p. 140, notes that immigrant Jews in America have been especially successful in adapting to an unfettered capitalist system. In particular, Glazer alludes to Abraham Cahan's story, 'The Rise of David Lavinsky', in which the young Jewish immigrant 'gets ahead' by producing clothes more cheaply than his established competitors. Glazer points out that 'only a rare businessman would not buy Levinsky's goods because of his accent'! Whilst this observation holds true for conditions in the USA, it might be observed of Europe that only a rare businessman would not see a Jewish competitor ruined by populist boycotts, or by wholesale expropriations of Jewish businesses and property! Hence it is not capitalism which guarantees the 'right of free competition', but the historical form of the state.
19 Again, Nathan Glazer has commented, in the case of immigrant Jews in America, that: 'The American Jew tries to avoid getting into a

situation where disrimination may seriously affect him', a most perceptive comment on the settlement strategy that has been adopted by Jews in the New World. ibid.

20 The quote, from *Trades Union Congress Report*, 1894, continues, 'and though they did not seem to earn any wages, they often in a short time were able to set themselves up in business. . .these people were incorrigible. . .they were either sweaters or sweated'. See p. 59.

21 Over 60 million souls according to Maurice Davie, *World Immigration* (New York, 1936), p. 12.

22 See Chapter 1, n. 5.

23 Figures from Bernard Weinryb, 'Jewish Immigration and Accommodation to America' in Sklare, op. cit., p. 4.

24 Quotations from the USA's German-Jewish leadership at the time of the 1881–2 pogroms in Russia, see ibid., p. 17. The Conference of the Managers of the Associated Hebrew Charities in 1886 condemned 'the transportation of paupers into this country [America]. . .all such as unable to maintain themselves should be forthwith returned whence they came' (ibid.). And indeed Jewish immigrants were returned to Eastern Europe by the Jewish Agent of the United Hebrew Charities at the Port of New York, sometimes on cattle-steamers.

Part II

CARIBBEAN SETTLEMENT IN BIRMINGHAM, 1939–1965

And the Lord God planted a Garden eastward in Eden.
(Genesis 2, 7)

7

PARADISE LOST

The West Indies have been shaped by the sea, and peopled by ocean wanderers. The islands were first settled by the Ciboney Indians, and later by the Arawaks and the Caribs, who sailed their canoes from the mainland of South America to the Caribbean islands during the first millennium AD. At the end of the fifteenth century, galleons dropped anchor off the shores of the islands, their Spanish crews seeking gold to plunder and souls to save. They were followed in the sixteenth century by English, French and Dutch seafarers, who came to pillage and loot the new-found wealth. In the seventeenth and eighteenth centuries came the traders in human cargoes. They landed slaves torn from Africa, loaded sugar, spices and rum, and returned to Europe with the holds of their ships stained black by blood and molasses. And as the nineteenth century drew to an end, the descendants of those same slaves set sail again, in ships that shuffled their human cargoes around the Caribbean in search of sugar plantations which offered work, and the promise of a better life.

SUGAR AND SPICE

In 1844 the English novelist Anthony Trollope visited the West Indies to report for the civil service. He concluded that 'if we could, we would fain forget Jamaica altogether. . .but. . .it belongs to us and must in some sort be thought of and managed and possibly governed'.[1] Trollope's report reflected a new attitude to colonial possessions, as the forces of English manufacture began to dominate British trade policy. For as the free trade lobby swept away tariffs and protectionism at home, swept away too were price guarantees for the West Indies staple crop – sugar cane. Indeed, long before the end of the nineteenth century, British imperialism was looking eastwards to the new 'jewels' of empire in Africa and India. The Caribbean became a backwater of colonial policy – its sugar industry in crisis; its local industries under-developed; its governance a matter of only slight significance for the British Crown.

For a time, at the turn of the nineteenth century, King Sugar reigned in Cuba, where American investment in new technology made estate production profitable once again. But within little more than a decade Cuba's sugar industry too went into decline. Unemployment soared. Jamaican migrants who had settled in Cuba were deported, although some 40,000 stayed to make their home on the island.[2]

In the years before the outbreak of the First World War, thousands more left their homes in the West Indies to build the Panama Canal. By 1912, over 40,000 black labourers, mainly from Barbados and Jamaica, were providing the muscle power for the massive project. Working six days a week for one dollar a day in temperatures that reached 120 degrees farenheit, the West Indian workers ensured that the canal was built on-time and within budget. But at a terrible human cost. The canal claimed the lives of over four thousand black workers – victims of disease, dehydration, mud-slides, crush-injuries and a succession of accidents involving unstable industrial explosives.[3]

Jamaicans also travelled to Costa Rica, where they built the Northern Railway, as well as to Venezuela and the United States. But international recession in the 1920s, followed by slump in the 1930s, led to restrictions upon immigration in both Venezuela (1924) and the USA (1929). For those left behind in Jamaica, the grim absurdity of colonial dependency and international crisis was clear:

> In the 1920s and 1930s there wasn't a lot of money. But we had food. Food to spare! Not even the pigs didn't want!
>
> But for instance my dad grew a lot of cane and banana, ginger and coffee, and cocoa, and all those things. And there wasn't any price for them. The price was penny farthing, penny ha'penny, twopence a pound for ginger and coffee.

And banana? You could take a couple of truck loads to the shipping station, and sometimes when you take it they are closed! You dump it some place 'cos you can't take it back. The price in them days was really shockin'. You see, Britain controlled the price and you take it or leave it. You have no say. Whatever price they say. You couldn't say you're going to take it and store it somewhere else. There was nowhere else to take it![4]

THE SECOND MIGRATION

During the Second World War the expansion of British and American military bases on the Caribbean islands provided new employment opportunities. Seven thousand West Indians joined the RAF as technicians and ground staff, and together with some 350 workers destined for the munition factories of Liverpool under the Overseas Volunteers Programme they journeyed to Britain to play their part in the war effort.[5]

In Jamaica itself, though, the cost of living more than doubled during the war years, and the immediate post-war period was a time of increasing hardship and political unrest. The early months of 1948 saw a rise in industrial militancy, with a bus workers' strike in March setting off a wave of bombings which threatened to explode into virtual civil war.

At the heart of the political crisis was the instability of the colonial economy and the insecurity of employment. Jamaica was once again guaranteed prices for sugar, bananas and citrus fruits by Britain. But under the Commonwealth Sugar Agreement approximately three quarters of the cane harvest was bought for a negotiated sum – itself determined by the world market price which fluctuated wildly from year to year. A cash-crop economy ensured under-development of the island's resources: Jamaica's import bill was double that of its export earnings.

Between 1946 and 1950 the sugar industry suffered from serious over-production. In Jamaica, sugar was the livelihood of thousands of peasant farmers who worked tiny family plots. The peasant farmers sold their sugar to estate farmers, whose factories processed and exported the peasants' sugar with their own. But at times of low demand, the market for the small producers disappeared. Small wonder then that many young people drifted from the land to the towns, seeking work as day-labourers, as drivers and dockers, or as clerks and messengers. Others were forced to sign short-term contracts as farm-hands in the USA:[6]

> We were in farming – yam, bananas. Just a small farm. . .for me, my parents, four sisters and a brother.
>
> So I went to the United States for three years. . .Farm work in Wisconsin, Florida, New Jersey, picking fruit. . .
>
> What they did – they gave some farm-workers' cards out in the vicinity. If you're well-known you get one and you go for a test – in Jamaica, by the Ministry. What they do is they sell a contract going out for three years. They took perhaps twenty, thirty men to pick citrus.[7]

The work was hard, and the memory of it lived on in the family:

> My Dad first went over to America for a couple of years in the fifties. He worked in Florida. . .in total for about three years. . .He said it was hard, it was hot and he had to work all day. But at that time there was hardly any work in Jamaica.[8]

For these migrant workers, the United States meant more than long hours of work and isolation. It was also a bitter introduction to racism:

> One thing I remember was the atmosphere of racial tension in America. . .In those days, in certain parts you just can't go. In Georgia, when we were travelling on a coach from Florida, we had to have our refreshments pushed through a pigeon-hole.
>
> When the Americans came out to Jamaica, we all mix like one. But when you get there it's a different thing. It come as really a shock.[9]

In 1952 the Colonial Report on Jamaica summed up the achievements of British colonial policy on the island:

> Every year some 6,000 attain school-leaving age without entering a school and join the mass of illiterates. . .the national exchequer cannot carry the burden of extending the present standard to the 50,000 who have no standard at all. This briefly is the perennial problem for Jamaican education.[10]

Wage rates on the island were also detailed. Workers in the sugar industry, when they could find work, earned from 6s. to 9s. 6d. a day – perhaps £2 to £2 10s. (£2.50) a week. A woman domestic servant would earn 16s. 6d. (82 pence) a week. Indeed, for women the problem of unemployment was even more severe:

> I left local school [in Jamaica] when I was 15 with the First Year exam. I wanted to become a teacher. I trained for a year, but it was hopeless. I had no chance of a job in Jamaica . . .in fact I never really had a proper job before coming [to England] to join my husband.[11]

THE NEW MIGRATION

Among the West Indians who worked in Britain during the Second World War, many opted to stay on, realising that their technical skills could bring them employment in the peace-time economy. Those returning to the West Indies discovered that the islands were no place for heroes. Promises of help and financial assistance for the Jamaicans who had served in the British armed forces during the Second World War rapidly evaporated. Seven years after the end of the war only 236 had been granted either financial or educational help, whilst 1,247 still awaited 'resettlement'.[12] Despairing of government help, some took ship and returned to Britain. A Colonial Welfare Officer in England drily noted that 'in consequence of conditions prevailing in the West Indies, men previously repatriated by this department have returned to this country'.[13] A 38-year-old Jamaican charged in Bristol with stowing away on a ship put his position more eloquently:

> We had to get work or starve. The economic conditions in Jamaica are deplorable and there is absolutely no work. I am married with five children and I have been unemployed for three years. My life savings are diminished and I have parted with all my belongings.[14]

Of course, economic and social conditions varied from island to island. The unemployment situation in Jamaica was worse than elsewhere. On average about one quarter of Jamaica's population were unemployed in the late 1940s and 1950s: a figure four times higher than that of Barbados, Trinidad and

89

Tobago.[15] Among the smaller islands, emigration in the mid 1950s and early 1960s actually created a labour shortage, especially of skilled workers.

THE *WINDRUSH*

Early on 24 May 1948 the *Empire Windrush*, an old Nazi 'Strength Through Joy' cruiser which had become a British prize during the war, sailed into the Royal Mail Wharf at Kingston. On board were some 200 Jamaican airmen, demobilised from the RAF and returning to their homeland.

Three days later the *Windrush* sailed for Mexico, to land a band of hopeful Polish emigrants, and after that she docked in Bermuda before setting out on the homeward journey. On board were ten stowaways and some 400 Jamaican migrants bound for a 'new life' in England.

In London the telephone lines were soon humming with the news of the Jamaican emigration. The Minister of Labour, George Isaacs, complained that:

> The arrival of these substantial numbers of men under no organised arrangement is bound to result in considerable difficulty and disappointment. I hope that no encouragement will be given to others to follow their example.

On 16 June, under a deluge of enquiries about what would happen to the West Indian migrants in Britain, Creech Jones, the Colonial Secretary, announced that: 'We recognise the need for some vetting, but obviously we cannot interfere with the movement of British subjects.' And he added: 'It is very unlikely that a similar event to this will occur again in the West Indies.'[16] On both counts Creech Jones was to be proved wrong.

During the night of 21 June the *Windrush* edged up the Thames and weighed anchor off Tilbury. On board 400 young men from the West Indies caught their first glimpse of England from the quays of Tilbury Docks. Unlike the tens of thousands of poor Jewish immigrants who had thronged the docks at Tilbury some fifty years earlier, the West Indians were 'coming home' to England. They were citizens of the British Empire, and England was the 'Mother Country'.

NOTES

1 See Joyce Egginton, *They Seek a Living* (London, 1957), p. 31.
2 ibid., p. 36.
3 Again, many thousands stayed on to become Panamanian nationals after the completion of the canal.
4 Interview in Birmingham, 4.11.1988.
5 See E.J.B. Rose *et al.*, *Colour and Citizenship* (London, 1969), p. 66.
6 This was the legacy of the McCarran–Walter Act in 1952, restricting Jamaican emigration to the USA to 100 per year. During the Second World War about 50,000 farm-workers were recruited from the West Indies to work in the United States. Ibid., p. 67.
7 Interview in Birmingham, 23.5.1988.
8 Interview in Birmingham, 17.5.1987.
9 Interview in Birmingham, 23.5.1988.
10 Egginton, op. cit., p. 48.
11 Fircroft Survey, 9.5.1955.
12 Egginton, op cit., p. 49.
13 ibid., p. 53.
14 ibid., p. 54.
15 See Ceri Peach, *West Indian Migration to Britain: A Social Geography* (London, 1968), p. 24, for details of 1943 and 1946 censuses. Conditions in Jamaica may have been 'deplorable', yet between 1953 and 1962, at the height of the emigration, Peach notes that Jamaica experienced 'one of the world's highest rates of economic growth' (ibid., p. 27).
16 Egginton, op. cit., pp. 60–1.

CASE STUDIES

Seeking work

Len Bailey * interviewed 16.8.1988. (Here and throughout * denotes fictionalised name. See Bibliography, 'Ethnographic Material', pp. 206–7.)

I couldn't see myself achieving or getting anything where I was in St Kitts. I left school at nearly 16 and I taught for about two months. My work was unpaid, but I did it, hoping the headmaster would hire me as a full-time teacher. But he didn't!

My father died when I was 14 and my mother was very ill. She died when I was 15. So I left home and went to work in Caruso and St Thomas. But I needed a work permit and I never had one of those.

I told my family, my auntie, that I was going to Caruso to look for work, but I secretly bought a ticket from Caruso to St Thomas. When I got

91

to St Thomas, I didn't know anybody. . .Everywhere I went, I wrote down the street name, but I still got lost.

The first person I met there was the Immigration Officer. He told me I could not work, only have a vacation. So if I saw there was work, for one hour even, I couldn't take it! He said if I was caught, then I'd end up in jail. The jail was on the seafront, and all the time you could hear the prisoners bawling that the water was hitting them, and that they were hungry.

Eventually I met a wonderful woman who allowed me to live in one of her rooms. She cooked for me, and washed my clothes for me, and only when I started working did she take rent from me. I could have cut cane, but she made me wait until I got a job driving a tractor. When anybody asked me how long I had, I didn't tell them I had twenty-nine days, I told them I had six months. You see there was a group of men from St Lucia who had permission to vacate in the country for six months – not to work, you see – but like me, they worked cutting cane and building.

Now the Immigration men used to travel round in trucks. But you could always distinguish them, because they had white number-plates. No other cars had white number plates! When they came for anybody working illegally I could see men run into the cane, just scatter, run anywhere, anyplace! One man, Marcel, ran into the sea up to his neck; and he couldn't swim!!

I never run, because I had become really cool and realised if I didn't run, I wouldn't draw attention to myself. . .How I got caught was when a man who was working with me told. His wife had an affair with one of the working men from St Lucia. So, out of revenge, he reported me.

I was called to the Immigration Department. . .When I got there, the officer said to me, 'Aren't you the man I spoke to before?' I said, 'I think so, I'm not certain.' He said, 'I'm certain!'

From there, I went back home to where I'd lived before. . .There was nothing there that I could do, so I decided to go to England.

A childhood on St Kitts

Douglas Thomas* interviewed 2.9.1988.

It was a carefree life. We used to go down to the village to have a shower . . .in the middle of the village, every morning, you know!

Everyone used to have a khaki [school] uniform, because it was hard-wearing. You used to take your own chair or stool to school. The books were yours, and you had to buy your exercise books. There were a couple of white children there too. The plantation owners used to send *their kids to the same school. The others used to send their kids to town. . . You didn't take much notice. All you knew was that they were slightly richer than you. I mean, there were some black kids who had more money than the average, and they used to get picked on just as much as the few white ones that were there.*

I was poor. . .but we had enough to keep us happy. We used to have a couple of sheep. We used to take them to the pasture in the morning. . . After school you'd go to the pasture and spend a couple of hours, come back and have a wash, sit around. . .At the weekend it was mainly church; that was the highlight of our week!

You couldn't starve on St Kitts, because of all the fruit that grew in the mountains. You didn't have to buy it, you just go and take it. Sort of mangoes, oranges. I mean, you name it! We used to bring back buckets' full and sit down and eat and eat. There was always someone who would give you something.

My grandmother brought me up, with partly the help of my auntie as well. My grandmother was having to bring up three boys. We got a lot of help from church members, things like that. . .

My parents left St Kitts round about fifty-eight [1958]. They came to England. They had to save up till they could afford to send for all of us, which they did gradually. They didn't send for us all at the same time. We younger ones were left till last.

My grandmother? Perhaps she had something to prove. She wasn't one to spare the rod and spoil the child. . .I can't remember what my father was like, but he mellowed a lot after he came to England. At least there was all the stories that you used to hear, about what he'd do if we did this or that. . .!

Getting ahead

Henry McCleod* interviewed 8.7.1988.

I was born in Jamaica. I leave the country part where I was born and went to live in the city. I was born in the parish of Claringdon on 10 October 1919. I leave school when I was 13. I could have gone on further, but as a matter of fact I didn't like school really. So I went to live in Kingston with an aunt of mine and I begin to work then. In those days if you got a job at three bob a week as a young boy you think that was good wage.

I was born into a family of eight, six boy and two girl, and two of the boy died at an early age. My parents were farmers. . .lot of land and

93

cattle, and a lot of food. I didn't like the farming life at all, but my Dad he was keen that I go into that line.

I went into Kingston and I start to work in small ways. . .I start off working with an Indo-Chinese food wholesaler, probably for a year, year and a half, but the money was too small and I move on to other wholesale place. In those days the Chinese were big business, and some areas in Kingston were controlled by Chinese – massive warehouses and wholesale places. So you can leave one and move to another. I have a bicycle with a carrier on the front and I pack it with small things to deliver, and I take it around different places. And I also work in the store packing things for people who have big orders, people from the country, you know.

Well I work in that line of business for quite a while – ten years or something like that. I move on to work at a bakery. This bakery does supply bread all over the country. . .so I have a driver and I do the delivering. I check in in the morning. Look out how much bun, bread, cake, you know, and probably get back at midnight. I work in that for a while until the war start.

[In our free time] we go to sports, cycle sports about three times a week – Wednesday, Friday and Saturday. It was a big sport like horse racing here. . .Bookmakers all round the place, and [you] put a bet on. . .We gone to clubs and the seaside. There was a lot of people coming and going from America, and that stimulated the music. . .everywhere you walk on the street you hear music. . .they hang it all on the trees, they call it Rediffusion. You go and you buy one for a couple of quid. Everywhere you walk it's blaring out!

Then I leave the bakery where I was working. When the war start I went to work at the Wills [cigarette factory] – they had a branch in Jamaica. Then in 1941 I went to work with the REME [Royal Electrical and Mechanical Engineers]. They were advertising for people to come and work in the army, so I went to work in the Textile Department, look after all the material, tents, leather-work, anything that the soldiers. . .kits that need repair – right in the camp. I worked there until the war finished then I went back to my firm – the cigarette firm. I worked there until I come to England.

The war opened up avenues for employment, because they had the airbase and various point that the army occupied, and the navy, both American and English. . .People mix with one another. I don't know of any instances of a racial issue. . .In the army you have black and white and I never came across any resentment. And I never know what racial discrimination is until I came into this country.

94

There were people coming to England, coming back from England. Some people that I have known, some lads, come and didn't spend more than six months and says, 'Oh no, that's not the place for me!' and then come back. Even chaps that were working in the same firm that I was working in, you know, we worked together, in six months' time they came back. They advise me, don't go there, it's not a nice place. That didn't go down well, but for some reason the feeling just develop in me to move on, to travel. I mean I need not. I work with a reputable firm. . .you get the highest wages. And when I put in my resignation, the manager of the firm, he's from Essex, the name was Thompson, and he call me and he said to me 'What are you going to England for?' He said, you have a job, and so forth. He said, 'England's not a bed of roses'. . .He said 'you're going to be sorry, because it won't be what you expect.' He couldn't persuade me either.

8

A CALL TO ARMS

When war is in the air,
West Indians will do their share.
That is why they came,
Not seekin' glory or fame.
They will fight, fight for victory.
Let us raise a cheer,
They will fight, fight and never fear.
Victory is near.

March, march, march to victory.
March, march, march to victory.
Fight land, sea and in the air,
On to victory.

(Song from 1939/40)

FIGHTING FOR FREEDOM

'Yes, I volunteered to fight! We were coming to the aid of the
Mother Country. We were fighting for freedom. But I didn't
have the vote!'[1] Thus the West Indian struggle against European
fascism and racism was summed up by one ex-serviceman.

For many West Indians volunteers, the war years evoke
bitter-sweet memories. Men and women alike answered the plea
of the Mother Country in her 'darkest hour'. They serviced,
armed and repaired the fighter planes that beat back the German
Luftwaffe in Britain's 'finest hour'. And they later flew the aircraft
and provided the technical assistance that inaugurated the
Second Front and brought forward the war's 'final hour'.[2]

Indeed when the West Indian air-crews arrived, they were

welcomed by the nation's leaders and feted by local people alike. Many life-long friendships were forged in those early months. Ken Darricot*, newly arrived in Lancashire from Jamaica, remembered the summer of 1940:

> I was friendly with this guy in our squadron. And when we was on leave he took me home with him, and I stayed with his family. They took me round, everywhere, with them. People were pleased to see us then. You go in a pub, and they'd come round you, offer you a drink, ask what's you doing.[3]

The British Central Office of Information produced a pamphlet entitled *West Indies Towards Victory*, which paid tribute to the invaluable work done by RAF technicians, and recorded the exploits of West Indian airmen in bombing raids over occupied Europe. In fact, many RAF air-crews believed that having a black flight engineer or pilot on board brought them 'good luck' on their missions.

Also recorded and publicised by the wartime Ministry of Information was the work of West Indian munition workers in Britain, especially those on Merseyside and in Lancashire through the Overseas Volunteers Programme. But West Indians worked in the Midlands too. The Midland Motor Company in Smethwick, for instance, employed workers from Jamaica, Barbados and India during the war years, beginning in 1940. Aproximately 70 per cent of the castings for the British army's tanks were supplied by this firm, and in 1954 the firm's Sales Director commented that 'if they [black workers] had not been available during the earlier part of the war, production would have been seriously impaired'. Birmingham Aluminium Casting Ltd in Smethwick also employed West Indian and Indian workers during the war years; they were engaged as machine millers, producing parts for aircraft engines.[4] Not so well recorded was the work of West Indian nurses in home and field hospitals, and the service of many West Indian women in various organisations active on the Home Front.

But as the threat of Nazi occupation passed, the official celebration of a popular struggle against fascism by 'all the peoples of the Empire' began to falter. The rhetoric of race and class began to creep back into government pronouncements. In

October 1941 Winston Churchill informed the boys of Harrow school that 'these are great days – the greatest days our country has ever lived; and we must thank God that we have been allowed, *each according to our stations*, to play a part in making these days memorable *in the history of our race* [my emphasis].'[5]

However, it was the arrival of American servicemen in Britain in 1942 that saw the greatest change in attitudes towards black colonial servicemen and workers, creating pressure to formalise segregation within institutions as diverse as the soldiers' mess, public swimming pools and dance halls. 'We the Negroes', wrote a West Indian munitions worker in 1942,

> had to suffer quite a lot. . .when we first came here, but now it's worse. The Americans have got some power over things that I can't understand. There used to be a few dance halls that we could go to after a week's work. . .Now when we enter these halls all one can hear is 'No Negroes'. When we ask why, this is always the answer, 'Well, you see, the Americans don't like the Negroes in the same place where they have fun.'[6]

Even black American GIs, accustomed to Jim Crow segregation within their own units, noticed that white American servicemen had 'poisoned the mind of the few British people', because they 'have tried to instill their ways and actions over here and try to make the English do things like they have done'.[7]

So by VE (Victory in Europe) Day 1945, getting a drink was not so easy for Sergeant Ken Darricot:

> I remember just after VE Day. I was in Birmingham, out with some of the guys celebrating. Well, it was a posh place, and when it was my turn to buy the round I went to the bar. The man looked at me and said, 'Sorry I can't serve no coloured folk in here – you'll have to go into the other bar.' That hadn't never happened before – but it happened many times after that.[8]

Indeed if the question most asked of West Indian servicemen in 1940 had been a friendly, 'Where do you come from?', as the war drew to a close this question became a terse 'When are you going back?'

In fact, the issue of 'going home' began to occupy the minds of many West Indian workers and servicemen as soon as it became clear that victory against the Nazi regime was merely a matter of time. Even at the end of 1944, the demand for labour in the munition factories was beginning to slacken. The overtime and bonus payments that permitted many West Indian workers to send money to their families at home began to dry up. For some, especially on Merseyside, the winter of 1944 brought the threat of redundancy. By 1945, semi-skilled West Indian workers were having to move outside Merseyside and Lancashire to find work. 'There is a tendency [for the West Indian workers]. . .to move away to the south of England', reported a Liverpool welfare officer in May 1945. 'This action is not encouraged, but it is difficult to intervene when. . .the men can seek and find their own jobs in their new surroundings.'[9] Above all, it was the Midlands that beckoned with the offer of work.

THE BEGINNING OF MIGRATION

Most of the technicians and ground crews who had served in the RAF in Britain were returned to the West Indies before being demobilised. Flight crews, on the other hand, were usually demobilised in England, and in many cases they were offered further training or courses in British education institutions.

The war years, however, had brought new experiences and created new expectations for all those who had made the journey to Britain. Those who returned to the islands could reminisce about their time in the Mother Country – which in the context of conditions in the Caribbean took on an added glow. Those who stayed in England kept up a correspondence, informing friends and relatives back home about their fortunes in the new land. There was now a pool of information about jobs and accommodation in Britain, and there was a network of pioneer settlements in many English cities. As such, the war years and service in the Mother Country had created the preconditions for a more substantial migration.

But although the network of pioneer settlements in Britain, and the lack of opportunity in the West Indies created the preconditions for migration, it was the shortage of labour in Britain in the early 1950s that set off the chain reaction of Caribbean emigration. The voyage of the *Empire Windrush* in

1948 was repeated by other ships bringing Caribbean migrants. But until 1950, less than 1,000 West Indians arrived in Britain each year – among them a number of stowaways who were sent back to the Caribbean anyway.[10] Even in 1953, only 3,000 migrants made the journey to Britain from the West Indies. After 1953, however, migration quickly gathered momentum, 'pulled' by the increasing demand for labour power in the industrial regions of England, and 'pushed' by Caribbean poverty and the imposition of new immigration restrictions in the United States.

In fact there is a consistent correlation between migration from the Caribbean islands and labour shortage in Britain during the 1950s and early 1960s. Between 1948 and 1968 there were four waves of economic expansion and recession in Britain. Boom periods peaked in the years 1951, 1955, 1960 and 1965. Recession bottomed out in 1953, 1958, 1962 and 1967, although even in these years unemployment remained historically very low. And it is significant that although West Indian migration, and black immigration in general, gradually increased in volume between the early 1950s and the early 1960s, year by year totals tended to reflect the cycle of economic expansion and recession, at least until the threat of immigration restrictions distorted the process in 1962. Thus migration from Jamaica reached a peak of nearly 18,000 per annum during the peak of the second boom cycle in 1955, dropping to just over 10,000 per annum in the recession year of 1958, and rose again to almost 30,000 per annum in the next boom year of 1960.[11]

Most of the early post-war Caribbean migrants settled in Greater London. The dominance of London as a centre of settlement was historical, for, with its vast financial and administrative infrastructure, the capital had always acted as a magnet for professional classes from the Caribbean.[12] But by the beginning of the 1950s, a new Caribbean capital was emerging in England, especially for Jamaican migrants. This was Birmingham – Second City of the Empire, and the capital of Britain's industrial heartland.

At the time, few West Indian migrants realised that Birmingham had already played its part in shaping their lives. Yet Birmingham's prosperity in the mid-twentieth century was built upon the triangular trade with Western Africa and the New World in the eighteenth and nineteenth centuries.

100

NOTES

1 Interview, 23.3.1988.
2 Speeches of Winston Churchill, 13.5.1940, 18.6.1940, 27.12.1944, in *Dawn of Liberation: Winston S. Churchill's War Speeches*, compiled by Charles Eade (London, 1945).
3 Interview recorded 14.5.1988.
4 Fircroft Survey. See Appendix A.
5 Winston Churchill, 29.10.1941, in *Dawn of Liberation*, op. cit.
6 Anthony Richmond, *Colour Prejudice in Britain* (London, 1954) p. 88.
7 ibid., p. 87. See also Peter Fryer, *Staying Power: The History of Black People in Britain* (London, 1984), p. 358, for details.
8 Interview recorded 14.5.1988.
9 Richmond, op. cit., p. 42.
10 Between 1945 and 1950, an average of 100 stowaways per year landed in Britain; 150 from Jamaica alone in 1950, 25 of whom were sent back. See Colonial Office Records.
11 Figures from Ceri Peach, *West Indian Migration to Britain: A Social Geography* (London, 1968), p. 106.
12 Even more obviously, London was the cultural centre of settlement, variously celebrated in the early 1950s by Lord Kitchener and Cyril Blakes' Calypso Serenaders ('Underground Train') and mourned by Grant-Lyttleton's Paseo Jazz Band ('London Blues').

9

CITY OF IRON

If we have no Negroes, we can have no Sugars, Tobaccoes, Rice, Rum &c. . .consequently the Publick Revenue, arising from the importation of Plantation Produce, must be annihilated: And will this not turn many hundreds of Thousands of British Manufacturers a Begging. . .?[1]

In the twilight of the Middle Ages Birmingham was little more than a market town of regional significance. But by the beginning of the seventeenth century the town was the centre of a burgeoning metal-working industry. Birmingham was unusual in being free of guild restrictions upon commerce, and fortunate in lying near the Tame valley which provided water-power for forges and mills. In 1610 the area was described as 'full of inhabitants and resounding with hammers and anvils, for the most of them are Smiths'.[2]

In 1619 the first African slaves were sold in the British American colonies.[3] Although English involvement with the slave trade was fitful at first, the elimination of African trade monopolies in 1698 put Birmingham into a unique position to exploit the markets opening up because of the triangular trade between Britain, Western Africa and the American colonies. In particular the inexorable growth in the demand for slave guns gave the Birmingham arms manufacturers, whose techniques of mass assembly and flexible sub-contracting undercut both British and continental rivals, a massive boost in profitability.

By the end of the eighteenth century some 5,000 Birmingham people were employed in the slave gun trade, sending on average some 150,000 guns each year to the African coast.[4] Such guns, however, were not used by the slave traders as weapons of war, but purchased en masse as barter for slaves along the African coast. Many slave guns were of appalling quality, harmless, according to one contemporary observer, 'except to the luckless wight who should load and fire them'.[5] And the slave trader John Newton confirmed that, in dealing with African traders for slaves,

> Not an article that is capable of diminution or adulteration is delivered genuine or entire. . .the natives are cheated, in the number, weight, measure, or quantity of what they purchase, in every possible way.[6]

None the less, the increasing price of slaves in the mid eighteenth century gave further impetus to Birmingham manufacturers. On his third slave voyage (1753–4) as master of the *African*, Newton recorded with alarm that 'Captain Boucher. . .tells me he has been obliged to give twelve guns, [and] twelve bags powder. . .to the amount of £19 sterling for a single slave, which I am resolved not to do upon any consideration.'[7] By the turn of the twentieth century aproximately 20 million Birmingham-made guns had been sent to Africa.

Apart from guns, brass and cutlery were also important Birmingham-made exports for the first leg of the triangular trade. But Birmingham was also developing direct trading links with the furthest corners of the Empire. Its metal-working industries produced goods for trade, exchange and colonial settlement – brassware, toys, rivets, buckles and buttons, etc. Rare stones and precious metals brought from afar provided the impetus to the Birmingham jewellery trade.

Nevertheless, the abolition of slave trading within the British Empire in the early nineteenth century created a hiatus in Birmingham's export trades. In June 1806 the renegade Quaker Samuel Galton, together with other Birmingham gun-makers, complained to the Board of Ordnance that with the abolition of the slave trade, they were prevented from dumping the 'Barrels' rejected by the Ordnance on the African market. They demanded – and received – a price increase for the quality Barrels that the Ordnance purchased. Indirectly, though, the abolition of the slave trade forced Birmingham manufacturers to improve quality and concentrate upon high-value production.

As the city developed new specialist trades, and the reputation of Birmingham-produced goods improved, so the heavier metal-working industries and forges tended to be lost to the Black Country. Birmingham's economy, by the mid-nineteenth century, was securely founded. Indigenous entrepreneurs built manufacturing empires upon the skills of local artisans. Profits were invested locally, first in the canal system and later the railway network. Birmingham became the hub of the Midland's industrial and transport infrastructure, and the most important centre for commerce and banking outside London.

By the end of the nineteenth century, Birmingham possessed a world-wide reputation for quality engineering. After the First World War, the bicycle, motor cycle and motor-car industries also gained in importance. By the 1930s, Birmingham was England's largest provincial city, with a population exceeding 1 million – a result of sustained immigration from outlying regions at the beginning of the century.

THE POST-WAR ERA

The Great Depression led to economic stagnation and a severe curtailment of migration into the city. But the Second World War saw a major economic revival, with much of Birmingham industry thriving on the munitions boom. The long-term effects of the war, however, were more serious, and it was not until the early 1950s that the economy of Birmingham and the West Midlands was able to extricate itself from the ravages of conflict and the years of constriction that followed.

The peak of the first major boom in the British economy in the post-war era was reached in 1951. In that year the great mass of Birmingham's working population was still employed in manufacturing industry. Engineering and metal goods industries employed one quarter of the city's labour force; motor vehicle and bicycle manufacture employed nearly 10 per cent, with another 5 per cent producing accessories.[8] Unemployment in Birmingham dropped to an all-time low of 0.3 per cent in that year, compared with the national average of just under 1 per cent. Male earnings in the city were about 5 per cent higher than the national average and women's employment was substantial in comparison to other regions. Basic wage rates were historically high, overtime was plentiful and, as a result, family incomes were over 10 per cent higher than the average for Great Britain.[9] Nevertheless, the booming metal and engineering industries demanded yet more labour, and the conditions were ripe for a new wave of immigration into the city.

CARIBBEAN PIONEERS

Although during the Second World War several hundred West Indian servicemen were stationed in the West Midlands, by 1948 perhaps only 100 West Indians remained in the Birmingham area. The majority were ex-servicemen, only recently demobilised, and unsure of their prospects back home. A few were munitions workers who had moved south from Merseyside.

In June 1948, just one week before the *Empire Windrush* docked at Tilbury, Creech Jones was questioned by Percy Shurmer, Labour MP for Sparkbrook, about the difficulties faced by 'students and factory workers from the African and West Indian colonies in Birmingham, who, on account of the shortage of accommodation, *plus the colour bar* [my emphasis], cannot get lodgings'.[10] Creech Jones replied that the 60 colonial students in Birmingham were being looked after by the university authorities and the British Council. The 'colonial workers', however, presented a different problem:

> These men have had accommodation difficulties because apart from the normal housing shortage, they have arrived in the city in batches and without warning. The prospects of employment have of course taken them to the Midlands.
>
> Notwithstanding the difficulties, these men have been made welcome.[11]

In fact almost all these 'colonial workers' were living in overcrowded hostel accommodation. Fifty West Indian workers were accommodated at the Causeway Green Hostel, and others found room at the Salvation Army Hostel and Rowton House. But the largest hostel in the city refused to take black residents, and another imposed a maximum quota of six; indeed some months earlier their plight had been such that a number had been put up in the Free Shelter at Winson Green.

Only as emigration from the West Indies gradually gathered momentum after the war did the small Caribbean population of

Birmingham begin to multiply. By 1951, at the height of the first post-war boom, there were several hundred West Indians living in Birmingham,[12] among them undergraduates, post-graduate students and a small number of doctors. Women from the Caribbean, especially nurses, were beginning to develop career structures in Birmingham, where Dudley Road Hospital and Yardley Sanatorium were recognised as centres particularly committed to the training of black professionals.[13]

By 1955, at the peak of the next trade boom, there were perhaps 6,000 West Indians living in the city.[14] The first systematic (if somewhat unreliable) census returns in 1961 estimate that 16,290 migrants from the British Caribbean territories were living in Birmingham, with another 10,000 resident in other parts of the West Midlands, out of a total Caribbean population of over 150,000.[15]

Above all, Birmingham was to become the English capital of Jamaica. About one quarter of all Jamaican migrants in Britain lived in the West Midlands, where they outnumbered other Caribbean islanders by four to one. By way of contrast, Jamaicans were only just a majority in London. Indeed, although London remained the centre of Caribbean settlement in the post-war era, by the mid-1950s the dynamics of labour demand had begun to exert a powerful influence upon the patterns of West Indian settlement in Britain. Skilled workers in particular were drawn to the West Midlands' engineering industries.

Len Pickard* from Jamaica had served for seven years in the RAF before arriving in Birmingham in 1949 at the age of 26. He chose Birmingham because:

> It was known as a centre of industry. I thought I could get a technical training for a better job, and I thought I would have the best chance of selecting employment here. I started work as a turner in Aston.[16]

And Michael Fitzwarren* remembered that:

> My father was a carpenter. . .He used to work on the building sites in Jamaica. His uncle taught him the trade. That's why he came over here, with those skills.
>
> He came straight to Birmingham. I asked him why he didn't go to London. . .the rest of my relatives are in

London. . .He said he had heard a lot about Birmingham, and decided to come here.[17]

Virtually none of the first Caribbean migrants came to Birmingham with the intention of staying longer than a few years. Most were aware that job opportunities would fade at a time of recession, and they frequently saw Britain as the first port of call on a longer journey. As John Vance* explained in July 1954:

> I have come to the United Kingdom in the hope of getting to America more easily. I have already been to the USA.
>
> I came to Birmingham because I had a friend who had prepared everything for me.[18]

But in the summer of 1954 business was booming in Birmingham. Outside the factory gates, the noticeboards offered work for all – whether skilled, semi-skilled or unskilled. Labour

Table 9.1 Percentage registered unemployed in June

	Birmingham	Great Britain
1948	0.8	1.4
1949	0.5	0.9
1950	0.4	0.9
1951	0.3	0.9
1952	1.0	2.0
1953	1.1	1.3
1954	0.4	1.1
1955	0.4	0.9
1956	1.6	1.0
1957	1.0	1.1
1958	1.2	1.8
1959	0.9	1.7
1960	0.5	1.3
1961	0.9	1.1
1962	2.0	1.6
1963	1.8	1.9
1964	0.7	1.3
1965	0.5	1.1
1966	0.6	1.0
1967	2.1	2.0
1968	2.1	2.2
1969	1.7	2.2
1970	2.8	2.4

Source: Anthony Sutcliffe and Roger Smith, Birmingham, 1939–1970 (London, 1974), p. 176.

market figures for Birmingham show just how severe the labour shortage was in the city, falling consistently to half of one per cent or less at times of boom, and rarely rising above 2 per cent even at times of recession (see Table 9.1).

For Len Spencer*, newly arrived from the Caribbean:

There was jobs goin' begging! Everywhere there seemed to be shortages. The evening paper had pages of adverts. But I knew what I wanted – I wanted a job as a turner. . .that was what I had done back home. . .

And right outside this factory was a noticeboard. I can see it still. 'Vacancies. . .for fitters, millers and lathe operators.' I thought, right Len, all you have to do is walk right through them gates, and the job's yours.[19]

NOTES

1 Malachy Postlethwayt, 'The African Trade, the Great Pillar and Support of the British Plantation Trade in America' (1745) – quoted in Peter Fryer, *Staying Power: The History of Black People in Britain* (London, 1984, p. 17.

2 William Camden, *Britain, or a Chorographicall Description of the Most Flourishing Kingdomes, England, Scotland, and Ireland*, Part I (1610), p. 567.

3 This event is recorded: 'About the last of August came in a dutch man of warre that sold us twenty Negars'. See Winthrop Jordon, 'Modern Tensions and the Origins of American Slavery' in *Journal of Southern History*, vol. XXVIII (February 1962), p. 18.

4 Details of slave gun manufacture and trading from Fryer, op. cit., Appendix F, 'Birmingham, the Metal Industries, and the Slave Trade', pp. 417–18.

5 ibid., p. 418.

6 See John Newton, *Thoughts Upon the African Slave Trade* (London, 1788).

7 An extract from Newton's log of the voyage, ibid.

8 Other traditional industries such as the jewellery trade, small arms manufacture, battery production and brass-working remained important sectors of the overall economy, although their importance as employers of labour was declining. See Anthony Sutcliffe and Roger Smith, *Birmingham 1939–1970* (London, 1974), pp. 155–7.

9 For instance, male earnings were 5.5 per cent higher than the national average in 1958, according to Census of Production. Family incomes were some 13 per cent above average in 1963. ibid., pp. 169–70.

10 Written Answers to Questions, House of Commons, 9.6.1948.
11 ibid.
12 Sutcliffe and Smith (op. cit., p. 238) estimate 1,000 West Indians and Africans among a total black population of 4,600 in 1952, although the President of the African League in Birmingham estimated in 1951 that there were 1,250 West Indians and 500 Africans in the Birmingham region.
13 These institutions were named in contrast to the negative attitudes displayed by some other hospitals. Information from Dr Piliso, interviewed 2.6.1945. Fircroft Survey. There were, however, instances of racial harassment of black nurses in Birmingham nurses' homes. See Fircroft Survey. In general, an unusual feature of Caribbean migration was the number of single women who left the islands to seek work and training in the United Kingdom, so that even in the early years there was a near balance of male and female migrants, with men just outnumbering women (by five to four) until 1961, and virtual parity being reached in the mid-1960s. See E.J.B. Rose et al., Colour and Citzenship (London 1969), p. 105.
14 This estimate comes from respondents to the Fircroft Survey in 1954–5, and from Birmingham City Council's Lord Mayor, Alderman Gibson. See Dahni Prem, The Parliamentary Leper: A History of Colour Prejudice in Britain (Aligarth, India, 1965) p. 22.
15 Figures taken from Philip N. Jones, The Segregation of Immigrant Communities in the City of Birmingham, University of Hull Occasional Papers in Geography, No. 7, 1961, p. 3, and Rose et al., op. cit., p. 92.
16 Fircroft Survey, 23.5.1955.
17 Interview, 18.6.1988.
18 Fircroft Survey, 8.7.1954.
19 Interview, 30.6.1988.

10

IN THE FOUNDRIES AND THE FACTORIES

> Man for man, West Indians are slightly less intelligent than white workers. . .
>
> West Africans are dull-witted. . .
>
> The Indian workers smelled, were sly, tried to bribe. . .and unlike West Indians, wanted to marry white girls!
>
> Irishmen are lazy, trouble-makers and gamblers, but Irish women are more industrious than English girls. . .[1]

The migrants who came to England from the Caribbean shared a dream. They all hoped, one way or another, to 'better themselves', whether they intended to settle in Britain, to return to the West Indies, or to continue on to the United States. Those who came to Birmingham hoped, for the most part, to prosper in a city famed for its craftmanship and renowned for its highly developed engineering and construction industries. The ladder of labour, reaching from the factory floor to the skilled labour aristocracy, was there to be climbed.

THE LADDER OF LABOUR

It is difficult to estimate precisely the percentage of skilled workers among the West Indian migrants who settled in Birmingham in the 1950s. However, on the basis of a substantial sample, Roberts and Mills estimated that over 60 per cent of male migrants who left Jamaica between 1953 and 1955 were skilled workers.[2] As Birmingham was predominantly a Jamaican centre of settlement, it is reasonable to assume that a majority of Caribbean male migrants in Birmingham in the mid-1950s were qualified in some way for skilled work. Among women from the Caribbean, fewer migrants were recorded as being skilled. Even so, well over 80 per cent of women migrants who left Jamaica in the mid-1950s were in work when they left,[3] and as late as 1962 Francis records a substantial number of clerical workers (630), teachers (210) and nurses (162) among his sample of female Jamaican emigrants.[4]

However, skilled Caribbean migrants could not necessarily afford to await vacancies in their particular trade or occupation upon arrival in England. The cost of migration was nearly £100, and the realities of colonial economic dependency meant that most Caribbean migrants entered Britain already in debt. Almost all needed to pay off the cost of their passage, either to relatives who had loaned the money, or to loan sharks who had lent money at exorbitant rates of interest. These debts had to be cleared, in addition to the monies which settlers in Birmingham were sending home to support their families. Such financial responsibilities put extreme pressure upon migrants to find work immediately upon arrival in England, and to top up basic wages with overtime.

Most of the West Indian migrants interviewed in Birmingham in 1955 expected to stay in England for about five years.[5] Those without skills or formal qualifications, but with youth, motivation and ambition on their side, saw migration to Birmingham as an opportunity to gain vocational skills and educational qualifications which could improve long-term prospects in the Caribbean or in the United States. For those already qualified and experienced, the chronic labour shortage offered the opportunity to earn relatively high wages in the capitalist metropolis, and to re-invest their earnings at home, where hard currency could buy unthought-of comforts. Additionally some respondents indicated that they had come to Birmingham in the hope of circumventing the restrictions of the McCarran–Walter Act,[6] and they intended moving on to the United States.

So in looking at the 'ladder of labour' in Birmingham, it is useful to separate two categories of West Indian migrant workers: those who arrived in Birmingham with vocational and professional skills, and those without industrial skills, but with the potential for promotion into skilled or supervisory posts at a time of labour shortage. In both cases we shall see that employer (and employee) discrimination systematically denied black migrants opportunities to advance up the ladder of labour. But we shall also discover a small group of Caribbean migrants, mainly Jamaican wood-workers, who managed to evade the direct effects of discrimination and find well-paid, skilled work in the furniture, engineering and construction industries.

The black elite

Although London attracted the greatest number of West Indian migrants with professional qualifications, a Caribbean intelligentsia had become established in Birmingham by the mid-1950s. A small number of West Indians who held degrees from British and American universities were practising professionals, especially in medicine. Half a dozen black general practitioners working in Birmingham had flourishing practices with predominantly white clients.[7] There were also West Indian doctors, nurses and medical technicians at the Queen Elizabeth Hospital and at the Birmingham Accident Hospital, in addition to West Indian medical students and student nurses who were training in Birmingham.[8]

Among non-professional workers, it was the West Indian carpenters and joiners who emerged as the black labour aristocracy. In 1955 there were some fifty skilled West Indian wood-workers employed in the Birmingham area, concentrated in the building trade in the Aston and Handsworth districts. These wood-workers, almost exclusively from Jamaica, were a particularly mobile group within the migrant labour force. A number had practised their trade in the USA, and had come to Britain in response to a specific skill shortage in the civil engineering and building industries:

In them days you could earn real good wages, especially with all the overtime that was going because of the boom.

A lot of men came out then. Some worked on the building sites, and especially if you worked 'the lump', you could earn a lot of money. 'Course it was hard work; you more or less slept on the job. But it wasn't only the money. You learned the latest methods of building construction, which meant that you could earn better rates at home, or get work in the United States.

A lot of Jamaicans also worked in the engineering industry, where you didn't need so many of your own tools – mould-making, jobs like that. Very common in Birmingham.[9]

Jamaican wood-workers were highly union-conscious. The branch secretary of the Amalgamated Society of Wood-workers (ASW) in Aston, which counted 12 Jamaicans among its 107 members in 1955, reported that

> when they leave [home] they are told that the important thing to do is to join the trade union and the whole of them [sic] have come to my branch through the interest of their friends and coloured workmates already here. They are very keen on seeing that they get the wage conditions as laid down in the Working Rule Agreement for the Building Industry.[10]

Almost uniquely among the manual classes, West Indian wood-workers generally found skilled work on equal terms with their white counterparts, and an attitude of generosity and acceptance from the craft union, the ASW. An ASW official in Kings Heath confirmed:

> We have two coloured members of Jamaican nationality whose entrance into the Society was necessitated by the fact of their employ. In the one case TASCOS which. . .is a closed shop, and the other a well organised building site. The report as to their being capable craftsmen is good. Whether they experienced any difficulty in seeking employ into a craft such as Carpentery and Joinery I could not say.[11]

Clearly some wood-workers did experience problems in finding skilled work, given the widespread assumption that black workers would not be up to European standards. 'The small number [of black wood-workers] we have are very amicable fellows', reported another ASW official, 'but the standard of craftsmanship are [sic] very much below ours.'[12] Naturally, standards of craftsmanship must have varied, but in general it is clear that the skills of black wood-workers were on a par with those of their white colleagues. A Birmingham cabinet-maker, who was an ASW branch secretary, observed that:

113

At present there are two [West Indian] members at CWS Cabinet Shirley, where I am. There is. . .no colour bar whatsoever. . .I understand from what I have been told [they] are real good workers.[13]

On the other hand, the very mobility of Caribbean wood-workers did create problems for the ASW. In Handsworth it was reported that the union had intervened successfully to ensure that one Jamaican wood-worker was paid the full rate for the job, but since then he had not been heard of, and he was behind with his union dues! Indeed their particular skills seemed to have lent them a mobility which was denied to other black migrants who became trapped in England. One Jamaican wood-worker informed a white colleague that he had come to the United Kingdom to save enough (£125 was mentioned) to go to the USA, since he was unable to migrate direct from Jamaica. And indeed, at the first signs of recession, which came at the end of 1956, these 'birds of industrial passage' seemed to have taken flight, moving on to warmer climes in North America.[14]

The foundry worker

For the great mass of the Caribbean migrants who found employment in Birmingham during the 1950s, however, wage labour involved long hours of tedious menial work in the foundries, factories and assembly plants which had made the city a household name throughout the world.

Work in the foundries was especially unpleasant. As the post-war economic boom gathered momentum, foundries worked around the clock to meet soaring demand for castings for the engineering industries. Ron Melly*, who arrived in Birmingham from Jamaica in 1952, remembered his first shift at the foundry:

It was like a vision of hell! I'd come from this quiet place in . . .(Jamaica) and here was this huge hall, glowing red and yellow, with the smell of burning. . .[and] figures who looked like they was shovelling the lost souls into a great fiery furnace.

No preacher ever described Satan's Kingdom to me better than that place! You know, it scared me so much that I prayed extra at night that I'd never end up in hell!

Ron worked as a caster at the foundry for ten years:

> We called it the 'hospital run', when you took the big ladles
> round. One drop of water – condensation, or sweat – and
> bham! Molten metal flying all over the place. If it hits you,
> it's straight through your clothes and into your skin. There
> was people in that place looked like they'd been in a war.
> Bandages on their faces, arms, legs...
> 'Course they didn't send you to hospital – that would have
> brought in the health and safety people, and they'd probably
> have closed the place down.[15]

In many cases Caribbean workers worked in segregated gangs,
although the method of segregation varied from plant to plant.
Sometimes they worked with other black migrant workers from
India or West Africa; at other times they were rigidly separated
from them:

> I worked at [a firm] in Stechford for a time. The work was
> real hard – lugging the finished castings out on to the lorries.
> All by hand of course – not even a trolly! And they weighed
> a...ton!
> Anyway, at first we was in a gang with some blokes from
> West Africa – Nigeria I think. But later they formed a
> Jamaican gang, and the blokes from West Africa were simply
> given the push. I reckoned they drop us next, so I look for
> another job – you could in them days – and I got a job with
> the corpy working first as a conductor, and later as a driver.
> The money wasn't so good, but the conditions! I mean,
> you got back home late at night, but at least you could still
> stand up![16]

The bus worker

By the end of 1953 shortages of labour within Birmingham's
municipal transport system had become chronic.[17] At a meeting
on 5 January 1954, Birmingham City Transport Committee
heard details of the severe shortages of operating and
engineering staff. Bus services were only being maintained 'with
considerable difficulty by members of staff working long hours
and frequently on their official day off'.[18] There was a shortage
of 1,160 posts. Vacancies included:

115

Drivers	553
Conductors	481
Skilled employees	15
Semi-skilled employees	93
Unskilled employees	18
Total	1160

On 16 March the Transport Committee sanctioned the recruitment of 'coloured labour for platform staff' and gave authority to the General Manager to engage 'suitable personnel'.[19] Recruitment of black workers began immediately.

By the end of October 1954 it was reported that 257 'coloured workers' were employed within the public transport section;[20] 197 were West Indian, with Indian and Pakistani workers the only other significant group.[21]

Among those taken on was Peter Francis*, who came to England from Trinidad in 1954. Born in Port of Spain in 1924, Peter left school at the age of 15 and later worked as a clerk. He arrived in London in 1954, and after unsuccessfully seeking a clerical post, he took a job on a building site before moving to Birmingham in the hope of finding new work:

> One evening I saw an advert in a paper, and called at the firm the following morning. I tapped on the window marked 'Enquiries'. Before I'd uttered a word, the girl behind the window said, 'Sorry, no vacancies!'

Peter Francis was still without work when, a week later, he happened to pass the bus depot in Selly Oak:

> I thought I'd have a try there, and was successful. The Depot Manager offered me a job straight away; to start working two days later. He treated me very cordially and gave me a dozen or so free vouchers for bus travel. 'Now you take these vouchers and use them until you come to work', he said. 'In the meantime, go and find suitable digs and settle down.'

Like all applicants, Peter Francis had to pass a test of arithmetic and demonstrate his ability to deal with the intricacies of pounds, shillings and pence, as well as to fill out an accident form. He was also subjected to a Transport Department test which looked in particular for flashes of temper when put under pressure!

There were already about a dozen black workers at the bus

116

depot when Peter Francis started work. Wage rates were apparently the same for both black and white crews, and for bus conductors with the necessary seniority it was possible to apply for training as a driver.[22] Such was the shortage of drivers in 1954 that this level of seniority was reached after a few months' service. For platform staff, this was a desirable promotion. Drivers not only received better pay; they were also spared the problems of handling cash and dealing with aggressive passengers.

However, Peter Francis's experiences in Birmingham left him doubtful about the wisdom of the journey from Trinidad to Birmingham, despite the encouragement of the Depot Manager to seek promotion:

> The Depot Manager, he's been good to me. I don't have to work evening shifts because I attend classes, and the union has got an agreement to do that.
>
> But I regret coming really. I can see that us folk are not welcome in England. I see it every day, and you read about it in the papers.
>
> I was in a pub in Balsall Heath, and they wouldn't serve me. I refused to take no for an answer, and argued with the barmaid. Some British workers who were in the pub overheard the argument and called out 'Oh, he's all right, we don't mind him. Come on Charlie.' They said to me, 'come and join us'. I got a drink, but felt humiliated.
>
> English people should be taught in schools about geography and the social and economic conditions in the West Indies. I've been amazed at their ignorance in these things.[23] #

The skill bar

Unlike Jewish migrants arriving in the East End, West Indian migrants arriving in Birmingham in the 1950s could not turn to kith and kin to provide them with work. Instead, they were entirely reliant upon finding work in the 'English' labour market.

During the 1950s the English labour market was still 'controlled', and, at least in theory, each person seeking work had to be placed through the Ministry of Labour. In practice, however, the general shortage of labour meant that the majority of workers simply changed jobs at will, and then had their new job 'confirmed' at the local Labour Exchange which issued the necessary permits. Peter Francis, for instance, should have applied to the local Labour Exchange for work; instead, he applied direct to the City Transport Department. Only after he had been placed in the job by Head Office at Congrave Street was he sent to the Labour Exchange for the necessary card.

But although many Caribbean migrants found work directly from employers, frequently with the help of a friend or 'middleman' already employed,[24] this system did nothing to help them 'break into' new areas of work. Black workers were therefore far more reliant upon the local Labour Exchange to help them if they were seeking skilled positions. So for the well-qualified West Indian worker, the attitude of the local Labour Exchange was crucial.

The Labour Exchange

The attitude of Labour Exchange managers towards black migrant workers in Birmingham is recorded in the Fircroft Survey carried out in 1954 and 1955. The manager of one youth employment bureau complained that it was difficult to place West Indian applicants because 'they go about in flocks. . .wear extraordinary clothes and behave like children'.[25] In the central Birmingham area, Labour Ministry officials strenuously denied that Birmingham firms operated a 'colour bar', although they confirmed that most employers preferred local men and that in the inner city, where small firms were predominant, it was virtually impossible to find work for black applicants![26]

Labour Exchange officials also tended to be sceptical of black applicants who claimed to be skilled workers. One senior official at the Aston Labour Exchange commented upon the fact that a 'fairly large number of [Jamaican] carpenters' had recently obtained employment in the area. But he added: 'the work on which they are engaged does not require a high standard of proficiency'[27] – a judgement that flew in the face of the craft union's positive assessment of the Jamaicans' capabilities. Such attitudes ensured that many qualified black migrants were 'filtered out' of the skilled labour market before they could even begin to look for work, and forced to take the unskilled labouring work that Labour Exchange officers believed was commensurate with their capabilities. 'Coloured migrants', asserted one Labour Exchange official in May 1955, '*invariably* [have] no trade; or lower standards than are required in Great Britain'.[28] Other Labour Exchange officers showed a greater understanding of the needs of black workers, and were more forthcoming about the nature of discrimination. In Smethwick, where 800 black workers were employed in local firms by 1955, the Local Manager was aware that 'the great mass of coloured workers have dirty, hard uninteresting jobs not wanted by whites'.[29]

Of course, the judgement of Labour Exchange Officers about the suitability of black applicants for skilled work reflected more than personal prejudice. Their views about the 'difficulty' of placing skilled black workers also reflected their experience of sending qualified black applicants to job interviews, only to have them return to the Exchange to report that they had failed to gain employment.[30] Experience had taught them that the reaction of management and personnel officers to black labour was, at best, tolerant, and, at worst, implacably hostile. They were also aware that different firms would accept or reject black applicants on the basis of management perceptions of a 'racial hierarchy'.

The employers

In the early 1950s, senior and middle managers (especially personnel officers) tended to be recruited from the senior ranks of the armed forces. Some had served only during the war years, and had gone into industry upon demobilisation. None the less, they saw service not only in Europe, but also in the British colonies. Others were career officers who, in the post-war era, became involved in the suppression of independence movements in Africa, India and the Far East. Indeed, a number of personnel officers in Birmingham firms had been career officers in colonial regiments or the imperial civil service in the 1930s. The invariable domination enjoyed by white officers over black soldiers or civilians, as well as familiarity with the hierarchies of caste within a colonial empire, instilled rigid views about the 'racial order' in the minds of these officers. Such views were not shed when the service uniform was exchanged for the manager's suit.

119

The Personnel Officer of one Birmingham foundry employing some 700 workers in 1955, almost half of them black, had been a British officer in an Indian regiment for nineteen years. He prided himself on being regarded as the firm's 'expert on coloured workers' and it was he who dictated the firm's policy towards black labour. West Indians, he opined, were 'Golliwogs – Negro types', and he was convinced that they were coming over to Britain to claim National Assistance. As a result the firm employed some 250 Indian workers, but only three West Indians.[31] Yet the Superintendent of a factory in Walsall employing over 700 workers assessed his 'coloured workers' differently. He asserted that:

> Pakistanis are 'a dead loss'! They play on their poor know-ledge of English, pretending not to understand when hard work is about. . .they can be incredibly unintelligent, and. . . are always pressing to get extra overtime.
>
> Jamaicans are better, but still inferior. Low skill, slow tempo. You have to keep them moving. Some of them are very good, but one was found sleeping on the job.[32]

The Senior Manager of MacKenzie Tube Manufacturers* believed that he detected a hierarchy among West Indians: the urban type and the 'slower' rural type. None the less, he believed that all of them were 'slightly less intelligent than white workers'.[33]

The firm with the most positive attitude towards West Indian workers was Burman & Sons in Kings Norton, who employed 54 black workers, mostly Arab and West Indians, among a workforce of 1,000. Almost all the Arabs were employed in labouring jobs, whereas several Jamaicans were doing semi-skilled machine work. The Labour Manager assessed the Jamaican workers as 'exceptionally good, much better than the Arab workers', although he too maintained that the Jamaicans required 'greater supervision than the whites'.[34]

BLACK EMPLOYMENT – THE PATTERN OF DISCRIMINATION

In effect, then, Caribbean migrants faced two forms of barriers to finding work in the 1950s. Many firms totally barred black recruitment, whilst others practised forms of selective, discreet, although certainly not secret, discrimination. At times the two policies could become indistinguishable, for, having initially taken on black labour, some firms took fright at the consequences and blocked further enrolment.

Johnson and Parker* in Stechford first took on black workers in 1950. For a time the management considered putting 'a coloured overseer' in charge of a department which would contain 'only coloured workers'. However, the firm's Director blocked the measure for fear that the department would become earmarked as 'a Black Department'. In consequence, the firm 'rationalised' its black labour force. By 1954 the firm had only 10 black workers, whereas in 1950 it had employed many more.[35] Other firms, employing only one 'racial group' (variously West Indian, Indian, African or Arab) in a particular factory, automatically barred the recruitment of other black workers.

Trade union officials confirm the selective pattern of discrimination and the prevalence of a colour bar in the mid-1950s. A district official of the National Union of General and Municipal Workers (NUGMW), which acted as an agency for the Ministry of Labour, and at the time numbered 'hundreds' of black workers among its members, reported that many employers refused all 'coloured labour'. Often no reason was given, but sometimes employers justified their action by reference to the 'unreliablity' of black workers, or stated that they would not employ black male workers because they already employed white women.[36] A senior Transport and General Workers' Union organiser confirmed that 'some firms are known to employ only West Africans because they preferred them, similarly with other firms and Jamaicans'.[37]

Of course the caste hierarchies that senior managers imposed in their factories cannot simply be traced to the effects of exposure to colonial culture. Their 'images' of black workers were woven into a broader tapestry of class prejudice, male chauvinism and nationalist pride. Managers who accepted black labour, but none the less barred black male workers from working in the same department as white women, frequently retailed lurid stories of the sexual appetite of black male workers in justification of their policies. Yet such attitudes drew as heavily upon stereotyped perceptions of 'their' white women as upon colonialist fantasies of black men. Thus the Personnel Manager at one Birmingham stoving company confidently asserted that it was 'the general ambition among coloured men to own a white woman'. He, like many other managers refused to allow white women workers to mix with black workers for fear of 'trouble'. In consequence the company employed only a handful of black workers, although business was severely affected by the labour shortage.[38] Yet in a number of Birmingham foundries, women core-makers were in close contact with black labourers who fetched the cores. A senior official of the Amalgamated Union of Foundry Workers reported in March 1955 that this had created 'no special problems'.[39]

Black women too faced a process of exclusion from certain workplaces, especially where it was considered that their presence would 'lower the tone' of the establishment. Not only were Caribbean women systematically denied skilled work, especially in offices, but they were often refused even traditional low-paid 'women's work', as shop-assistants or cleaners, because this almost invariably involved contact with the public. The experience of May Spencer was typical of many.

The stenographer

May Spencer was a short-hand typist, who had qualified as a stenographer in Jamaica. She registered at the Labour Exchange for work as a short-hand typist in 1955:

At the time there were lots of vacancies for short-hand typists. The [Labour] Exchange had cards for jobs in at least half-a-dozen firms. I showed the [Labour Exchange] man my qualifications, and did a short test.

I was sent to this firm on the Saltley Road*. I was shown into a big office, but there were only white women working there. They all looked very prim and proper, and when I walked in, they just looked straight through me – as if I didn't exist!

Eventually, after a long wait, I got up the courage to tell one of them – she seemed to be in charge – that I had come about the job. 'Oh right dear', she said, 'you want to see Mr So and So' – I don't remember the manager's name – 'He'll be down in a few minutes.'

Anyway I waited ages, and still nothing happened. It was

obvious that they were just hoping I'd go away, because no-one made any attempt to fetch the manager. In the end I did go – I wasn't going to be humiliated any longer.[40]

A similar case, involving three Jamaican stenographers, occurred in May 1954. The three women were interviewed by a firm in Aston. Far from being offered employment, the company suggested to the women that they would be best advised to take jobs as bus conductresses with the City Transport Authority.[41]

DE-SKILLING

However, although there is overwhelming evidence that skilled black workers faced systematic barriers in *finding* work in Birmingham, a process of 'de-skilling' was even more apparent *within* the workplaces where black migrants were employed. Here again, discrimination took two forms. On the one hand, Caribbean workers were denied technical promotion, for instance from semi-skilled to skilled machine operator. On the other hand, they were denied promotion to shop-floor supervisory grades. In practice, the two forms of discrimination usually went hand-in-hand.

In May 1954 MacKenzie Tube Manufacturers* employed 31 black workers among a total labour force of 900, although previously the firm had employed 80 to 90 black workers. All but one of the black workers were West Indian, this being a result of the firm's conscious decision to employ only one 'national group' of non-white workers. The firm was non-unionised, despite the fact that much of the work was semi-skilled, but the company organised its own Works Cooperative Committe. It was this Committee which management 'consulted' before deciding to employ black labour.

The Works Cooperative Committee agreed to the employment of black labour on two conditions:

1 'Coloured workers should go first in the event of redundancy.'
2 'Coloured workers should not be promoted if white labour was available.'

As a result, West Indians were taken on 'in batches of 12–15' for group integration. There was to be no segregation within the works.

123

Having clearly set out their ground rules, management announced themselves 'highly satisfied with their coloured workers'. Some hostility on the part of foremen was noted, but all black workers were on semi-skilled work; indeed one was in charge of a £100,000 machine, with two white assistants. The management also employed one black assistant draughtsman in the firm. The Personnel Manager even expressed his indignation over the colour bar on West Midland buses, asserting that 75 per cent of the bus workers were Irish, who had 'no right to exclude coloured workers who had fought side by side with the English in the war'.[42] Yet the firm's discriminatory promotion policy was openly acknowledged, and the management were aware that some of their best black workers were leaving for better opportunities elsewhere.

MacKenzie Tube Manufacturers is remarkable not so much for the fact that they entered into a formal agreement with the white workforce over redundancy and promotion, but for the fact that, despite this agreement, most of their black workers were employed in semi-skilled positions, with one or two carrying out highly skilled work. In the light of the Works Committee agreement, this can only be explained by the sheer scale of the labour shortage, and the lack of alternative white labour.

In other firms, discrimination, in terms of promotion and redundancy policies, was equally effective, if less formalised. Central Precison Castings* in Smethwick had two black workers in skilled positions, a turner and a checker, out of a black workforce of 85. The black workforce was itself segregated between Indians and West Indians. The Personnel Manager explained that the firm was reluctant to promote black workers to skilled or supervisory positions, because of the 'short duration of their employment'.[43] Whether this was a reference to the migrant status of black workers, or simply a statement about the firm's long-term aims, is unclear. The assessment of senior management at Electrical Products Ltd* in Witton was much less ambiguous. There were no black workers in highly skilled jobs, since 'none have shown the ability for highly skilled work',[44] although there had been some upgrading of black workers from shop-attendants (labourers) to machine work, particularly within the Press Shop.[45] Parkinson Stoves* had already reduced the number of black employees in June 1954, when one senior manager remarked: 'I would be very reluctant to ever put a coloured worker in charge of white workers. I would resent it myself as other white workers would'.[46]

THE TRADE UNION RESPONSE

The management announced their intention of employing coloured workers for fetching and carrying, and put out tentative feelers about the union's reaction. The reply was simple. We have no colour bar like some misguided organisations. All workers are treated on equal terms and provided our coloured friends join the appropriate union, work for the same rate for the job and obey the rules, they will receive the same consideration as anyone else.[47]

Such a forthright statement by shop stewards about the rights of black workers in Britain in 1955 stands in marked contrast to the prevailing attitude of many trade unionists towards black labour. Certainly some trade union officials recognised the long-term political consequences of black immigration, and understood its roots in the process of labour migration from Britain's under-developed colonial empire to the metropolitan centre. But such an awareness did nothing to change the climate of opinion in Britain, especially in Chamberlainite Birmingham, where the legacy of social imperialism lingered in the popular culture of the middle and working class alike.[48]

In practice, the response of trade union leaders and the rank and file towards black workers ranged from cautious hospitality to forthright hostility. Indeed, individual attitudes often bound together the contradictory tendencies of acceptance and rejection. Black immigrants might be accepted as 'workers' in a particular firm or industry, but black people were not seen as belonging to the 'English working class' – a class whose culture had been forged in the *industrial* confrontation between labour and capital. Thus many trade unionists measured black workers against the values of a white, male-dominated labour aristocracy, and, at best, viewed them as unreliable elements of a provincial 'lumpenproletariat'.[49] An official of Birmingham Trades Council expressed a typical viewpoint, when he claimed that:

In Birmingham we have many skilled men with real skill in their fingers. These men are going to other countries – but only under certain conditions; skill, someone to house them or vouch for them and [they must be] under a certain age.

Coloured workers – unskilled – come to Birmingham ad lib.[50]

Additionally, the labour movement was torn between the strategy of organising black migrants to maximise wage rates during a period of economic expansion, and exploiting the discriminatory practices of employers to gain systematic advantages for indigenous workers.[51]

These contradictions are expressed in many of the statements made by trade union officers and officials about Caribbean and Indian migrant workers in the mid-1950s. There was a begrudging acceptance of the need to take action to uphold a common 'workers' front' against employers attempting to exploit black labour, especially if this was at the expense of the white working class. But at the same time, shop-floor racism was accepted as an everyday and 'natural' reality. Thus the decision by Birmingham City Council to introduce black crews provoked a furious reaction from bus drivers and depot staff. They demanded a ballot to decide the issue, against the advice of officials in the Transport and General Workers' Union. It was only when an interim agreement was struck to limit black crews to 10 per cent of the workforce that the drivers backed away from demanding strike action.[52] And despite the TGWU's stand on the principle of accepting black crews, one regional secretary acknowledged that the basis of opposition lay in the belief that 'white busmen are afraid that the status of the job will be lowered . . .that it will become a nigger's job'.[53] Indeed trade union officials would recount instances of shop-floor racism with much shaking of heads and protestations about the scrupulous fairness with which *their* union dealt with black workers, but tended to see the victims as responsible for their own problems because they failed to conform to accepted working-class cultural norms: 'if only coloured workers didn't contract out of society and live in colonies. . .if only coloured workers didn't work so much overtime. . .if only coloured workers were less excitable' are common themes among the views expressed by trade union representatives in the mid-1950s.[54]

126

In many cases, the 'threat' posed by a black presence within the workplace was only one part of a wider critique of black immigration. The severe post-war housing crisis, the 'threat of undercutting' posed by black migrant labour and a populist imperialism merged into this Amalgamated Engineering Union (AEU) branch official's view of 'little England':

> First, to put it mildly, it would appear to be an insane policy to allow uncontrolled influxes of coloured, or for that matter white also, into a town where the housing problem is so acute as it is in Birmingham.
>
> Secondly, the fear that our general standard of living may be brought down by virtue of the fact that the coloured people may be used as a source of cheap labour.
>
> Thirdly, and this could be unjust, it would appear that the people who talk glibly about the colour bar being operated, if any criticism is made or action taken in any way against the coloured people, are usually housed well away from the proximity of the groups of coloured citizens. . .the place to employ coloured people is on [sic] their natural environment, and taking a long term view, the only chance of survival for this country is to populate our colonies and reduce the amount of population in this island, not increase it.[55]

Interestingly, this official represented a branch that had nearly 350 members, none of whom were black.

Of course, actual contact with black workers did much to reassure white workers and remedy fears that black immigrants would reject trade unionism and undercut wages. An AEU branch official in Birmingham Area no. 7 reported that:

> At Wolseley Motors. . .from the reports of Shop Stewards, they find black workers most eager to join the union. Unfortunately they are on shift-work, and it is usually about once in every eight weeks that they are able to attend branch meetings. . .but are always good at paying their contributions.[56]

Unlike the AEU, which only organised a small number of black workers, the NUGMW had 'hundreds' of black members. As a result, the union's district leadership took a far more positive attitude to black labour in Birmingham, and assessed black workers' capabilities far more accurately. Wesley Perrins, the District Secretary, noted that Jamaicans were highly respected by their co-workers because of their good manners and high initiative. He quoted the case of a Jamaican worker who helped alleviate a growing atmosphere of ill-feeling in the foundry where he worked by demonstrating that all the friction really flowed from the haphazard way his shop was laid out and the failure to ensure a rational flow of work. Elsewhere, the group bonus system was thought to be an important factor in breaking down 'colour prejudice'. The District Secretary quoted cases where mixed gangs with a predominantly white membership preferred their black colleagues to other white workers who were not so quick and efficient. Where a group bonus was concerned, and this could represent an extra 20 per cent in the week's wage packet, it seems that white workers could be quite colour blind![57]

Overall, the attitudes adopted by both trade union officials and the rank and file, tended to be informed by a mixture of cultural prejudice and personal experience. A small minority, with a political awareness of imperialism and colonialism, viewed black workers as fellow victims of capitalist oppression. One NUGMW official had formed a deep friendship with a Jamaican comrade during the war, and this, together with his political awareness of colonialism and its consequences, meant that the NUGMW in Birmingham operated with a far more enlightened attitude than most other unions. Further evidence of this comes from a NUGMW branch at one of Birmingham's major power stations. Although there were no black workers employed there, the Branch Secretary reported on the 'race hatred and anti-Semitic propaganda leaflets' distributed by a skilled white worker at the power station, who supported the 'fascist. . .British National Movement'. He intended to 'deal with this'.[58]

Elsewhere, and in other unions, this political consciousness was lacking. Instead, class consciousness was expressed through notions of regionalism and nationalism, drawing sharp distinctions between 'the British working man' and 'foreign', especially non-white, workers, whose innocence and naivety made them the potential dupes of employers. Thus *in principle* the notion of worker equality *against the employer* was accepted, in order to protect wage rates, but in practice nothing was done to break down the barriers of discrimination against black workers for fear of 'stirring up shop-floor opinion'.

A district organiser in the AEU typified the attitude of many when he spoke of the need to defend the principle of 'last-in, first-out', regardless of colour, since once broken:

> this would prove a stick for the employer to beat the union with. If an employer tried to sack a coloured worker before a white worker, the union would be prepared to make a fight of it.[59]

In fact, 'making a fight of it' where a black worker's rights were concerned was little more than a pious hope given the fact that employers and white workers alike were prepared to ignore this principle. A shade more honest, was the reaction of the TGWU official who thought that 'the union had to accept, in deference to its white members' attitude, that the last-in-first-out principle of redundancy did not apply to coloured workers'.[60] Furthermore, the great majority of black workers were employed in foundries and engineering shops that were either un-unionised, or else only unionised in the skilled sections. In such cases, black workers were entirely at the mercy of employers, and 'agreements' which privileged white workers in cases of promotion, wage rates and, above all, redundancy.

Finally there were trade union leaders who were prepared to espouse racism openly for short-term advantage. John Lord*, a full-time official of the TGWU, not only advocated the need for immigration control but also proposed that preferential treatment for white workers with regard to promotion should be enshrined in law. On the Midlands Advisory Council for Industry, Lord continually carped about 'coloured workers' in Birmingham. But he was especially critical of Birmingham City Council's decision to employ black workers on the buses. He claimed that the introduction of 'coloured workers' had failed to remedy the chronic labour shortage, since even more white employees were now leaving in protest at this policy.[61]

AND AFTER THE BOOM?

In 1954 and 1955 there were five job vacancies in the Birmingham employment area for every registered unemployed person in the district. But in 1956 the situation changed dramatically, as unemployment quadrupled to 1.6 per cent and the number of unemployed rose above the total number of job vacancies.[62] Yet even at the height of the boom in 1954 and 1955, most employers foresaw that recession would follow, especially in the volatile steel industry where most Caribbean migrants were employed. The consequences of recession for black workers were also clear.

From the outset, capital was nervous about the likely long-term consequences of employing black workers in the metropolitan centre. In the views of those employers who were interviewed in 1954 and 1955, the employment of black labour was undertaken reluctantly – it was a short-term measure to ease a short-term problem. At Associated Castings* in Smethwick, where over 250 black workers were employed, senior management anticipated the next recession. In the event of lay-offs, the firm's policy was clearly spelled out by the Personnel Manager – 'you can't let down your own brothers!'[63] At Birmingham Auto Castings* the Labour Officer asserted that the 'last-in, first-out' principle would apply to all workers, regardless of skin colour. But he was contradicted by the Sales Manager, who warned 'Don't tie us down to that!' He believed that this was a 'national problem' to be solved at the highest level.[64] And at Campbell-Hansons*, although the Personnel Officer announced that he would be guided by instructions from the directors, he thought that the order of dismissal should be 'coloured workers first, then any foreign labour, then Irish, Scots and finally non-Birmingham labour'.[65]

In fact there is evidence that during the limited recessions of the late 1950s and 1960s, black workers were dismissed before white labour, regardless of the last-in, first-out principle.[66] But the general buoyancy of the Birmingham economy tended to disguise the effects of institutionalised racism in industry and commerce until the end of the 1970s, when the storm of recession and unemployment broke with a vengeance.

NOTES

1 Senior Manager at MacKenzie Tube Manufacturers*, Birmingham, 19.5.1954, Fircroft Survey.
2 See G.W. Roberts and D.O. Mills, 'Study of External Migration

Affecting Jamaica, 1953–55' in *Social and Economic Studies* Vol. VII, No. 2, 1958. G.E. Crumper ('Working-Class Emigration from Barbados to the UK, October 1955' in *Social and Economic Studies*, Vol. VI, No. 1, 1957) estimated that the proportion of skilled workers among those leaving Barbados in October 1955 reached 70 per cent.

3 Roberts and Mills, op. cit.

4 See E.J.B. Rose *et al., Colour and Citizenship* (London, 1969), p. 51.

5 For details, see interviews carried out with West Indian workers in the Fircroft Survey.

6 See Chapter 7, n. 6.

7 These doctors were also the acknowledged representatives of the black population in their early dealings with the City Council and voluntary agencies.

8 The Birmingham doctor D.R. Prem records the case of a doctor from Edinburgh University being offered employment in a city hospital by Birmingham City Council during the Second World War. However, when it was discovered that this doctor with 'an imposing English name' was in fact West Indian, the Chairman of the Hospital's Committee announced that 'a clerical mistake' had been made and was unable to offer the applicant the position. See Dahni Prem, *Parliamentary Leper: A History of Colour Prejudice in Britain*, (Aligarth, India, 1965), pp. 7–8.

9 Interview, 6.9.1988.

10 Secretary ASW, Aston, Fircroft Survey.

11 Report from ASW, Kings Heath, ibid.

12 Report from ASW, Birmingham 8th District, ibid.

13 Report from ASW, Birmingham 3rd District, ibid.

14 Interestingly, the Secretary of the Regional Branch of the ASW expressed concern about the employment prospects of black wood-workers in the event of recession. See report, 8.11.1954 ibid.

15 Interview, 12.7.1988.

16 ibid.

17 In 1951, less than 10 per cent of the population of Birmingham owned a motor vehicle. The standard, and above all the price, of public transport was therefore an issue of major political sensitivity in Birmingham. The labour shortage could have been alleviated by increasing the crews' wages. But the net effect would have been a highly unpopular rise in bus fares in a city where journey-to-work distances were already high, since the Labour-controlled City Council refused to subsidise bus fares through the general rate fund.

18 Minutes of Birmingham City Transport Committee, 5.1.1954.

19 Minutes of Birmingham City Transport Committee, 16.3.1954.

20 Of the total, 191 were male and and 66 female – accounting for aproximately 5.5 per cent of the workforce.

21 During this period some forty 'coloured workers' left the job after being taken on, although this may not have been exceptional at a time of extremely high labour turnover. It was also discovered, with apparent surprise, that the Engineering Department had been

employing both male and female 'coloured' labour since 1947, and that these workers constituted about 10 per cent of the workforce. However, all were either 'cleaners or second-class mechanics'. Details from Fircroft Survey.

22 At the end of 1954 it was reported that among Birmingham City Transport Department's black employees, only eight were drivers, although another sixty were in training to become drivers.

23 Information from an interview conducted on 25.2.1956. Fircroft Survey.

24 This system was obviously open to abuse. A District Organiser of the Amalgamated Engineering Union (AEU) was aware of a case in which a white foreman had extorted money from black migrant workers in a bicycle works in return for the promise of better paid work in the factory. The AEU pursued this matter with the management, and as a result the foreman was dismissed. ibid. 29.6.1954.

25 Interview, 13.5.1954. ibid.

26 Interview, 19.5.1954. ibid.

27 Interview, 1.6.1954. ibid.

28 Interview, 28.5.1954. ibid.

29 For details of firms employing black labour in Smethwick see Fircroft Survey, 'Coloured Workers employed in Smethwick', Summer 1955.

30 For example, see the Case Study, 'The Chocolate Factory, p. 134 below.

31 See interview, 26.5.1954. Fircroft Survey. The interviewers also reported that the company was strongly anti-union, and unionisation was very weak within the factory. The work was reported as extremely heavy and the works overbearingly hot. The very high number of workers with bandaged limbs also suggested that the foundry was a dangerous place to work.

32 Interview, 12.2.1955. ibid.

33 See n. 1 above.

34 Interview, 11.6.1954. ibid.

35 Interview, 10.6.1954. ibid.

36 Interview, 24.6.1954. ibid.

37 Interview, 27.5.1954. ibid.

38 This practice is confirmed by a report from an NUGMWU official. See ibid., 24.6.1954.

39 Interview, 17.3.1955. ibid.

40 Interview, 12.9.1988.

41 Fircroft Survey, 1.6.1954. One firm in the Birmingham area did employ an Indian woman 'from a high caste' as a short-hand typist, but another Indian woman trained as a stenographer was forced to take unskilled work in a factory.

42 Fircroft Survey, 19.5.1954. This comment demonstrates how the experience of colonialism itself generated contradictory attitudes towards black (especially West Indian) workers. In this particular

case the allegiance of black colonial subjects to Empire apparently outweighed the 'disadvantage of colour', at least in comparison to the Irish who had 'rebelled' against British colonialism. In the eyes of many employers, the Irish migrant worker also featured on the 'racial hierarchy'. A senior manager of one firm employing some 10,000 workers in Birmingham expounded the view that 'coloured workers and country Irish' were 'too rough' to be employed in his firm (interview, 8.7.1954), whilst another manager asserted that the Irish were 'the worst workers in the factory and unhygienic in the widest sense' (17.6.1954).

43 ibid., 26.5.1954.
44 ibid., 12.1.1955.
45 The Branch Secretary of the AEU in Birmingham 11th District reported: 'we find that quite a few firms in Birmingham use coloured people for cheap labour. It came to my notice that this practice is frequent at Electrical Products* in Witton.' ibid.
46 ibid., 17.5.1954.
47 Report of National Union of Vehicle Builders shop stewards at Nuffield Metal Products. See *Birmingham Journal*, the newspaper of Birmingham Trades Council, June 1955.
48 This is discussed by P. Rich, 'The Politics of Race and Segregation in British Cities With Reference to Birmingham, 1954–76' in S.J. Smith and J. Mercer, *New Perspectives in Race and Housing in Britain* (Glasgow, 1987), pp. 72–106.
49 For discussion of the historical origins of this divide between 'rough' and 'respectable' elements among the Birmingham working class, see Carl Chinn, 'The Anatomy of a Working-Class Neighbourhood: West Sparkbrook, 1871–1914', PhD, University of Birmingham, 1986.
50 Fircroft Survey, 24.5.1954.
51 It should be borne in mind that such privileges for the indigenous working class were negotiated by the trade unions and written into the formal labour contracts of many East European workers in the late 1940s.
52 See *Your Business*, No. 82, February 1954, and Birmingham Trades Council Annual Report 1954–5, p. 29.
53 Fircroft Survey, 27.5.1954.
54 See in particular a report of discussion at a branch meeting of the AEU. ibid.
55 AEU, King's Norton. ibid.
56 Written response from AEU, Birmingham Area No. 7. ibid.
57 ibid., 21.1.1955.
58 Report from NUGMW official at Hams Hall Power Station. ibid.
59 ibid., 29.6.1954.
60 ibid., 27.5.1954.
61 ibid., notes from interviewers.
62 See p. 108 for details.

63 Fircroft survey, 26.5.1954.
64 ibid., 17.6.1954.
65 ibid., 21.3.1955.
66 See newspaper cuttings in Birmingham Central Library, Local History Section, entitled 'Problems of Coloured Immigration' [sic], for details.

CASE STUDIES

The chocolate factory [1]

At the beginning of 1955 nine black workers were employed by Belmonts*, a large commercial bakery and confectionery manufacturer on the outskirts of Birmingham city centre. Three of these workers were migrants from India, the others were West Indian, mostly from Jamaica. One Indian worker, Peter Alam*, and a Jamaican, John Snape*, had been working at the company for three or four years. The other seven, all women, were relatively new to the job, and had only been with the firm for a short time.

None of the women were employed in a skilled or semi-skilled capacity, and none of the black workers held supervisory grades. The female workers were employed as machine operatives, chocolate-packers and cleaners. However, one of the two Indian women was well-educated, with Cambridge qualifications, and had worked for a year as a stenographer in India. She had been forced to take work at Belmonts because of systematic discrimination in her search for office work:

> *I have been refused at least eight jobs, even though I applied with a Labour Exchange card. At one plywood factory they openly admitted they did not employ coloured people. [At a chemist] I telephoned at one o'clock to change the appointment to five. The man I spoke to said that was OK, but as soon as I appeared he told me the job was filled. So I asked why they had not told me when I phoned. They didn't make an excuse, just said they were sorry.*

> *My brothers were unemployed in Bradford for three weeks. . .They are both well educated. They came to Birmingham, and the only jobs they could get were as labourers – at the gas works. Now they are [bus] conductors with the City.*

I now work here as a chocolate-packer: it was the only other work I could get. There are nine other coloured workers here, and we get on well with the white workers. But occasionally workers make remarks like, 'why do you come to England to take our jobs?'

The two black male workers had also experienced discrimination, although in different ways.

John Snape from Jamaica had originally worked for a tyre manufacturer in another West Midlands town, but had left his job after a dispute with a chargehand over the way he drove his fork-lift truck. Snape claimed that the chargehand had lied about him, falsely accusing him of driving too fast and neglecting his work. In the end, Snape preferred to leave the job, rather than argue at it – a 'solution' that was at least feasible during a period of high employment. He had found work at Belmonts after two weeks without work; yet twice during the period of his employment at Belmonts he was imprisoned, apparently for debt. On each occasion he was given his job back by the firm, although he had been warned that this was his 'last chance'. Snape regarded Belmonts as 'the best firm I ever worked for' and he believed that his job in the biscuit division offered the possibility of promotion to skilled work. 'If I want, I will probably become a baker', he asserted, remarking that he had an excellent relationship with the foreman who showed him how to bake biscuits.

Peter Alam from Digha in India had experienced far more direct discrimination. He had served a five-year apprenticeship in India as a locomotive engineer, and had worked for East India Railways as a qualified fitter for a further five years. Despite his skills and his formal apprenticeship certificate, he had been refused work as a mechanic in England:

I came to Birmingham because I thought that there were opportunities for engineering here. I applied at the local Labour Exchange for a job as a mechanic. They told me that there were vacancies for mechanics at British Railways.

When I arrived, I handed in the card and my apprenticeship forms. They gave me both back and told me there were no vacancies. But the next morning the jobs were still being advertised in the morning papers, as they had been the evening before.

So I went back to the Labour Exchange, where the vacancies were still on the board. I gave my card back to the man behind the counter. He asked me why I hadn't got the job. I told him I didn't know; only that they had told me there were no vacancies. The officer at the Exchange asked me if I thought it was 'because of the colour bar'. I said I didn't know. They gave me another card, and I was sent along to the gas works. There they told me they had vacancies, but for gas fitters, not locomotive fitters.

In the end he had found his present job through friends, although he cherished the hope that he would be able to get back to his trade by continuing his studies to become a qualified mechanical engineer in Britain.

Typical of the West Indian women were Diane Salmon* and Del Prior*, aged 19 and 20 respectively. Diane Salmon had left school in St Andrew in Jamaica at the age of 15. She had worked as a dress-maker in Jamaica for three years, learning the trade and hoping for a regular job. But in 1954, effectively out of work, she acted upon a friend's advice and came to England. She expected to stay for two years or so:

> *I was out of work from 15 December 1954 until 22 January 1955, before I got [this job] scraping the chocolate from the moulds.*
>
> *I looked for work in London [during that time] and got some general work at the laundry in Gordon Road, south-east London.*
>
> *I was originally in another department here, but the other workers gave me their work to do and laughed at me. I asked the forewoman for a change, and it's been better since then.*

Del Prior also left Jamaica because she was unemployed. She had a sister in Birmingham who was training to become a nurse:

> *I got a job with the buses for two weeks at the beginning of November, but it was too cold, so I left.*
>
> *I got this job through friends who knew someone here. I started on 23 November 1954. I hand pack chocolates in the confectionery department.*

The oldest of the West Indian women was Eileen Green*. She was 27 years old, and had originally come to England to join her boyfriend, who was working as a brick-layer. Eileen Green had previously worked as a hand-press operator in the metal and plastics department of a large

Birmingham manufacturer, before getting work at Belmonts as a machine operator in the confectionery department. Unusually, she preferred the white workers to her fellow Jamaicans, feeling that she could not 'get along much with folks from the same place'.

Although the black workers at the bakery were not all West Indian, their experiences were remarkably consistent and follow the trend elsewhere. Those without skills or experience were easily able to find work as unskilled workers at a time of chronic labour shortage. They were even able to change jobs quickly, either because they disliked the work or because of hostility from white foremen or fellow workers. But clearly there was a skill bar. Despite experience and qualifications, neither the Indian stenographer nor Peter Alam were able to find work to match their skills. Trapped as unskilled labourers at the bakery they were thus potential victims of any downturn in the economy or rise in unemployment. As for the chance of promotion within the bakery, the Production Manager was quite adamant about the company's policy: there was no chance of any 'coloured worker' becoming a supervisor since 'they would not be here long enough to gain the necessary experience'.

The chiropodist

Interview, 3.9.1988.

I got a job with Reliance Tubes*. That was my first job. But in the early part of '57 the jobs went down, and they have this system, last-in, first-out. That affects me, 'cos the people who came in last had to go.

I went to the Post Office and applied for a job – that is, the Post Office Supply, not the letter, the supply side. They sent and called me for an interview. I had the interview, and they said, 'yes', I could have the job. A labouring job, what they call Pack and Porter. And I should start on the Monday.

But I got a message from the foreman where I used to work; there was a job back at Reliance. So now I had to decide which one of these two jobs I should have. By now I had moved and had a room with some coloured folk in Small Heath. . . .And they said, 'Look, it's a government job. You might go back to that other job and the same thing might happen again. So think it over, our advice to you is to take this job.' It was sixpence more. £7 6d.

137

So I started with the Post Office. That was the early part of '57. . .The job wasn't very good. The money was very small. You had to do endless overtime to make up your money.

Well anyway during the time I worked in the Post Office I decided I was going to take up a career. And I saw an advert in the paper for the Institute of Chiropody in Leatherhead. And I wrote to them and asked if I could enrol – you could do it in parts, part correspondent. You could go there at weekends, in holidays and what have you. So I worked in-between, travelling on the train, for a little over two years.

Then I went to the Coop – they have a big chiropody surgery. And they offered me a job. But I didn't intend to give up the job that I had, and as I was off [work] for two weeks I said: 'Before I do anything I'm going to try it out.' So I went there for a day.

I tell you, people just stared, you could see the racial. . .it was so tense. Then again the wage was not so good. So I decided to stay on [where I was]. And I moved up in grade, because if you show a bit of potential, and there are some supervisors who give you a chance – there was some where you didn't have any chance – they would give you a good appraisement. I did make it up to a storekeeper. . . .

Dr Pilgrim, Dr Piliso and Dr Lloyd – these people were advocating for equal rights and justice. That was all we were asking for! All the jobs you could have were labouring jobs, a bus conductor. . .there was no such thing as promotion for a coloured person. And it was Pilgrim and Dr Pilso and some of our lads who got together and had meetings. And we would protest bitterly against, you know, the attitude. The government had to do something.

And unionism. I knew what unionism meant. When I came here, I came here with a union card, because the firm I was working at in Jamaica was unionised. So I knew about unionism from home. And I said wherever I get work, I got to join the union.

When I first went to Reliance I joined the union, the Transport and General. And at the Post Office too. But I found that the type of union that we were looking for did not exist. Well you see the meaning of it: the brotherhood of man! But they had more racialism in the union than anywhere else. We were disappointed. But although we were disappointed, it was better to be in the union even so.

138

NOTE

1 Reconstructed from from interviews carried out in the Fircroft Survey, 27.1.55; 31.1.55; 10.2.55.

11

SETTLING DOWN

In the early 1950s, there was no Caribbean 'ghetto' in Birmingham; no piece of 'back home' to shelter the immigrant in a new and strange land. For a fortunate few, a scrap of paper, with the address of a friend or relative in the city, offered hope of a welcome and a place to stay for a few days. But for Len King*, disgorged on to New Street railway station in the early hours of a bitter February morning, the welcome was bleak indeed:

> Looking at that empty platform. . .all the hopes I had suddenly drained away.
>
> It was right in the middle of the winter. . .there was the shock of being so cold. I had nothing to keep it out. And snow! That was so different from what I had known in Jamaica. . .
>
> I wondered what on earth I'd come to Birmingham for.[1]

For Len King, the cold weather only accentuated his most pressing need – accommodation. But if Birmingham had jobs a plenty in the early 1950s, the city's housing shortage had reached crisis point.

SOMEWHERE TO LIVE

In the post-war era much of Birmingham's housing could best be described as decrepit. The lack of war-time investment and the ravages of the Luftwaffe had taken their toll, but underlying the crisis of housing in the 1950s was the deterioration of the pre-war housing stock.

In 1946 some 81,000 houses were without baths and 35,000 were without separate WCs. A further 29,000 houses were back-to-backs, crammed into the heart of the city and far too small for the needs of most families. But it was not only the overcrowded, back-to-back terraces that were decaying. In January 1949, Alderman Roberts observed that the traditional terraced slum was being superseded by the 'London type of slum' – 'a house which became a ruin'.[2]

Alderman Roberts was referring to Birmingham's Victorian villas – vast emporiums of light and space, impossible to heat economically, and hugely expensive to maintain. During the 1930s and 1940s, their original owners deserted the Victorian city for the outer suburbs. They sold to a new breed of inner-city landlord, who converted these villas 'with varying degrees of competence and legality' into flats for the new proletariat who were flocking to Birmingham from the English provinces, and from Wales, Scotland and Ireland.[3]

Indeed, largely as a response to this tide of provincial and Irish immigration, and the critical shortage of accommodation, the City Council imposed the 'Five-Year Rule': a minimum qualification of five years' residence in Birmingham for applicants for municipal housing. By 1950 the problem of homelessness was so severe that the Council operated seven municipal hostels, and throughout the early 1950s the Council was forced to shuffle the homeless into sub-standard houses awaiting demolition and redevelopment in the central zone.[4] But homelessness was still a problem in the mid-1950s, and there was widespread public anger at the inability of the City Council to solve the housing crisis effectively.

But if the chronic housing shortage and the Five-Year Rule created an accommodation crisis for provincial migrants, black migrants suffered further problems due to the widespread discrimination of private landlords. This was recognised by Percy Shurmer, Labour MP for Sparkbrook, as early as 1948:

> a large number of students and factory workers from Africa and West Indian colonies in Birmingham and district. . . cannot get lodgings on account of the shortage of accommodation, plus the colour bar, so that several of them often have to occupy one small room that is just enough for two persons.[5]

The evidence of a colour bar in housing was unequivocal. West

Indians and Indians alike were denied accommodation by private landlords and frequently refused admission to hotels in Birmingham.[6] An opinion poll in 1956 found that nearly 74 per cent of local people considered that a colour bar operated in Birmingham, and over 98 per cent said that they themselves would be unwilling to take a 'coloured' lodger.[7] So for West Indian migrants in the early 1950s:

> It was very, very hard to get accommodation. Absolutely hard! Because the natives, they wouldn't have you. They would not have you!
>
> Anyway before I came to Birmingham I wrote to one of my schoolmates who was here. . .and asked if he could secure a room for me. He got this room from some Salvation Army people. . .because the Salvation Army were very helpful.[8]

Indeed, it was mainly through organisations such as the Salvation Army that the first West Indian migrants eventually found local people willing to offer them longer-term accommodation:

> My friend, and me, and some other lads, used to go to the Salvation Army Church in Small Heath. So we have a talk with this lady, and she said 'Yes, she could put us up' because she had some other boarders as well.[9]

More often, though, it was the longer-established Asian settlers in Birmingham who bought property and provided accommodation for the pioneers of Caribbean immigration. Indeed, many West Indians discovered that 'It was only in those Asian places that you could get accommodation.'[10] Such houses, however, were more like hostels than homes; for with so many migrants working night-shifts, 'those houses were also on two shifts. . .the night-shift go out and the day-shift come in – using the same bed'.[11]

Precisely because of landlord discrimination, and a dire shortage of affordable rented family accommodation throughout Birmingham, house purchase and owner-occupation became a favoured option for most Caribbean immigrants. But there were formidable obstacles to be overcome before the dream of 'a home of your own' could be realised.

First of all it was necessary to save enough for a deposit – a particular problem for those supporting families in the West Indies. Secondly, discrimination against black applicants by building societies and private institutions forced Caribbean migrants to take loans from non-commercial organisations, usually at heavily inflated rates of interest. Mortgages at lower rates of interest were available from the municipal authorities, but only on old properties in the city's middle-ring, in areas where the housing stock was already in a delapidated condition.[12] Thirdly, for buyers on the 'open market' it was necessary actually to find someone prepared to sell their house to a black buyer:

> Well I saved a bit of money. I had some money that I took with me from home, put it in a bank and tried to save as much as I can. Then in 1960 I decided I was going to get a little place for myself – a home.
> So I went around looking. That was really the time when I came up against racial discrimination. I tell you it was bad. I went to some houses where once they open the door, they just look at you and close the door! And those who didn't close the door were polite enough to say 'Oh I'm sorry. It's sold. Somebody just bought it. Somebody bought it before you!' And some said 'Look, as far as I'm concerned I could sell you this house. . .but my neighbours. . .my neighbours asked me not to sell it to any coloureds.'[13]

By the end of the 1960s it has been estimated that some 40 per cent of black migrants in Birmingham were owner-occupiers; a proportion far greater than the average for the city, although clearly this did not indicate higher levels of black affluence.[14] For most, buying a house was the first essential step in forming a family, or, more usually, in reuniting family and relatives from the West Indies. Inevitably:

> it was a squash in the house, because we had other relatives come to live with us as well, until they saved up enough to get a place for themselves.
> I slept in a bed, there was three of us in it. It was a three bedroomed house, that's all. 'Cos there was so many in our house I shared the bed with the others.[15]

Towards the end of the 1950s a pattern of West Indian settlement in Birmingham became apparent. This pattern was dictated primarily by the limited availability of housing; although it was also constrained by the fact that black migrants mainly worked in industries which were concentrated around the old city perimeter.

There were virtually no black families living in the inner zone of Birmingham, with the exception of Newtown Aston. This inner zone, which included the worst of the 'classic slum' properties in the city, came under the control of the City Council as a result of compulsory purchase in 1946 – the first step in a huge programme of post-war urban redevelopment. Vacant properties in this inner zone were used as temporary accommodation for families on the City Council's housing list. However, few black families had been resident in the city for long enough to be eligible to be rehoused by the City Council before the central zone's redevelopment was complete in 1970.[16]

The main area of West Indian settlement was in the middle ring, sandwiched between the city centre and the expanding outer suburbs. In the north and east of the city, the housing was dominated by late Victorian and Edwardian terraces (about 20 to 30 houses per acre). In the south and west, large detached and semi-detached Victorian villas were predominant (between 1 and 6 houses per acre) set beside parkland and along tree-lined avenues. In these areas, black settlement tended to be ribboned along main roads, where property was cheaper and where access to the main bus routes was easy.[17] It was also concentrated in areas of leasehold tenure where leases had only a few years to run. Such 'fag end' leases on large Victorian villas were generally unattractive to property companies; they were therefore available for 'quick cash sales'. The villas were bought up by small-scale speculators, who sub-divided the properties into flats for rent. Despite being badly converted, badly maintained and badly managed, such property was none the less attractive, 'for the property speculator on the one hand, and the desperately needy on the other'![18]

In effect, then, the pattern of West Indian settlement in Birmingham was determined by a mixture of economic deprivation, urban geography and racial discrimination. Denied access to the old terraced housing in the inner ring and to the new municipal estates in the outer ring because of the Council's policies, and unable to buy into the private housing in the suburbs because of low incomes and institutional discrimination, West Indian migrants were forced into the 'middle ring' together with Indian and Irish immigrants.[19] But even so, West Indian settlement was more concentrated than that of other black groups. Thus Asian migrants, although clustered in similar areas to Caribbean migrants, were more thinly and widely spread.[20] The northern wards of the middle ring – Rotton Park, Soho, Lozells, Handsworth and Sandwell – accounted for more than half (50.2 per cent) of the total West Indian population in the city.[21] The 'new suburbs' were almost bereft of black faces. (See Appendix II, Map 2.)

However, the geography of early West Indian settlement tells us very little about the way in which most Caribbean migrants lived their lives and experienced the housing crisis in Birmingham. Indeed for the early migrants, and especially for their children, it was the *particular* four walls which surrounded them, *their* house and *their* street, which were the boundaries of their lives – not the 'segregation' quadrants and lines drawn by social scientists on the Birmingham city map.

GROWING UP

Silvia Day was born in Sparkbrook, in the centre of what the local press liked to call 'the black ghetto':

> I remember the first house – it was old, and even though it was clean, from the outside it looked shabby, 'cos it was in the middle of Sparkbrook.
>
> It was behind a betting shop. It had a cellar, and at the back a door that went through to the betting shop. We didn't have a front door to the house – just a path that went through to the entryway. Then upstairs was Mum and Dad's room and the three of us girls used to sleep in a side room. . . We had an outside toilet. My dad owned the house. . .it was in Anderton Road.[22]

Indeed Sparkbrook itself was anything but a 'black ghetto', since what distinguished it for Silvia was that:

> there was *so many* mixed races. . .everyone used to get on, black, white, Indian, Chinese – you know? I can remember

145

when we walked to school an Indian lady taked us and her two
boys. Mum and her used to chat and get on really well.[23]

Certainly Sparkbrook could seem like a haven of tolerance in
comparison to living elsewhere – 'When I lived in Sparkbrook I
was never called a nigger, or a black bastard.'

Yet the effects of poor housing in Sparkbrook uprooted Silvia
and her family from an economic ghetto that tolerated ethnic
diversity, and propelled her into a new suburban estate where
she was forced to confront entirely different attitudes:

> My sister got TB, so we had to be moved out of the area 'cos
> she caught it there. So we moved up to Hollywood, sort of in
> the country, 'cos there wasn't much houses and whatever
> about there then, so she could convalesce and get fresh air. . .
>
> We moved into a more or less white area. There was only
> one other black family on the whole estate. I were the only
> black kid in the school. . .and I had a lot of hassle. It really
> upset me at first, 'cos I had never had it before, and didn't
> know how to deal with it. . .I used to go home in tears
> because people had called me a black bastard and things.[24]

Perhaps because there was no true ethnic ghetto, to create a sense
of imprisoned security, Caribbean life in Birmingham rarely
spilled out on to the streets in the carefree manner of the Jewish
East End. As a result, West Indian children often found
themselves imprisoned in the family home:

> We had all that we wanted. . .but my Dad was very strict. He
> didn't like us to go out to play. He built a tennis court in the
> back yard and we used to play tennis. He never wanted us to
> go out at all.
>
> If we played on the street it was on occasion. Like on
> Sunday; we played for two hours and then went back in. We
> had pocket money, but we wasn't allowed to spend it. . .The
> only thing [Dad] used to do was send us all to the pictures on
> a Saturday to watch cartoons. He sent all the family. I think
> it cost sixpence.[25]

Indeed in a low-waged household, where both parents worked,
a sense of social isolation crept into the lives of many children:

> We never got out of Birmingham. We'd go to the park, and

the pictures on Saturday. I never went abroad or to other parts of England. My other friends used to go abroad. But we couldn't afford it.

But my Mum and Dad always explained to us that life was hard in Jamaica. They sort of indoctrinated us. . .and if they had anything, they'd give it to us.[26]

A WOMAN'S JOB

The lack of affordable child-care facilities in Birmingham was a problem for all working-class parents. But most West Indian parents lacked any extended family in England whom they could call upon to look after young children whilst they went out to work. This dilemma faced the Jamesons, saving to bring over the eldest daughter from Jamaica to reunite the family. Stephen Jameson recalled:

My Mum didn't use to work. She was a housewife. . .But I had a bigger sister, she's a lot older, and she was over in Jamaica. So my Mum got a job in the kitchen of a big hotel in Birmingham. . .

But my Dad didn't like my Mum to work. He thought that we could live off his wages alone. Well my Mum didn't see it that way. She wanted to save enough money to send for my big sister.

Now she thought we was old enough to look after ourselves. We wasn't unruly. We didn't mess about. But my Dad wouldn't have that. So he told the local authorities. And they came round, and seen that my Mum was leaving us to go to work – we were 6, 7 [years old] at the time. My sister was looking after us – she was 8.

They came and they said, 'Is anyone at home?' I said, 'No. My mum's gone to work and my father's gone to work.' And they said, 'Would you like to come for a ride?' I didn't know where I was going at the time. It was me who answered the door. I told the rest of my brothers and sisters, 'Would you like to come for a ride with this lady who's come to the house and asked if we want to go for a ride?'. . .They was very nice to us, but I didn't catch on to what was happening.

They took us away – put us in a home for two weeks. That was in Halesowen. I didn't like it at all. We was split up. I had

147

my bigger sister with me and my other sister was at another place and my brother was at West Bromwich.

Then my mother came to the home, and like she was crying and saying it was my Dad's fault. After two weeks we just went back, 'cos my mother lost her job coming up all the time, and she said she'd stay at home. But my other brother couldn't stand it at the other place and ran away. He was the only black kid there and had to share a bedroom with the other white kids. It was too much.[27]

In the Patterson family the burdens of caring for smaller children at home fell on to the much older sister; a form of child-care common to many white working-class families in Birmingham. However, where the older child had been separated from the parents for some years, this extra burden was much resented. Sonia Patterson recalled:

My Dad was always in work. My Mum got a part-time cleaning job at the Queen Elizabeth Hospital. I think she just thought of me as a baby sitter. I've found that a lot of girls who were born in the West Indies and came over [after their parents had migrated] they don't sort of have any close relationship with their parents. . .

Thinking back on my mother now. . . .she had pressures from everywhere. My Dad was working on the building sites. And me coming over would make four kids, and she later had one more. She had part-time work – there was no nursery – so I used to have to look after the kids when I first came over. I suppose she didn't have time to give me much love, given that I didn't know her.[28]

Indeed, for Sonia's mother, the schedule of domestic tasks to be accomplished, before and after going out to work, was daunting:

Mum used to be up at five o'clock to get me Dad's breakfast, then she'd be out at six, leaving us our sandwiches or whatever for school on the kitchen table.

She got home at five, picked us kids up from the child-minder's, fed us, and then started cooking me Dad's tea. He'd come home at about ten to six and at six o'clock dinner would have to be on the table. Then about six-thirty he'd go out, to the pub or the pictures, and me Mum would put us kids to bed.[29]

SCHOOLING

Whereas the schooling of Jewish immigrant children in the East End was dominated by the overbearing presence of the Jew's Free School, and Jewish children were concentrated in a small number of local schools, Caribbean schoolchildren in Birmingham were dispersed among a comparatively large number of junior and secondary schools throughout the city.[30] In fact most West Indian children were educated in schools where they formed a small minority.[31] And for the first black children in all-white institutions, school became an unrelenting battleground in which they had to prove their worth to white kids and teachers alike:

> I went to an infant and junior school right in the middle of a big council estate. It was known as quite a good school, and there wasn't many black kids – just a handful of us. . .
> I had lots of aggravation – that's one of the things I still remember, going through school fighting for myself, being very aggressive – I had to stand up to a lot of kids who just picked on me for my colour. They called me all sorts of names. . .I got into a lot of fights, and got into a lot of trouble for it.[32]

At secondary school the adult world began to impinge more forcefully:

> When I started at secondary school I was a bit of a rebel. . .I was never suspended from school or anything like that. I always seemed to get away with it! I can remember, once though, I had the slipper – I hit this Indian chap. . . Unfortunately the wood-work teacher came out and saw this – he used to be a boxer and everyone was afraid of him. As soon as I saw him I thought, 'Oh shit. I know what's going to happen now!' He pulled me over and asked me to wait. He asked me whether I wanted the cane or the slipper. I said 'could I have the slipper?' I should have asked for the cane, 'cos I'm sure he put something in the slipper, a wooden block or something. It hurt like hell! After that, I was always wary. . .

Where the school is, or was, is by an estate called Russell's Hall. The National Front was influential in that area. A lot of the kids in that area used to be members of the National Front. There used to be quite a few disturbances. . .Having said that, though, there was only a small minority that blew it, made it difficult for the majority of people at the school.[33]

Despite the difficulties faced by the first generation of black pupils at school, parental pressure to succeed academically was intense. Most West Indian parents saw education as the only realistic escape route for their children from the low-skilled, poorly paid work that had become their lot in Britain. This pressure often exacerbated feelings of isolation:

I always did well at school because I was pushed by my parents to do my best. If you didn't you knew about it when you got home. Your report had always to be good, and your marks high at school!

After school it was basically back home – children should be seen and not heard sort of thing. I had a very strict and restrictive home life. I had one friend who lived across the road. . .my parents thought they were OK, so I could play with him. But it was very difficult to go out and play, late-ish, with other kids. I was always having to have a book in my hand, and reading. . .bettering myself. . .stay in and study sort of thing.[34]

Yet even when black children proved themselves as academically able, the arbitrary punishments doled out by teachers could still take on distinctively racial overtones where black kids were involved:

One thing I remember distinctly – it was when I first noticed the injustices of school – was an incident where two of us were chewing gum in class. The white kid next to me – the teacher just asked him to spit it out. But he turned round and thumped me across the face, for chewing, for the same thing![35]

For children arriving in Birmingham to join parents they scarcely knew, the cultural shock of starting school in a city was enormous. And the school system's lack of understanding had far-reaching consequences for the children's lives:

150

In Jamaica, like, it took nearly half the day to get to the school – so you didn't learn much, especially when you had to help out on the farm and whatever. . .

Anyway I went to secondary school [in Birmingham] – this was after being here a year. . .And the other kids used to laugh at me. . .the teacher realised that I couldn't read or write; they had to teach me how to form letters.

I used to go with the girls next door. They were born in the West Indies and we could sort of relate to each other, although their parents were totally different from mine – that's when I had problems at school – and I don't think me Mum could take it really, 'cos I started giving her trouble.

I remember the teacher, Mrs Caldwell, she used to get really annoyed with me. I used to talk a lot, and do silly things. . .I was sent to see a psychiatrist. And she referred me to this other school. . .

So I ended up in one of those ESNs – Educationally Sub-normal Schools. I was going on 13. I was there until I was 16. I was boarding during the week, and at the weekend I had to go home. But I didn't want to go home! There was some kids that didn't have to go home, so I used to try and make out that me Mum's got a lot on. . .'Can I stay here?'. . .I used to like it. I used to have friends, whereas at home they didn't like me.

There was no black staff there. Some of them were nice. My Home Mother was German. She really took a liking to me – I got on well with her. One time she said she would take me to Germany with her for the summer. But she said, 'How can I take you with me to Germany, if when we get back you are still a cheeky little girl to me?' Oh, I was really cheeky you know![36]

Yet fate could play peculiar tricks. Brought up in the heart of the city, and expecting only the worst that the education system could throw at her, Janice Sinclair was diagnosed as diabetic:

Well, I get diabetes. So I was sent to Croftwood School 'cos I wouldn't take the injections – every opportunity I got I was eating sweets. I kept going into comas, really messing myself up.

So they sent me to boarding school, which really freaked

me out, because it wasn't what I expected. It was a typical middle-class boarding school. I thought there would be a load of rough kids there, and we could all be bad together! But it wasn't for rejects and whatever. It was, you know, for well-off posh people. Not like me![37]

BREAKING AWAY

In Birmingham, children of West Indian parents shared with white children the economic and social deprivation of growing up in declining inner-city districts. But they often lacked the escape routes that white children had into the world beyond the city. Black families did not have an extended family living in the countryside. Bank holiday outings to the seaside were virtually unheard of. It was therefore institutions such as the Baptist Church, or the Girls' Brigade, which provided them with their first taste of life beyond the confines of home or the local park:

> They took us camping, to Reading. I went twice. That was a new experience for me. I'd never really been away or been on holiday or anything. The first time about ten people went from my church – all the Baptist churches organised it. The next year when I went, my brother came. I was about 10 then, 10 or 11. . .
>
> The camp was sort of on a farm – with tents and a marquee where you had a meeting, and wash tents. . .We went walking, went on day trips, hikes, running, played games.[38]

And once free of parents and school, the teenage years, especially during the early 1960s when high employment bought bicycles for the older children, could be a time of freedom:

> Most of the friends that I used to hang around with lived in the same area. We used to play football, we used to go cycling.
>
> All of us had bikes. Come weekends we used to go down to Kinver, about fifteen miles away – up and away for half a day like. Sometimes we used to go fishing. I could never see the point though. I used to go because we had a few cans [of beer] around. Well, one can with a straw. That was cheap![39]

Some youngsters were also aware that they had a freedom that other African-Caribbean children could not take for granted:

My family never really tied me down. . .My Mum always used to say that she wasn't going to bring her children up like what her Mum used to do. . .it was the same for my brother within reason.

Even when I was at school I could go to the disco. But none of my black friends could go – not one of them.[40]

But of course, plentiful work meant that children left school and went straight into work. In the 1950s and 1960s, further education was a luxury that few could afford when an extra pay-packet could secure some degree of comfort for all the family:

I left school at 16. . .because my father thought that I ought to go out and earn a living, instead of staying at school and getting some qualifications, even though my teachers were pushing for me to stay on.[41]

Stephen Jameson became a butcher:

I was a butcher. I just wanted some money, some money coming in. . .But I didn't like it. All I could see was blood everywhere.

I was kept in the back actually. I wasn't allowed to serve on the till – I was the only black person serving there, and I don't think they liked the idea of a black serving at the till. That's what they told me anyway.[42]

When Sonia Patterson left school her mother found her a job in a sewing factory in Winson Green, making trousers:

It was piece-work and, coming from school, finding that you had x-amount of trousers, of seams to do, before you got your money. . .I mean it was boring, really boring.

I remember the manager threatening to sack me. . .and I daren't get the sack 'cos me mother would go mad – I didn't know what she would do![43]

A few, though, like Errol, were fortunate enough to find work that gave them satisfaction and the opportunity for advancement:

I stayed on at school till I was 16. But I had no qualifications – CSE grades 3 or 4, that's all. But I knew basically what I wanted to do was to go into engineering. . .

So I spent a month dossing around. Then a friend of mine said, 'I think you should get a job now.' So what I did, I got the Yellow Pages, looked at engineering firms section, and the first one I came to was Invincible Electrical Engineering. I phoned that place up. This was on a Thursday. Phoned the boss. 'Are you available for an interview?' 'Yes.' 'When?' 'Now!' Went up there. Interview. 'Have the job today. Start Friday.'

I was an electrical mechanical fitter. I really enjoyed working there. . .I was 18, and the youngest person to be in charge of the night-shift. You had to make decisions for yourself. We were repairing electrical motors. . .the gaffer took time to teach me. . .When I started there was ten working there. There was three gaffers. Two of them started on the factory floor and worked their way up. . .It was very close-knit. There was two other black people there – one was an electrician, the other a winder.[44]

Errol lost his job on 12 December 1981. Earlier in that year the census recorded that over 15 per cent of the workforce were unemployed in Birmingham, but for people of Caribbean descent the rate of unemployment was over 26 per cent.

It was six years before Errol found work again.

NOTES

1 Interview, 27.3.1988.
2 *Birmingham Gazette*, 25.1.1949.
3 Anthony Sutcliffe and Roger Smith, *Birmingham, 1939–1970* (London, 1974), pp. 237–8.
4 ibid., p. 245.
5 Written Answers to Questions, 9.6.1948, House of Commons.
6 See Dahni Prem, *The Parliamentary Leper: A History of Colour Prejudice in Britain* (Aligarth, India, 1965), p. 7–8.
7 Additionally, over 80 per cent wanted Commonwealth immigration to be restricted, with 13 per cent wanting it stopped altogether. Only 17 per cent thought they had a responsibility to help the 'coloured' worker in Birmingham. See John Darragh, *Colour and Conscience* (London, 1957), p. 21.
8 Interview, 12.5.1988.
9 ibid.
10 ibid.
11 ibid.
12 Birmingham began a municipal mortgage scheme in 1959, but

although aproximately 2,000 mortgages were granted to black people between 1959 and 1966 (*Institute of Race Relations Newsletter*, February 1966, p. 16), these mortgages were usually offered only on properties around existing centres of black settlement. In 1968, the City Council estimated that 40 per cent of the council's mortgages were advanced to black people, but over half of these were given to immigrants 'on the older type of property' (General Purposes Sub-Committee, 16.7.1965).

13 Interview, 12.5.1988.
14 Sutcliffe and Smith, op. cit., p. 381.
15 Interview, 16.5.1988.
16 The population of this inner zone was reduced from 100,000 to 50,000, 'although those involved are entirely white'. See Philip N. Jones, 'The Segregation of Immigrant Communities in the City of Birmingham'. University of Hull Occasional Papers in Geography, No. 7, 1961, p. 25.
17 ibid.
18 ibid.
19 Thus in 1961, over 80 per cent of black migrants lived within the pre-1918 boundaries of the city of Birmingham.
20 Jones estimated the 'index of segregation' to be 10 points higher for West Indians *vis-à-vis* settlers from the Indian sub-continent (55 per cent compared to 45 per cent) See Jones, op. cit., p. 7.
21 Within this area, Handsworth and Soho accounted for more than 10 per cent of West Indian settlers in Birmingham.
22 Interview, 21.5.1988.
23 ibid.
24 ibid.
25 Interview, 3.7.1988.
26 ibid.
27 Interview, 17.7.1988.
28 Interview, 3.5.1988.
29 ibid.
30 Not that this fact could be gleaned from contemporary press reports. Even the liberal press raised the spectre of Birmingham as the city with 'the problem of schools with too many immigrants', claiming that this 'critical and growing problem' was 'fast getting out of hand'. *Guardian*, 11.2.1967.
31 The real 'problem' facing Birmingham schools was a lack of resources to make necessary provision for all the city's children, albeit black immigration added about 1,000 children to the school population by the end of the 1950s, rising to 7,500 in the mid-1960s. This was under 8 per cent of the total. For an appraisal of the politics of 'immigrant' school numbers and the issue of 'integration' see Sutcliffe and Smith, op. cit., pp. 383 ff.
32 Interview, 8.5.1988.
33 Interview, 9.2.1988.
34 Interview, 23.5.1988.

155

35 ibid.
36 Interview, 3.5.1988.
37 Interview, 12.11.1988.
38 Interview, 15.10.1988.
39 Interview, 3.5.1988.
40 Interview, 15.10.1988.
41 Interview, 23.5.1988.
42 Interview, 17.7.1988.
43 Interview, 3.5.1988.
44 Interview, 9.2.1988.

12

SHAPING THE FUTURE

THE WEST INDIAN WORKER IN BIRMINGHAM

In the 1950s and early 1960s we have seen that the great majority of Caribbean migrants in Birmingham were employed in the heavy industries which ringed the inner zones of the city. In the foundries and factories, where the workforce often numbered many hundreds, social relations between management and the workers were distant and formalised. Hiring of labour was officially controlled by state agencies, although in practice local networks usually provided an alternative 'labour exchange'. Conflicts between capital and labour were 'managed' through institutionalised contact with trade union officials. Redundancies were agreed after formal consultation with shop stewards and trade union representatives. In non-unionised workplaces, issues relating to promotion and redundancy might be discussed by the Works Committee.

But in seeking to understand how a black working class emerged in Birmingham in the 1950s and 1960s, it is necessary to explore how social relations of production which *de facto* placed Caribbean workers side by side with the English working class as labour power for industrial capital were fragmented as:

1 the English bourgeoisie sought to introduce *within the metropolitan factory* forms of domination which it had enjoyed in the colonial periphery; and
2 sections of the indigenous working class exploited the ethnic fragmentation which flowed from discriminatory employment practices, to gain material advantages in terms of higher wage rates, promotion and better job security.

157

I propose to examine these two issues separately, although, in practice, they are inter-linked. Thus management decisions which discriminated against black workers were justified as a response to the assumed hostility of white workers to 'coloured' labour. On the other hand, many union officials and shop-floor workers, although critical of racist practices by management, and concerned about 'splits' within the workforce, tacitly accepted discriminatory practices of hiring, promotion and redundancy, when this advantaged white workers.[1]

1 Colonial caste in the metropolitan factory

In the mid-1950s, the attitude of Birmingham managers towards the employment of black labour can best be characterised as erratic and contradictory. Despite chronic labour shortages, many firms flatly refused to employ any black workers. Some firms employed Indian or Pakistani migrants whilst rejecting West Indians as 'Golliwogs – Negro types'.[2] Others avidly recruited West Indians because 'some of them are very good', but refused Pakistani workers because they were 'a dead loss'.[3]

Among employers who employed black labour, many refused to allow black workers into sections where white women worked, hence limiting their scope for promotion; although others did so, and found 'no special problems'. Equally, whilst some foundries employed black workers only in segregated sections, others discovered that a group bonus system led to the breakdown of all-white gangs, as most white workers preferred a competent black colleague to a white worker who was less efficient.

Yet even firms with policies which offered some degree of opportunity to their black workforce were adamant that their role was limited to that of labouring: 'I would be very reluctant to ever put a coloured worker in charge of white workers. I would resent it myself as other white workers would'!, remarked one senior manager at Parkinson Stoves*.[4] Indeed, most industrialists believed that in the long term, there was no role for black workers in their workforce because there was no future for black people in Britain. In the event of recession, black workers were to be laid off first, since 'you can't let down your own *brothers* [my emphasis]!'[5] 'Coloured labour' was viewed as a short-term expedient for a short-term problem.

Overall, therefore, the 'typical' response of capital to black labour was one of exclusion – either total exclusion *from* the factory, or exclusion *within* the factory from all but the least skilled sectors of employment. And this (even disregarding the tendency of some white workers to formalise discriminatory practices with management) raises questions about the motivation for such employment practices. For those firms which excluded black workers at a time of labour shortage, and even those firms which dismissed black workers before white workers at a time of recession, could scarcely have been profiting from their discriminatory employment practices.[6]

In Birmingham in the mid-1950s, therefore, it seems that the attitude of industrial capital to black migrant labour was influenced not by a calculated approach to the profitability of industrial capital[7] but by the historical experience of British imperialism. And in particular, the 'erratic and contradictory attitudes of managers towards the employment of black labour can be traced to their quite specific experiences of the hierarchy of empire and their familiarity with caste structures in the colonies.[8]

2 Workers and immigrants

Just as the attitude of capital to the employment of black labour was erratic, so we have seen that white workers could hold curiously contradictory views about West Indian migrant labour in Birmingham. Whilst some connived with employers to import neo-colonial structures of segregation and discrimination into the workplace, or else actively sought to exclude the black migrant workforce from the labour market, others accepted the presence of a black proletariat in Birmingham (with varying degrees of enthusiasm and understanding) as the consequence of British colonialism and imperial policy. In effect, what we are witnessing in Birmingham in the mid-1950s, is the unfolding of a struggle within the working class; a struggle about the role of colonial workers in metropolitan society, and in consequence an ideological conflict which was to 'renegotiate' the meaning of nation and race in the metropolis.

Perhaps the most significant factor in the unfolding of this struggle was the existence of an entrenched hierarchy of labour

159

within the working class, dominated by 'men with real skill in their fingers'.[9] In Birmingham especially, sections of this labour aristocracy held markedly chauvinistic attitudes towards women, unskilled immigrants from other parts of the United Kingdom, and Irish migrants, long before 'coloured workers' were introduced into Birmingham industries. And indeed some initial working-class reactions to West Indian workers in Birmingham, mixed sexist, labourist and colonialist stereotypes into a series of panics about the 'threat' black workers posed: the fear that 'their women' were under threat from black male sexuality; that wage rates would be undercut by 'immigrant strike-breaking'; or that West Indian migrants had come to 'sponge off the welfare state'.[10]

On the other hand, the fact that Jamaican carpenters and cabinet-makers found a more ready acceptance among their white colleagues because of their 'real good work' and their trade union awareness should warn us that the mid-1950s were a time before the issue of race took on what Ira Katznelson refers to as a 'predictability' of meaning for the English working class.[11] Indeed, within the labour movement in Birmingham the debate raged over whether black migrants should be actively welcomed and integrated into the trade unions as fellow proletarians, or whether, by default or intention, the interests of the indigenous working class would be 'better served' by allowing *de facto* segregation and a stratification of the labour force along the lines of 'colour'.[12]

In the mid-1950s this debate had only just begun to wrack the Labour movement. In Birmingham the NUGMW's policy of enthusiastically organising black workers stood in stark contrast to the efforts of at least one senior official within the TGWU to formalise workplace apartheid. And whilst some trade unionists could draw upon the spirit of the anti-fascist struggle to oppose organisations trying to divide the political power of the working class on lines of race,[13] few were able to escape the insidious effects of social imperialism, and place the struggles of an emerging colonial proletariat on to the agenda of the labour movement 'at home'. On the contrary, the very process of employer discrimination tended to harden indigenous workers' attitudes towards 'coloured' labour. Observing that black migrants rarely held skilled positions, believing that only a tiny minority had experience of industrial work and trade union organisation, and assuming that black workers in Britain would return home at the first sign of recession, white workers were encouraged to regard 'coloured labour' as technically incompetent to serve capital, and as culturally incompetent to resist it. It was but a short step to some form of 'biological' determinism.[14]

So perhaps it is significant that Dr Prem, an Indian general practitioner and a vociferous campaigner for Indian independence, was chosen as a Labour Party candidate in the municipal elections in Birmingham in 1945, when the black population of Birmingham barely reached a few hundred. Dr Prem won the seat. But after he stood down in 1948 no other black candidate was elected to the City Council for thirty-one years. The successful candidate, in 1979, was Egbert Carless, a Jamaican-born Post Office engineer, who had settled in Birmingham in 1954.

A CARIBBEAN PETITE BOURGEOISIE?

We have seen that the small elite of West Indian wood-workers in Birmingham who found work as carpenters and joiners were able to establish themselves on conditions of relative equality with indigenous craftsmen. Undoubtedly the chronic shortage of skilled construction labour provided these workers with the opportunity to gain skilled work. But it would seem that on building sites, where most workers were sub-contractors or independent craftsmen, and where institutionalised systems of hiring, management and control were lacking, the skills of individual black workers were recognised and rewarded.

Interestingly, on the building sites, the social relations of production were remarkably akin to those of the East End sweatshops at the turn of the century. Certainly the lack of factory organisation and its managerial discipline, and the absence of personnel officers obsessed with colonial caste-structures, allied to a system of sub-contracting that 'paid by results', opened up the only 'window of opportunity' for skilled black workers in Birmingham during the 1950s.

As such, there was a potential here for the development of an independent Caribbean business class, which could have built up sub-contracting businesses in the wood-work and construction trades. The fact that these wood-workers 'moved on' to better paid work in the USA, or returned to the Caribbean as recession began to affect the building trade in Britain, is testimony to the importance of colonial under-development in the making of a Caribbean working class in Britain. For the loss of this West Indian elite meant that the Caribbean community in Birmingham was being drained of expertise and accumulated capital, and was losing a potential petite bourgeoisie in what was becoming a land of settlement. At this point therefore, the relationship between Birmingham as a metropolitan centre and the West Indies as an under-developed colonial periphery comes into focus.

For the Caribbean emigrant, accumulating capital as a wage labourer in the metropolitan economy was (or seemed to be) a far more realistic proposition than remaining in the West Indies to work the family land or to seek employment in the town. Yet a small capital investment in land, machinery or property in the Caribbean could offer a returning migrant some promise of comfort and security in later life. So for those able to accumulate capital in the metropolis, their prospects upon returning to the islands seemed rosy indeed.

But in practice, the cold economics of under-development actually obstructed the 'return' to the Caribbean. The cost of passage to England was high. Most families' limited resources were locked into land and property in the Caribbean. In some cases this capital was pledged against the cost of migration; but in any event, land and property could not be sold to provide the migrant with cash for the journey, as well as capital to invest in Britain, without destituting remaining family members at home. Hence the high costs of migration had to be 'paid off' in the metropolis, which, given the limited earning power of the Caribbean worker, left little or nothing for reinvestment – either in the Caribbean or in Britain. In Birmingham in particular, whatever money could be saved tended to be dissipated on essential investment in housing in order to counter landlord discrimination and the chronic shortage of accommodation in the rented sector.[15] This 'investment' in housing in Birmingham in turn encouraged the migration of further family members, with the attendant costs of passage.

Hence the growth of a Caribbean petite bourgeoisie in the

1950s and 1960s in Britain was severely limited. There was no Caribbean equivalent of the Jewish cabinet or slop shop in Birmingham: in part, because investment in property offered a far more secure return than entrepreneurship, but also because the Caribbean community tended to lose its capital and human resources to the Americas. Even the general availability of employment throughout the West Midlands in the 1950s and 1960s, notwithstanding the peaks and troughs of recession, seemed to support the viability of a 'wage earning strategy', and further constrained the accumulation of entrepreneurial capital and the growth of a Caribbean business class in Birmingham.

ON COLONIALISM, UNDER-DEVELOPMENT AND THE MAKING OF THE BLACK WORKING CLASS

The initial response of English capital and labour to West Indian immigration can therefore only be understood in the context of the development of British colonialism and the ideological impact of Empire within the metropolis. Or, to use Paul Gilroy's morphological metaphor, cultural forms secreted in Empire redeveloped and combined with new forces in the metropolis, to 'renegotaite' notions of race and class in the bus depots of central Birmingham and on the streets of Smethwick.[16] So in exploring the experience of Caribbean migrants in Birmingham during the early period of settlement, we are confronted with a migration which has both a colonial and a metropolitan dimension.

Under-development created the preconditions for the waves of emigration that have punctuated the history of the British West Indies in the post-emancipation era. But in the 1940s and 1950s, it was the colonial relationship which made possible, and indeed encouraged, emigration from the Caribbean to the Mother Country. Of course, West Indian migrants, like Polish and East European volunteer workers in the immediate post-war era, were moving to the developed metropolitan centre in search of work. But unlike East European migrants, Caribbean migrants were 'guaranteed the right' of employment and domicile by the accident of Empire. Yet, from the outset, the newly arrived Caribbean migrants competed in a labour market where Empire had made the meaning of 'race' and 'colour' significant, and where the English bourgeoisie, even as 'the sun set on the

Empire', sought to reimpose the social relationships of colonialism in the metropolitan factory.

However, de-skilling, segregated work practices, unfair dismissal agreements and the denial of promotion to black migrants not only created its own cycle of deprivation in the short term; it also *exposed black migrants in the long term* to the threat of *structural unemployment*. This threat emerged initially from the effects of cyclic recession, as black workers were sacked before their white colleagues.[17] But the threat was also present at times of economic growth, as mechanisation and rationalisation eradicated the very jobs – foundry labouring, machining, press moulding – which black migrants had filled. Between 1951 and 1966, there was a 10 per cent decline in the manufacturing labour force, especially marked in unskilled and semi-skilled work, which was due to increased capitalisation and specialisation. In Birmingham, 'more new capital equipment was introduced into [local] industry after 1945 than at any other time in its history'.[18] Small firms, able to specialise in new forms of production, managed to hold their share of a contracting manufacturing base; but few black workers were employed by small firms. On the other hand, service industries, traditionally under-represented in Birmingham, increased their labour force by one quarter between 1951 and 1966. Building and civil engineering, insurance, banking and finance, the professions and public administration all experienced major expansion.[19] But these sectors were virtually devoid of black faces until the 1970s. Indeed, if the structural characteristics of the British economy (themselves rooted in Empire and colonialism) initially 'brought' West Indian migrants to Britain, and to Birmingham in particular, then those same structural characteristics – the decline of manufacturing industry, the proneness to stop-go economic performance, and the entrenched pattern of boundary management by the unions and capital – played no small part in denying them opportunity to prosper in Britain.

EMPIRE AND DIASPORA

Whether answering the plea to defend the Mother Country in 1940, or simply coming to 'better themselves' in the 1950s and early 1960s, Caribbean migrants entered Britain through the door of Empire. Indeed, as Nicholas Deakin has observed, the early immigrants, inspired by the high ideals of Empire and Commonwealth taught in the West Indies, 'took their British citizenship seriously'.[20] Even in Britain, just four years before the passing of the restrictionist 1962 Commonwealth Immigration Act, Caribbean migrants could draw comfort from the words of David Renton, the Joint Under-Secretary of State at the Home Office, who insisted that 'this country is proud to be the centre of an inter-racial Commonwealth...the greatest assortment of peoples of all races, creeds and colours the world has seen'.[21]

Hence 'Empire' had significant political, social and even psychological implications for the early Caribbean migrants. The colonial education system celebrated a white-led Eurocentric world, which implicitly encouraged migration to Britain as a form of cultural, as well as financial, 'advancement'. And early migrants in particular, seem to have been heavily influenced by a vision of the 'Mother country' which had given the world democracy, fair-play and cricket.[22] At the very least, the first generation of African-Caribbean migrants fully expected that the Mother Country would respond to the 'sons and daughters of Empire' with a degree of hospitality and fairness, if not outright joy. Their genuine mystification when faced with hostility and discrimination, is constantly recorded in the contemporary testimony of West Indian migrants in Birmingham.

And here, comparison with the experience of Jewish immigrants is instructive. For even Judaic orthodoxy, contemptuously dismissed as medieval hocus pocus by sophisticated Anglo-Jewish society, played its part in easing the pain of settlement in England. Orthodox religious ritual, and the daily celebration of Jewish custom, helped to shield the Jewish immigrant from the hostility of the 'goy' world, and acted as a buffer against the psychological trauma of rejection. For West Indian migrants, England was a shattering of illusions. The 'shared heritage' of Empire, language and religion proved to be nothing of the kind. Moreover, by suppressing the African roots of Caribbean culture, and by denying the common heritage of black struggle against slavery and imperialism, Empire destroyed the cultural and psychological 'buffering mechanisms' which might have allowed the early migrants to anticipate white hostility, and organise autonomously in the new land.[23]

It is significant, too, that the African diaspora has shaped emigration from the Caribbean in a quite different pattern from that of Jewish emigration from Eastern Europe. For the communities of the Jewish diaspora clung to Europe through centuries of persecution and attempted genocide. With the rise of capitalism, a new Jewish bourgeoisie came into being, which wedged itself into the political and economic structures of the emerging nation states. It was this Jewish bourgeoisie which 'policed' Jewish emigration at the end of the nineteenth century. And, at least in the case of Britain, it manifestly stemmed the tide of immigration and influenced the eventual pattern of settlement.

Conversely, the African diaspora has been haunted by the brutal experience of slavery and colonialism. In the New World, an independent black leadership was systematically annihilated. The cultural heritage of Africa was all but obliterated. The power of the written word was taken away, and the capacity of the black community to achieve sustained economic growth was undermined.[24] Thus, when the children of the African diaspora once again set ship, this time en route to England, there was no powerful or wealthy Anglo-Carribbean elite to guide their way in the new land – even if only to re-export them as unwanted guests. For 'friends' and 'protectors' the African-Carribbean immigrant could count not upon an oligarchy of financiers, industrialists and politicians whose influence within the state administration was considerable, but rather upon a whimsical coalition of Empire loyalists, free-marketeers and socialists who believed variously in the duty of the Mother Country, a free trade in labour and the brotherhood of man. None of these 'friends and protectors' stood the test of time; although it is fair to say that some sold out more abjectly than others.

So the mass movement of Caribbean peoples to Britain is much more than a moment in the history of Third World labour migration. More significantly, it is a chapter in the story of the African diaspora. And Birmingham, city of Iron and Empire, is inextricably linked to that story. For in the seventeenth century the ships that left the great ports of England for Western Africa were loaded with 'textiles made in Lancashire and muskets, brass rods and cutlery made in Birmingham'.[25] For almost two hundred years these ships traded the 'Matters of our own Manufactures, for...Gold...and Negroes', the latter being indeed 'the best Traffick the Kingdom hath, as it doth...give so vast an Imployment to our People'.[26] Emptied of their iron goods, these ships loaded human cargoes along the West coast of Africa, and carried ten generations of Africans to slave and die upon the plantations of the New World.

The African slave trade was the largest forced migration in history. Allowing for those who perished on the voyages, and in the slave stockades, 'the volume of traffic to the New World', according to Joseph Holloway, '...may well be over forty million' souls.[27] By the mid-nineteenth century one-third of all people of African descent lived outside of Africa.[28] The triangular trade between England, Africa and the New World made the fortunes of many Birmingham merchants. The sugar, cocoa, rum and tobacco produced by the slaves made the fortunes of many a Birmingham entrepreneur.

Birmingham radicalism played its part in the black slaves' emancipation. In 1789 the freed slave Olaudah Equiano gave thanks to the people of Birmingham 'for the favours and the fellow-feeling that they have discovered for my very poor and oppressed countrymen', and for their support for the abolitionist cause. In Birmingham the Jamaican cabinet-maker, William Davidson fought successfully to place the abolitionist cause on the agenda of domestic radicalism, and link the cry for the liberation of the black slave to the demands of the English proletariat for democracy and justice. Davidson died on the scaffold with four white comrades in May 1820.[29]

In the twentieth century the descendants of the freed slaves volunteered to join the common people of Britain in their struggle against Nazism and fascism. After victory some stayed; and in later years many more came, to make a home in England's Second City. The wheel of history has turned full circle. Birmingham now stands at an inter-section: of black history and white history; of diaspora and Empire; of slavery and freedom.

NOTES

1 See, for instance, pp. 125–9.
2 See p. 120.
3 See p. 120.
4 See p. 125.
5 The Personnel Manager at Associated Castings* in Smethwick. See p. 130.
6 Such systematic discrimination between different ethnic groups is only a profitable option for industrial capital in the metropolis if practised within a controlled system of labour migration, whereby a general depreciation of labour costs is achieved by minimising the social costs of the reproduction of labour power. Whether such policies actually benefit capital in the long term is a complex and much debated issue. Analyses of the German and Swiss migrant labour systems in the post-war era have reached divergent conclusions. For a discussion, see Stephen Castles and Godula Kosack *Immigrant Workers and Class Structure in Western Europe*, 2nd edition (Oxford, 1985), pp. 385ff. Castles and Kosack conclude that 'it seems impossible to say whether immigration improves or harms productivity' (p. 408).
7 The issue of wage rates is critical here. Although many black workers were employed in jobs which white workers were unwilling to take, the trade unions, out of their own vested interests, seem to have maintained wage parity between black and white workers *in the same jobs*. Castles and Kosack believe 'it is not possible to detect a downward pull on wages' as a result of immigration into Britain the post-war era (ibid., p. 424).
8 See Chapter 10, especially pp. 119–20 for details of these experiences. It is perhaps significant that few (if any) of these metropolitan managers had experience of running commercial organisations in the colonies. Their views were moulded by the political structures of Empire, particularly through service in the army and the colonial civil service.
9 See p. 126.
10 These comments are consistently recorded by the Fircroft Survey. For example at an AUEW branch meeting reported upon on 28 January 1956, hostility was directed against 'Jamaicans marrying British girls' and 'immigrants who won't go home in a recession hereby becoming a burden on the rest of us'.
11 Katznelson notes that in the 1950s, 'race questions were not only unpleasant, but in political terms were anomic and unpredictable'. By the early 1960s a new 'predictability, irrespective of party political allegiance, was becoming apparent'. See Ira Katznelson, *Black Men, White Cities* (London, 1973), p. 130.
12 This conflict is mirrored in the formal political field in the split between Birmingham Trades Council and the Labour Group on the City Council over housing policy for black migrants. See pp. 188–94.

13 See pp. 128–9 for details of one trade union's attempts to counter racist organisations in the workplace.

14 The widespread failure of English radicalism to embrace the struggle against colonialism and imperalism has left the English working class especially vulnerable to the appeal of social imperialism. For a discussion, see J.M. Mackenzie, *Imperialism and Popular Culture* (Manchester, 1986).

15 The historical decline in the private rented sector is also significant here. In 1914 some 90 per cent of the national housing stock was in the private rented sector. Seventy years later that had dropped to 9 per cent. See Sally Smith, *The Politics of Race and Residence* (Cambridge, 1989), p. 52.

16 Thus Paul Gilroy notes that 'culture is not a fixed and impermeable feature of social relations' and 'its forms change, develop, combine and are dispersed in historical processes'. See Paul Gilroy, *There Ain't No Black in the Union Jack* (London, 1987), p. 217. Robert Colls and Philip Dodd also make the point with regard to specific symbols: '[the fact] that symbols and ideas recur does not ensure that their meaning is the same. Meaning is. . .a matter of present context and practical life.' See Robert Colls and Philip Dodd in Preface to *Englishness: Politics and Culture 1880–1920* (London, 1986).

17 See press cuttings in Birmingham (Central) Reference Library, Local Studies Department, entitled 'Problems of Coloured Immigration' (sic), for details.

18 See Anthony Sutcliffe and Roger Smith, *Birmingham, 1939–1970* (London, 1974), p. 165. Equally significant was the emergence of the new international division of labour in the post-war era, with heavy manufacturing industries developing in the Third World.

19 ibid., pp. 163–4.

20 See Nicholas Deakin *et al.*, *Colour, Citizenship and British Society* (London, 1970), p. 283.

21 David Renton, speaking as Joint Under-Secretary of State at the Home Office, in the House of Commons, 5.12.1958.

22 To a certain extent this was a self-regulating process. Pioneer migrants who chose England as their destination are likely to have been strongly influenced by the ideology of Empire.

23 Hence, at least in Birmingham, it was not until the mid-1960s that black community groups began to organise semi-autonomously outside the 'conventional' political system to obtain better housing conditions. John Rex notes that in 1963 he and Robert Moore 'found that the party surgery held in the Labour Club. . .was primarily concerned with considering and processing the housing claims of the native-born and Irish workers and their families. Many others, however, native as well as immigrant, found increasingly that their needs were only likely to be considered by their own social organisations working through a new community association that had come into being'. See John Rex, *The Ghetto and the Underclass: Essays on Race and Social Policy* (Aldershot, 1988), p. 53.

24 Gilroy comments that black cultures 'have been produced over a long period of time in conditions of the most terrible oppression. They have been created inside and in opposition to the capitalist system of racial exploitation and domination, by those who experience subordination at its most vicious and degrading'. Gilroy, op. cit., p. 159.
25 See Peter Fryer, *Staying Power: The History of Black People in Britain* (London, 1984), p. 14.
26 John Cary, 'An Essay on the State of England. . .' (Bristol, 1695), p. 75.
27 Joseph Holloway (ed.) *Africanisms in American Culture* (Bloomington, 1990), p. 1.
28 For an analysis of the statistics, and a review of the issue in dispute, see Philip Curtin, *The Atlantic Slave Trade: A Census* (Madison, 1969).
29 For details see Fryer, op. cit., p. 110 and pp. 214f.

Part III

IMMIGRATION AND THE POLITICS OF RACE

But Lord! to see the absurd nature of Englishmen, that
cannot forebear laughing and jeering at everything that
looks strange.

(Samuel Pepys, *Diary*, 27 November 1662)

13

THE FIRST ACT

At the turn of the twentieth century, notes Bernard Gainer in his study of the origins of the 1905 Aliens Act, 'there was not a single society or organisation in East London devoted to pressing for restriction or control of immigration'.[1] This situation, however, owed little to a tradition of good natured tolerance within the East End, and rather more to an organisational hiatus in anti-alien sentiment at the end of the 1890s. But the turn of the century marks a turning point in the nature and scope of anti-alienism in Britain, as the issue moved from the salons of the nobility on to the streets of the capital. For, by 1901, this organisational vacuum had been filled by the formation of the British Brothers' League, which was to lead the people's protest against 'the East End of London...becoming the dustbin of Europe into which all sorts of human refuse is shot'.[2] It is the changing nature of anti-alien sentiment, and above all its transformation from High Tory to the national popular, which is the theme of this chapter.

THE ORIGINS OF THE ANTI-ALIEN MOVEMENT

Prior to 1900, two organisations, the Society for the Suppression of the Immigration of Destitute Aliens (SSIDA) and the Association for Preventing the Immigration of Destitute Aliens (APIDA) formed the vanguard of resistance to unrestricted immigration into Britain.[3] Founded in 1886, the Society for the Suppression of the Immigration of Destitute Aliens enticed a collection of noble lords and ladies to its high offices, but made only a minor impact upon the national scene, and none at all upon the 'impoverished workman. . .[the] victim of alien competition' for whom they claimed to speak.

However, among the array of titled office holders in the Society was Captain J. C. R. Colomb, Honourable Member for the East End constituency of Bow and Bromley. It was largely at his instigation that a Select Committee of the House of Commons was set up in February 1888 to advise on alien immigration. And although the Select Committee stopped short of recommending legislation to control immigration, it 'contemplated the possibility' that legislation might be necessary in the future.

In 1891 many of the stalwarts of the Society for the Suppression of the Immigration of Destitute Aliens recommenced their agitation, under the guise of a new organisation, the Association for Preventing the Immigration of Destitute Aliens. Once again Captain Colomb, ably assisted by Colonel Howard Vincent and the journalist Arnold White, sought to raise the spectre of the 'alien menace'. But although there was undoubted hostility towards the influx of Jewish migrants within the East End, the Association made no headway in its attempt to exploit this resentment. Even the East End *Evening News*, a paper capable of discerning a mass uprising of native East Enders in the breaking of an immigrant's window, lamented the lacklustre response that was occasioned by the cry of 'aliens out' in 1891.[4]

However, working-class indignation at the 'dilution' of the labour market by 'alien competition' was certainly rife, especially among trade unions who could claim that Jewish immigration affected their members' living conditions. The London Trades Council and the Dockers' Union passed resolutions against 'aliens' in 1891.[5] In 1892 the Trades Union Congress passed a resolution to restrict 'foreign pauper labour', since, it was asserted 'we must protect our own starving work-people by refusing asylum for the paupers of Europe'.[6]

But the collection of earls, dukes, lords and ladies (not to mention the captains and the colonels) which headed the Association's Executive Board did nothing to recommend APIDA to working-class Londoners. Nor did the Association have any real roots in East End society. For although Captain Colomb and Sidney Buxton (the MP for Poplar) were Association supporters who represented East End constituencies, neither constituency was seriously affected by immigration in the early 1890s.

Conversely Members of Parliament for the areas really affected –
Whitechapel, Stepney, Mile End, St George's – were notable only
by their absence. On the board of APIDA only the Rev. G.S.
Reaney and the Bishop of Bedford (previously Rector in the
Spitalfields district) could claim any close connection with the
areas of Jewish settlement.[7]

In effect the Association was a High Tory cabal, concerned to
promote the cause of anti-alienism from the vantage point of
privilege, in the vague expectation that this would strike a chord
amongst the lower orders. And of course the Association hardly
needed the support of the popular classes to bring their plans to
fruition. They could count upon their followers to instigate
legislation directly in the Lords or the Commons. The support of
'the people' – especially when half of the male population, and all
females, were disenfranchised – seemed to be of little
consequence.

It was not until the General Election campaign of 1895 that the
alien issue flared again. This time the Unionists made a more
concerted attempt to woo working-class support by pinning
anti-alienism to the promises of Joseph Chamberlain's social
programme.[8] And although the total programme was never
endorsed by the Conservative Party, the package 'served the
Opposition by-election candidates well' during the next three
years, and certainly played some part in the return of a
Conservative–Unionist administration in 1895.[9]

With Lord Salisbury once again in power, the prospects for
restrictionist legislation seemed favourable. However, a series of
government ministers found reasons to avoid bringing forward a
Bill, and until the turn of the century there was an apparent lull
in anti-alien agitation. None the less, the seeds of the British
Brothers' League, and a more populist anti-alienism, were sown
during this time.

A NEW DIRECTION

In 1892 James Silver became proprietor of the Stepney-based
weekly, the *Eastern Post*. Silver used the *Post* to promote his
personal brand of conservative politics, but in particular he used
its pages to press the case for restrictions upon immigration. In
1901 the *Eastern Post* trumpeted the convening of the Stepney

Housing Conference, which Silver (now an Alderman) hoped would finally set the issue of Jewish immigration alight. In fact the Conference was a fiasco. Scarcely fifty people attended the meeting, while many of the vociferous opponents of restriction mobilised from nearby Toynbee Hall.[10] Outmanoeuvred, but still undaunted, Silver promptly presented a resolution to the St George's Board of Guardians which identified alien immigrants as the source of 'excessive rents, overcrowding and consequent impoverishment of our own people'. This resolution, 'a mandate from the people', was discussed by the eleven members present and passed by a majority of one.[11] Boosted by this victory he pressed a resolution at Stepney Borough Council asserting that immigration was the cause of the housing crisis, and control the key to its solution. The eventual acceptance of this resolution was, according to Silver's *Eastern Post*, acclaimed 'with loud cheers'.[12]

On 22 December 1900 the *Eastern Post* carried a letter signed 'Anti-alien' which raised the idea of an anti-alien 'league'. Simultaneously (and possibly not without connection), William Shaw founded the British Brothers' League. Shaw, unlike his more illustrious predecessors, sought to create a populist movement. He asserted that immigration, although affecting all classes, most directly concerned 'the working man. . .Consequently, it was to the Working Men of East London that I first appealed'.[13] Combining the organisational skills of Major Evans-Gordon, and the propaganda vehicle of Silver's *Eastern Post*, the British Brothers' League grew rapidly. Mass meetings and public rallies were organised throughout the latter half of 1901. In January 1902 the Brothers' League packed the People's Palace in Mile End with some 2,000 members (plus another 2,000 in the hall and another 2,000 outside) to press the claim that alien immigration and gross overcrowding were part and parcel of the same problem; restriction was its only solution.

The British Brothers' League maintained a spurious claim to put nation above party politics. But in reality the League had strong links with the Conservative Party's organisation in the East End. Thus the Conservative and Unionist agent for Bow and Bromley organised the mass rally at the People's Palace, together with the Chairman of Stepney's Conservative and Unionist Association.[14] Even the 'membership' which the League claimed – according to the *Jewish Chronicle* some 12,000 in the latter half of 1902[15] – was more of a fiction than a reality. The vast majority of 'members' merely signed the League's roll and paid no dues to the organisation.[16]

None the less, the League was a significant factor on the local political scene, not only for its success in mobilising popular resentment against the Jews, but also for its strategy of creating links between a working-class constituency and the Tory establishment. Indeed, Colin Holmes suggests that 'it makes no sense to discuss the movement in isolation. . .it was really one rung of an inter-locking ladder'.[17] At the foot of the ladder was the BBL and the Londoners' League;[18] at the centre, the east London Conservative Associations; and at the top of the ladder stood the Parliamentary Alien Immigration Committee at Westminster. And like most ladders, this had a practical function; for by linking the housing crisis to the issue of alien immigration it was hoped to save Tory seats as the franchise was widened, especially in working-class areas.[19]

Certainly the worst outbreak of violence against Jews in the East End, which occurred in Bethnal Green in June 1903, arose out of the claim that immigrant Jews were displacing local people in the housing market. By then, however, anti-alien Tory MPs were attempting to distance themselves from involvement with the BBL, alarmed by its descent into rabid anti-Semitism. Instead, they began to channel their activities through the more 'respectable' Immigration Reform Association which was founded in February 1903 under the Presidency of the ubiquitous Earl of Donoughmore. The Immigration Reform Association's publicity carefully avoided mentioning the ethnic origin of pauper immigrants, whilst associating 'destitute aliens' with criminality and overcrowding.

As for the BBL, its activities began to taper off towards the end of 1903, and it held only one indoor meeting throughout 1904. Yet the techniques of mobilisation it employed – its members organised in military-style cohorts of 100 men; mass rallies with aggressive 'stewarding'; the whipping-up of anti-Jewish sentiment and nationalist xenophobia – were to become the hallmark of fascist organisations twenty years later, and were to reappear on the streets of East London with Mosley's Blackshirts in the 1930s.

THE ALIENS ACT

On 29 January 1902 Evans-Gordon moved an amendment to the King's Speech in which he sought to link the precipitate housing crisis in London to the theme of immigration control. 'Not a day passes', he thundered,

> but English families are ruthlessly turned out to make way for foreign invaders. . .rents are raised 50 to 100 per cent and a house which formerly contained a couple of families living in comparative decency is made to contain four or five families living under conditions which baffle description. . . It is only a matter of time before the population becomes entirely foreign.

And displaying a touching concern for the plight of the lower orders, he continued:

> The working classes know that new buildings are erected not for them but for strangers from abroad;. . .they see the schools crowded with foreign children and the very posters and advertisements on the wall in a foreign tongue. . .a storm is brewing which, if it be allowed to burst, will have deplorable results.[20]

Although the predicted storm never arrived, the appointment of a Royal Commission on the 'Aliens' Question' seemed to set the seal upon the anti-alien campaign. Yet when the Commission reported in the summer of 1903, it exposed the claims of the anti-alien lobby as popular fictions. The Commission not only punctured the myth of an alien invasion, finding that far less than 1 per cent of the British population were aliens (0.69 per cent), but it also unhinged the issue of immigration from the housing crisis, by pointing out that the worst overcrowding in London was in the wards of St Margaret and St John, where no aliens were resident!

But the terms of the Commission were limited soley to the question of immigration and its possible restriction – the wider questions of housing policy, employment legislation and social welfare, which were identified as the panacea for the real problems of the East End, were outside its jurisdiction. The majority report, signed by five of the seven-man inquiry team, found in favour of restricting immigration where the immigrant was deemed 'undesirable', either on the basis of criminality or because the immigrant was without visible or probable means of support. For the first time, as Paul Foot remarks in *Immigration and Race in British Politics*, the 'demands for rigid control of immigration were no longer merely the outpourings of a reactionary Tory rump'. They were now enshrined in the recommendations of a full-blooded Royal Commission.[21]

When the King's Speech of 1904 promised legislation to deal with the 'evils consequent on the entry of destitute aliens', Vincent, Evans-Gordon and the growing Unionist protectionist lobby centred on Joseph Chamberlain finally scented victory.[22] However, the vigorous opposition of the Liberals on the question of restricting the right of asylum kept the Bill off the statute books during 1904. When it was reintroduced the next year, it appeared to proclaim anew the right of asylum and to restrict the power of control over 'destitute aliens' to those arriving on 'immigrant ships' – defined as vessels carrying more than twenty third-class passengers. Another parliamentary row ensued, with Hayes Fisher, the Conservative Member for Fulham, likening 'pauper and diseased alien immigrants' to 'a river of sewage', whilst Keir Hardie, the leader of the Independent Labour Party, attacked the Aliens Bill as 'fraudulent, deceitful and dishonourable'.[23]

Eventually, in August 1905, the Aliens Bill became law. Even from the point of view of the restrictionists the Aliens Bill was flawed, for in practice it did little to restrict the total number of immigrants entering the United Kingdom. From the point of view of the poor of the East End the Bill was irrelevant. No new houses were built, and the old houses continued to decay and fester. No new jobs were created for 'British workmen', although the sweatshops of the East End continued to exact their toll of disease and misery without favour of religion or nationality.

But the campaign which the anti-alienists had waged was to leave lasting traces upon the face of British politics. For through the British Brothers' League and the Londoners' League, the Tory Party had been able to build up grass roots organisations in eastern London which appealed directly to the material interests of labour. And although this agitation frequently met with blank indifference, and increasingly with downright hostility from socialist leaders, even the spasmodic successes of the campaign suggested that, at worst, anti-alienism could be a spoiling tactic to undermine traditional appeals to Liberal radicalism in London. At best, it could form a populist plank for a corporate imperial strategy, such as that being advanced by Joseph Chamberlain and the tariff reformers.[24]

True, many senior Tories were appalled at the antics of the anti-alienists, fearing that restrictionism in England threatened retaliation against the vastly more considerable volume of British emigration to the USA and the dominions. Others baulked at the demagogy of Evans-Gordon and his cohorts of Brothers, believing that anti-alien xenophobia could unleash a a *Judenhetze* in the East End and bring a revolutionary mob on to the streets of the capital.[25]

Ironically, the Aliens Bill of 1905 marked a watershed in British politics. A year later the Tories were swept from power, after two decades of virtual supremacy, by an opposition electoral victory which brought over 50 representatives of 'Labour' to the House of Commons (30 Labour men and a further 24 Lib-Labs). Tory strategists had many years in the political wilderness to ponder the lessons of their crushing defeat.[26] Those who regarded the party's descent into anti-alien xenophobia with distaste could point to the sharp demise of the Liberal Unionists and the electoral trouncing of a number of anti-alienists. Set against this was the palpable evidence that Evans-Gordon and Vincent held their seats, whilst Claude Hay, a prominent restrictionist, actually increased his majority in Shoreditch against the national swing.

ANTI-ALIENISM AND ANTI-SEMITISM

In looking at the genesis of the anti-alien movement and the struggle over the Aliens Bill, a question inevitably arises which engaged many commentators at the time. Namely, was anti-alienism a campaign purely dedicated to the restriction of alien immigration, as its protagonists claimed? Or was it, as many of its detractors asserted, part of a conspiracy to exploit resentment against overcrowding, sweating and poverty in the East End for broader anti-Semitic purposes?

Inevitably, evidence about the extent of anti-Jewish feeling among native East Enders at the turn of the century is anecdotal rather than scientific.[27] Clearly there was resentment against the immigrant Jews, a fact reported in the Jewish as well as the Gentile press. However, local newspaper accounts also confirm a lack of interest in the aliens' campaign, at least before 1900; whilst the Earl of Dunraven, a perpetual agitator for the cause of restriction, was forced to concede in 1892 that 'immigration *ought* [my emphasis] to stand at the level of a great national concern' – but by implication it did not.[28] He was echoed by Arnold White, who constantly bemoaned 'the disinclination of every Englishman worthy of the name to harass the persecuted Russian Hebrew' and the failure of the country at large to engage seriously with the problem of alien immigration.[29] In fact the campaign for the Aliens Bill sparked a popular response (at least in terms of mobilising a mass movement) only during the brief flaring of the British Brothers' League – between 1901 and 1904, at a time when the housing crisis in the East End was at its height.

The tension between the need to retain 'respectability' in the eyes of the political establishment, and the populist demands of the rank and file for 'action' against the Jews, is reflected in the desperate efforts of William Shaw and Evans-Gordon to distance themselves from charges of anti-Semitism, without distancing themselves from the aims of the movement.[30] Moreover the fact that both leaders were forced to condemn 'agitation' which could be 'used as a cloak for religious passion or racial animosity' (Shaw)[31] indicates that the BBL's street propaganda, far from 'dispassionately' advocating the 'logic' of immigration control, in fact frequently descended to rabid anti-Semitism.

Therefore the anti-alien movement can best be characterised as a movement which oscillated between two extremes. On the one hand, it had to conform to the demands of high politics, where the campaign for restrictive legislation was fought and won. On the other hand, the fleeting success of the British Brothers' League in mobilising popular sentiment against the Jews offered the vision of a new style of movement which could build support among the lower and middle classes for Tory and Unionist policies.

Hence full-blown anti-Semitism, on the model of anti-Semitic movements in Russia or even Germany, was an option which simultaneously excited and repelled the movement's leadership. It excited because of its potential to mobilise the rabble – not to mention respectable London shop-keepers. Thereby it offered a basis for right-wing populism in an era of creeping democratisation and opened a corridor to Westminster for a new breed of populists such as Captain Colomb and Major Evans-Gordon. Yet anti-Semitism repelled precisely because the rabble was volatile and it was not respectable, especially in high society, to espouse anti-Semitic views.[32]

Certainly the campaign against immigration at the end of the nineteenth century was, with a minor detour to condemn Italian immigrants ('every one with a knife', according to Evans-Gordon in a parliamentary debate in 1902), a campaign against *Jewish* immigration. The dividing line between anti-alienism and an agitation that could spark off verbal or physical attacks upon any Jew in Britain was therefore thin. The meeting places, the homes and the workplaces of immigrant Jews were also those of Jews who had been resident in England for generations. The shouts of 'Wipe them out' that greeted the speeches of the 'respectable' men at the People's Palace also suggest that, to many of the rank and file, the distinction between aliens and immigrants, rich or destitute, was irrelevant – providing that they were Jews. Whatever their motives, individual or collective – and the restrictionist movement included many cranks and eccentrics – White, Evans-Gordon, Vincent and all the worthy Lords and Commoners who leapt to their feet to support the Aliens Bill must have known that the Jewish/alien spectre, once raised, could not be exorcised at will.

The anti-alien movement at the turn of the nineteenth century also faced two ways. In one sense it looked back: mirroring forms of anti-Semitism which were widespread in Russia, Austria and Germany in the nineteenth century, and encapsulating a style of patrician arrogance which had been the hallmark of the British ruling class throughout the eighteenth century. Yet it also looked forward to an era of mass politics in which the hegemony of the ruling classes could no longer be 'taken for granted'. To this extent the anti-alien movement was exploring a new political landscape. And its attempts to exploit popular resentment against immigrants who were 'driving English people out of their native parishes',[33] its flirtation with the politics of 'race', and the para-military style of mobilisation employed by the British Brothers' League, clearly point the way into the twentieth century.[34]

NOTES

1 Bernard Gainer, *The Alien Invasion: The Origins of the Aliens Act of 1905* (London, 1972), p. 60.
2 *East London Observer*, 11.5.1906.
3 In this context Irish settlement in England does not constitute alien immigration since it was within pre-war national boundaries. Clearly, however, the emergence of a populist anti-alien movement at the end of the nineteenth century needs to be seen in the context of earlier anti-Irish sentiment. For a discussion of the political response to Irish immigration in the 1840s, see 'Class, Ethnicity and Popular Toryism' in Neville Kirk, *The Growth of Working-Class Reformism in Mid Victorian England* (Beckenham, 1985).
4 *Evening News*, 17.6.1891.
5 Gainer estimates that more than forty-three unions and trades councils had passed anti-alien resolutions by that year. See op. cit., p. 95.
6 *Trades Union Congress, Report*, 1892.
7 The Jewish Harry Marks, MP for St George's-in-the-East, was a Conservative exclusionist, and was rebuked by the *Jewish Chronicle* on 26 July 1895 for his attacks upon pauper aliens, but apparently he was not a member of APIDA.
8 Chamberlain first demanded that the immigration of 'pauper aliens' should be controlled in his programme of popular reform and social legislation of 1892. See Chamberlain's article in *The Nineteenth Century* (November 1892).
9 See S. Maccoby, *English Radicalism 1886–1914* (London, 1953), p. 141.
10 Gainer, op. cit., p. 65.
11 ibid.
12 *Eastern Post*, 30.11.1901.
13 ibid., 23.11.1901.
14 Gainer, op. cit., p. 70.
15 *Jewish Chronicle* 31.10.1902.
16 Aproximately 1,500 paid dues according to the *Jewish Chronicle*. ibid.
17 Colin Holmes, *Anti-Semitism in British Society, 1876–1939* (London, 1979), p. 91.
18 The Londoners' League was formed in 1901, also to press for immigration restriction. According to Holmes, 'it was the Londoners' League which ultimately controlled the management aspects of the BBL meeting in 1902 at the People's Palace'. ibid., p. 91.
19 ibid.
20 Evans-Gordon in the House of Commons, 29.1.1902.

21 See Paul Foot, *Immigration and Race in British Politics* (Harmondsworth, 1965), p. 92.
22 As the Member for Birmingham West, Chamberlain had direct experience of the alien problem. Birmingham was plagued by 121 aliens in 1902, although this dropped to 89 in 1904.
23 Foot, op. cit., p. 98.
24 For details of the struggle over trade and tariff reform, see G. D. H. Cole, *British Working Class Politics 1832–1914* (London, 1941).
25 Fear of the 'revolutionary' potential of the London residuum was especially widespread at the end of the nineteenth century, reaching a climax on Bloody Sunday, 13 November 1887, when mounted soldiers attacked a crowd of demonstrators marching along the Strand.
26 In 1900, 334 Conservative MPs and 68 Liberal Unionists had been returned. In 1906 the Conservative total shrank to 130, and the Liberal Unionists' total to 28. See Cole, op. cit., p. 179.
27 For a detailed snapshot of public discourse on the Jewish question at the end of the nineteenth century, see William Fishman, *East End 1888* (London, 1989).
28 See *The Nineteenth Century*, No. 180 (June 1892).
29 White's evidence to the Royal Commission on Alien Immigration, quoted by Holmes, op. cit., p. 106.
30 Shaw later pulled out, according to Garrard, at least in part because of the movement's increasingly anti-Semitic tone. J.A. Garrard, *The English and Immigration, 1880–1910*, (Oxford, 1971), pp. 63–4. But Holmes offers evidence to suggest that Shaw resigned because of personality clashes with other leaders. Holmes, op. cit., pp. 94–5.
31 Adding 'for [we] put ourselves in the wrong'. Garrard, op. cit.
32 Holmes notes 'the strength of liberal toleration and the aura of disapprobation which surrounded anti-semitism' in England at the turn of the century. See Holmes, op. cit., p. 106. However, he correctly sees this level of toleration as an historical development – not as a quintessentially 'English tradition'.
33 According to the *East London Observer* (11.5.1901), adding the aliens were 'literally taking the bread out of English mouths'.
34 Here there are major similarities with German pre-fascist movements, especially the Pan German League (ADV) led by Heinrich Class, which also attempted to build a popular basis for authoritarian politics prior to 1914. After the collapse of the autocratic Kaiser regime in 1918, and the establishment of a democratically elected National Assembly in 1919, the ADV became more active and gained considerable financial support from German industry, as well as support from the conservative establishment. In 1920, the leader of a small ultra-right-wing political party, one Adolf Hitler, journeyed to Berlin to meet Heinrich Class, and announced himself an avid disciple. See Simon Taylor, *Prelude to Genocide: Nazi Ideology and the Struggle for Power* (London, 1985), pp. 15–18.

14

THE ROAD TO SMETHWICK

The errors of a wise man make your rule,
Rather than the perfections of a fool.
(William Blake, 'On Art and Artists')

The arrival of the first ships carrying Caribbean migrants to Britain in the late 1940s prompted immediate calls for restraints upon 'coloured immigration' into the United Kingdom. Yet more than a decade elapsed before anti-immigrant sentiment coalesced into a coherent political movement advocating restriction. But whereas the anti-alien movement at the end of the nineteenth century achieved only local success in its attempts to popularise restrictionism, by the early 1960s the issue of 'controlling coloured immigration' had come to dominate English political culture at both local and national level.

Birmingham was to play a dominant role in the development of this anti-immigration sentiment. Unlike the anti-alien movement, political demands for the control of immigration in the post-war era spread upwards – from the street to town hall and on to parliament; and outwards – from Birmingham and the West Midlands to London. Significantly, the campaign was led not by lords of the realm, or ex-Indian army wallahs,[1] but by individuals such as Albert Mucklow, engineer and trade union member, who could claim, with at least some justification, to represent the *vox populi*.[2] Above all the campaign against 'coloured immigration' culminated in the defeat of the Labour Minister Patrick Gordon Walker at Smethwick in the General Election of 1964. He lost his seat to Peter Griffiths, completely against the national trend, in a campaign locally dominated by the issue of black immigration.[3]

MISSING THE WAY

The first campaign to exploit the issue of black immigration in Birmingham in the 1950s has an unexpected connection with earlier attempts to exploit anti-Semitism in the East End – in the person of Oswald Mosley and his British Union of Fascists. In February 1952, Mosley proclaimed that West Indian immigration was a pernicious influence upon the country, and that 'we must prevent the residence of Negroes in Britain'.[4] Indeed, sensing that his policy of enforced repatriation would get a more sympathetic hearing in Birmingham than in his old stomping ground of the East End, Mosley announced at a meeting in Sparkbrook, in March 1956, that Birmingham was the British Union Movement's 'greatest hope'.[5]

In the autumn of 1956 Mosley set off on a series of rallies across England, in the hope of raising the Union Movement from the ashes. Announcing 28 October as the date for his rally in Birmingham, he boasted that he would fill Birmingham Town Hall for the meeting. Mosley's action set off a wave of protest in Birmingham, with black community organisations and the Trades Council promising direct opposition to his provocation.[6] In the event, however, this counter-demonstration was called off, and Mosley spoke to an audience of some 500 people, policed by nearly 100 stewards who violently ejected a number of student protesters.[7]

In October 1958 Mosley again spoke in Birmingham, attempting to exploit the aftermath of racist rioting in Nottingham and Notting Hill. But by 1960, despite another large rally in Birmingham, it was clear that Mosley's Union Movement was still an isolated and despised fringe party. Events elsewhere, however, suggest that Mosley's failure had less to do with his slogan of 'racial hygiene' – 'Jamaica for the Jamaicans and Britain for the British'[8] – than with the taint of his fascist past. Indeed, the attack by hundreds of striking workers upon a Union Movement lorry sporting the slogan 'Mosley stands for Workers' Ownership' suggests that most working-class Brummies, who still remembered German air attacks upon the city, were not enamoured with Nazi fellow-travellers, whatever their message in the post-war era.[9]

THE LOCAL DIMENSION

Among those who went to Mosley's 1956 meeting, ostensibly to heckle,[10] was the Conservative councillor for Birmingham Acocks Green, Charles Collet. But whatever it was that Charles Collet went to heckle, it was unlikley to have been Mosley's denunciation of unrestricted black immigration from the colonies, for Councillor Collet was even then urging the Council to demand controls on the number of 'coloured immigrants' coming to the city.

At about the same time as Charles Collet began his agitation against immigration in the City Council, a letter appeared in the *Birmingham Mail* asking:

> Am I to understand that when jobless I, a ratepaying Briton whose forebears have inhabited these islands since before there was an England [sic], am I to stand at the counter of the labour exchange office on a par with these new arrivals? Or must I labour to keep the stranger on the dole – to pay for his food, housing and clothing?[11]

The letter came from one John Sanders, who eleven years later was able to claim as Chairman of the Birmingham Immigration Control Association that 'we can organise here in the West Midlands sufficiently to capture every marginal constituency by making immigration the decisive issue'.[12] Nor in the aftermath of Smethwick was this a totally idle boast.

The links between Charles Collet, the Birmingham Immigration Control Committee (later Association), John Sanders and Peter Griffiths have been well documented.[13] Suffice it to say that Councillor Charles Collet was elected President of the Birmingham Immigration Control Committee Association in 1960, with John Sanders as its Treasurer. The Association became the 'most powerful anti-immigration pressure group in the country', spawning a Smethwick Branch in March 1961. The Smethwick Branch, led by Donald Finney, rapidly attracted 500 members, among them senior members of the local Labour Party and many community activists. Although the Birmingham Association disintegrated after a dispute about its links with the Tory Party, a new association, the British Immigration Control Association, came to the fore.

On 6 March 1962 (just after the Third Reading of the Commonwealth Immigration Act) the British Immigration

Control Association was wound up. But by then the issue of immigration and race had become stitched into the fabric of politics in Birmingham. In the 1962 municipal elections, against a national swing to Labour, the Tories won three seats in Smethwick and Donald Finney (now a member of the Conservative Party) was elected for Spon Lane 'with the biggest majority the ward had seen since the war'.[14] Indeed when the Tories seized control of Smethwick Council in municipal elections in 1964, the prophecy that Gordon Walker would be defeated in the General Election was literally written on the walls.

Smethwick, of course, was the culmination of a far deeper shift in the social and political mood of Britain. As such it was a symbol, 'like Little Rock and Alabama',[15] of the arrival of 'race' as a significant issue in British politics in the post-war era. Indeed Stuart Hall has remarked that 'the defeat of a Labour Minister. . . revealed the degree to which. . .sectors of the working class were now clearly exposed and vulnerable to the construction of a popular racism'.[16] But why did Birmingham provide such fertile ground for the establishment of the immigration control associations, and for the growth of a popular racism?

THE POLITICS OF BIRMINGHAM PEOPLE

During the period of post-war Caribbean settlement in Birmingham, it was the Labour Party who held the reins of municipal power.[17] During this period of Labour domination, the Labour Group on the Council had two leaders: Albert Bradbeer, a congenial Quaker who led the group from 1952 to 1959; and Harry Watton, who led the group from 1959 to 1966 and 'built up a personal influence over Birmingham municipal affairs reminiscent of that exercised by Joseph Chamberlain in the 1870s'.[18] The period of Watton's leadership was also marked by serious strains within the Birmingham labour movement, as the Trades Council and many sections of the rank-and-file Borough Labour Party angrily denounced the rightward shift of the Group's policies and attacked Watton's authoritarian style of leadership. Not a few of these clashes occurred over the Labour Group's attitude towards immigration control and the evolution of the City Council's policy towards its black citizens.

The key issue in the evolution of this policy undoubtedly

concerned housing. The housing shortage in Birmingham in the early 1950s was indeed chronic.[19] The Five-Year Rule introduced in 1949 primarily to deter provincial and Irish immigration into the city meant that the Council's initial refusal to house West Indian and other black migrants in the 1950s was not a shift in policy based upon racial exclusion, but was an extension of the ethos that 'Birmingham people come first'.

In January 1954 – largely because of Bradbeer's single-minded determination to push the measure through against considerable opposition – the City Council appointed a Liaison Officer to serve the growing 'coloured' community. But the Labour Group also began to take the line that adequate provision could be made for black immigrants only if their numbers were controlled. Hence in January 1955 a Labour delegation headed by Alderman William Bowen called upon the Home Secretary, asking him to restrict coloured immigration into Birmingham and expressing 'extreme concern' at pressure on services and housing.[20] The move towards a restrictive policy broke the Labour Party's consensus on immigration policy, dividing the Labour Group against the Trades Council, who were supported by the Borough Labour Party and most local ethnic minority organisations. The Trades Council maintained its opposition to control until the passing of the Commonwealth Immigration Act in 1962.

In May 1959 Harry Watton replaced Bradbeer as leader of the Labour Group. Watton had none of Bradbeer's internationalist vision, nor did he have Bradbeer's contacts with local West Indian or Indian organisations. Yet although the drift towards a more overtly racialised response to Birmingham's housing crisis took place under his leadership, policy itself was also drifting on a gathering undercurrent of racist sentiment in the city.

THE RACIALISATION OF HOUSING POLICY

The immigrants are living in tight pockets turning inwards to themselves and it would seem intent on creating a 'little Jamaica' or the like within the city. . .I would emphasise that the integration desired by the Council is not being achieved except in a small way at the places where coloured people work.[21]

In 1959 Birmingham City Council publicised the finding of a survey which indicated that 3,200 houses in the city were occupied by 'coloured people' and that a sample check estimated that eleven people lived in each house. From this, the Council estimated that 35,000 'coloured people' were living in the city, of whom 24,000 were West Indians.[22] A year later the Council's General Purposes Committee appointed an ad hoc sub-committee to inquire into problems of overcrowding in Birmingham.

An interim report in December 1960, although recognising that overcrowding had generally declined, identified a concentration of overcrowding in areas such as Handsworth, Aston and Sparkbrook, etc., where tenants, 'mostly newcomers', were overcrowding 'a considerable but unknown number of houses'.[23] Conditions in these houses were described as much worse than in commonly termed 'slums', and evidence was produced of high infant mortality rates, as well as of TB and venereal disease among 'coloured immigrants'. It was also noted, with ill-disguised alarm, that 'coloured women' had high birth rates, and that women constituted some 40 per cent of the West Indian population.[24]

The report also focused upon the fact that 'coloured' immigrants faced extreme difficulties in getting municipal housing. The Five-Year Rule was now recognised as a positive barrier to black settlers becoming council tenants, and hence intruding into white housing estates. The Committee stressed that few immigrants could hope to be rehoused in prevailing conditions since they would only be rehoused after five years *if and when* (original emphasis) they had enough points.

The Committee's statement was displayed prominently on the front page of the Council's news-sheet, *Your Business*. Reporting that lodging houses in areas such as Sparkbrook could contain up to fifty tenants, the editorial assured its readers that only in 'cases of exceptional overcrowding' were coloured immigrants likely to qualify for an offer in the sixth year after their arrival in the city, and 'the number of such cases is comparatively small'.[25] Hence as the 1960s beckoned, and a brave new world for Britain's Second City was unveiled by the city's planners, the Labour leadership not only abandoned any suggestion that council policy should intervene to ameliorate the specific problems faced by black

190

immigrants, it now trumpeted the virtues of the Five-Year Rule as an effective method of 'containing' black immigration. Having isolated the infected zones, the Council set about 'curing' the disease.

The City Council could enforce the overcrowding provisions of the 1957 Housing Act to attack the problems of multi-occupation, ill-health and social stress which it now identified as being caused by 'newcomers' in Sparkbrook, Handsworth, etc.[26] But it was also recognised that if overcrowding was to be controlled, overcrowded families would have to be rehoused by the Council. Such a policy would throw a heavy burden upon the Housing Management Committee, which in 1960 could only allocate 5 per cent of letting to 'special priority groups' and about 10 per cent to homeless families. Yet if overcrowded families were not systematically rehoused, an attack upon multi-occupation would simply drive the problem from one ward to the next.

The fear that rehousing immigrant families would provoke a political backlash initially stymied any course of action.[27] In October 1961 the General Purposes Committee reiterated that no proposals were being considered that would specifically alleviate the housing problems of black people, in the face of persistent taunts by Councillor Collett that the city was preferring 'immigrants to the needs of Birmingham citizens'.[28] However, armed with the 1961 Housing Act, and later the 1964 Housing Act, as well as the 1965 Birmingham Corporation Act which was wrung from the newly installed Labour government, the City Council set about the problem of overcrowding with a vengence.

Unfortunately, their vengeance fell almost exclusively upon black landlords and their predominantly West Indian, Indian and Pakistani tenants.[29] The provision for registration of houses in multiple occupation, and in particular the powers to refuse registration in cases where either the landlord or the area were deemed unsuitable, were powerful instruments for containing the black population within the zones that poverty and landlord discrimination had already allocated them. Sanitary policy was directed at the edges of the so-called twilight zones in an attempt to control the spread of black tenancies into white areas. And even when black tenants were rehoused by the City Council, they were filtered through the mesh of the local authority's housing staff who systematically allocated them to the 'clearance houses'

191

in the middle ring on the basis of *their* assessment of 'different standards of housekeeping'.[30]

Certainly the creeping racialisation of housing policy was an implicit rather than an explicit process. As such every political and professional representative of the City Council eschewed any racist *intent* in the formulation of policy. But in February 1966 the Labour Group Leader explicitly revealed the ideological rationale for the Council's housing policy. After receiving a newspaper head-line 'Council houses for immigrants?', scrawled over with the message 'Look after our Birmingham people first!', Harry Watton explained:

> Birmingham people must come first – that is where I stand personally and that is where I hope the Labour Group will stand. I am not in favour of any form of priority for immigrant families.
>
> There are elderly people living only a stone's throw from my own house who have lived here all their lives, and who have helped to make this the second city, who still have to live in back to back houses and who in the snow this morning have to go to the end of the yard for a toilet.

He continued, in answer to a question about the fairness of the Five-Year Rule:

> Surely those who come from outside are lucky if they only have to wait five years. Many of the people I am talking about had to wait all their lives. I don't accept the suggestion that we should reduce the waiting period. It is not valid in Birmingham. You cannot ignore the seriousness and immensity of Birmingham's housing position.

Finally, asked about the Council's policy of rehousing black immigrants in 'slum' properties, Watton observed that: 'Many Birmingham people have to go into such properties. Immigrants will be rehoused and the rehousing will depend upon their housing need and *their own personal housing standards*' [my emphasis].[31]

Watton's views are especially poignant, for although he avoids the language of race, he none the less constructs an image of 'little England' – in this case its Second City – which is divided not by capital and class, or even by wealth and poverty, but by some vague ethnicity. In essence Watton draws upon a Chamberlainite corporatism to construct his vision of the great metropolis built by 'Birmingham people', who should now enjoy the fruits of their labour in old age. Yet these same Birmingham people who have made Birmingham the Second City, 'still have to live in back to back houses...and go to the end of the yard for a toilet'. Presumably the political irony was lost upon Harry Watton.

Watton's view, though, is characteristic of the much deeper shift in the social and political mood of post-war Britain, especially as it relates to the working class and the labour movement. For although Watton rejects the language of class in favour of a policy which gives pride of place to 'Birmingham people', his policy pointedly appeals not to 'Birmingham people', but to the 'Birmingham working class' who were the main beneficiaries of municipal rehousing policies.

Here, then, the creeping racialisation of housing policy reaches the point of critical mass. Watton's statement not only promotes the interests of a particular class fraction, (albeit expressed in the language of a local 'ethnicity'); it also privileges this class fraction in policy, for *in practice* the white working class is able to gain housing resources at the expense of Birmingham's emergent black proletariat. The solidarity of labour is disintegrating. The language of a class is replaced by forms of language which give significance to concepts of ethnicity within a class, as localism, nationalism and colour become the touchstones of municipal policy. For Watton knows that his appeal to the white working class (codified as 'Birmingham people') can deliver the necessary political support for his factional and personal power base within the Labour Group.[32] A population that shares a sense of 'cultural belonging' is thus in the process of being transformed into a political constituency.

Of course Watton is not creating this constituency – Smethwick demonstrates that it was already 'in the making'. But in attempting to snatch back this constituency for the Labour Group on the basis of chauvinism, not only is ideological credence given to the dichotomy between 'coloureds' and 'Brummies', but the dichotomy is given a 'common sense' logic. Ideological social relations and social action now reinforce each other. Thus political mobilisation *on the basis of race* is energised. For the native working class, being a white Brummie is not only a matter of cultural identification, it is now a matter of political privilege.

Being white becomes significant in terms of status and access to resources in employment, housing, education and leisure.[33] Indeed being white now *appears* to replace the historical category of class as an axis of struggle and as an indicator of privilege, especially in terms of social consumption.

Hence by the mid-1960s, municipal policy and political discourse identified black citizens in Birmingham not as a section of the working class, nor even as a specific group of migrant workers with special needs, but as a racial sub-group. Their rights – *vis-à-vis* the 'native' working class – were limited; indeed special legislation was needed to prevent 'coloured immigrants' from contaminating areas of white housing.

Certainly it is necessary to draw a distinction between the politics of racism and racialised politics. In Birmingham the controlling Labour group warded off concerted pressure to formally racialise the city's housing policy and exclude black immigrants from all municipal housing. Indeed, the Labour Group's capitulation to the politics of chauvinism and race was seen as a peculiarly local phenomenon. The leadership was clearly at odds with the rank and file of the Labour Party, especially over housing policy. At the time it was considered that the concentration of municipal policy-making in the hands of an inner clique and the emergence of a personality cult around the leadership were the real reasons why the racialisation of housing policy was possible under Labour.

But what happened in Birmingham was no isolated phenomenon. The creeping racialisation of municipal policy in Birmingham was evidence of a wider crisis of *Labour* politics in Britain in the mid-twentieth century.[34] Smethwick was a warning of the storm to come. That is why Stuart Hall has asserted that the crisis of the 1950s and 1960s was 'not a crisis *of* race' (emphasis in original), but 'race' was 'the lens' through which people came to perceive the crisis was developing.[35] The most obvious symptom of this crisis in the mid-1960s was that Labour was in danger of 'losing' its electoral hold upon its traditional working-class constituency. At the time, Watton and his group contended that a housing policy which discriminated in favour of the 'local' working class was justified as mere common sense. Such was the worldly wisdom of the Labour Group.

Yet there's many a wise man falls asleep, and wakens up a fool.

NOTES

1 Although their views were not without significance – see pp. 119 ff.
2 Mucklow founded the Birmingham Immigration Control Association on 13 October 1960. See Paul Foot, *Immigration and Race in British Politics*, (Harmondsworth, 1965), p. 195.
3 Griffiths won Smethwick for the Tories with a 7.2 per cent swing, compared to a national 3.5 per cent swing to Labour. ibid., p. 64.
4 Robert Skidelsky, *Oswald Mosley* (London, 1981), p. 508.
5 Possibly Mosley believed that some vestige of support still remained from his days as the Labour MP for Smethwick – he was elected in December 1926. John Darragh in the *Sunday Mercury*, 7.10.1956, estimated Mosley's Union Movement to have a mere 200 to 300 members in Birmingham.
6 All the major political parties, with the exception of the Conservatives, demanded that Mosley be denied the use of the Town Hall. The city's African-Caribbean Association called for a counter-demonstration. This proposal was initially supported by the Trades Council and other political groups.
7 *Birmingham Post*, 29.10.1956.
8 For instance in a speech reported by the *North Kensington Leader*, May 1959. See Skidelsky, op. cit., p. 509.
9 Mosley had tried to exploit industrial unrest in the Birmingham motor industry in the summer of 1956 to win recruits for the Union Movement. See *Birmingham Post*, 26.7.1956.
10 According to his statement reported in the *Birmingham Gazette*, 29.9.1956.
11 20.10.1954.
12 *Guardian*, 23.7.1965.
13 See Foot, op. cit.
14 ibid., p. 41.
15 See Dahni Prem, *The Parliamentary Leper: A History of Colour Prejudice in Britain* (Aligarth, India, 1965), p. 1.
16 Stuart Hall, 'Racism and Reaction' in CRE and BBC (eds) *Five Views of Multi-Racial Britain* (London, 1978), pp. 18–19.
17 Labour were in control of Birmingham City Council from 1952 until 1961, and headed a minority administration for a further five years.
18 Anthony Sutcliffe and Roger Smith, *Birmingham, 1939–1970* (London, 1974), p. 104.
19 See pp. 140–5 for details.
20 At this time the government view was strictly anti-interventionist, with the logic that no specific provision could be made for black migrants in order to demonstrate 'the equality of citizens from all parts of the Commonwealth'.
21 Report of City Council Liaison Officer for Commonwealth Immigrants, Birmingham City Council (BCC) Proceedings, 21.5.1959.
22 ibid. These figures, especially those for West Indians, would appear

to be over-estimated, since the 1961 census put numbers much lower. See p.106.

23 BCC Proceedings, 6.12.1960.
24 ibid.
25 *Your Business*, No. 157, December 1960.
26 In fact the 1966 census demonstrated that only 1.7 per cent of all houses in the city had been converted into lodging houses and only 2.8 per cent of the houses in the middle ring were multi-occupied. See Sutcliffe and Smith, op. cit., p. 244.
27 By October 1962 only 141 notices had been served to curb multi-occupation, whereas some 3,600 houses were known to be multi-occupied at the time.
28 Memorial introduced by Collett, at Birmingham City Council Meeting, 15.7.1961.
29 Indeed the Corporation openly stated that the main target of their campaign was the Pakistani landlord. See E.J.B. Rose *et al.*, *Colour and Citizenship* (London, 1969), p. 249.
30 See John Rex and Sally Tomlinson, *Colonial Immigration in a British City* (London, 1979), p. 141, where one housing visitor records that: 'We can't hide the fact that people have different standards of housekeeping. We don't want to offend people. We try to put people into neighbourhoods where they won't conflict.'
31 See interview with Watton in the *Sunday Mercury*, 13.2.1966. One week before this interview, the Birmingham Borough Labour Party had passed a resolution, by 87 votes to 63, attacking the Five-Year Rule and demanding a change in the City Council's housing policy, despite 'strong opposition from the Labour Group of councillors, and their leader Alderman Harry Watton'. ibid.
32 For an analysis of the development of 'codified' statements on race, without recourse to explicit racist language, see Frank Reeves, *British Racial Discourse* (Cambridge, 1983).
33 Municipal housing, education and leisure are all part of what Manuel Castells refers to as the process of 'collective consumption'. Such services in the case of Birmingham in the post-war era are 'objectively socialised [and] essentially dependent upon their production, distribution and administration on the intervention of the [local] state'. Significantly, this has come about because 'the development of the class struggle and the growing power of the working-class movement *open up breaches in the dominant logic along the line of least resistance* [my emphasis], thus affecting the relations of distribution rather than the relations of production.' See Manuel Castells, *The Urban Question* (London, 1977), p. 457.
34 This approach is stressed by Paul Gilroy in his article 'The End of Anti-Racism'. He writes: 'race cannot be understood if falsely divorced from other political processes. . .A more productive starting point is provided by. . .seeing "race" and racism not as fringe questions but as a volatile presence at the very centre of British politics actively shaping and determining the history not simply of

blacks, but of this country as a whole at a crucial stage in its development.' See Wendy Ball and John Solomos (eds) *Race and Local Politics* (Basingstoke, 1990) pp. 193–4.
35 Hall, op. cit., p. 31.

Appendix I

THE NEXT GENERATIONS

In 1929 *The New Survey of London Life and Labour* provided a snapshot of the changing structure of Jewish employment in the capital, one generation after the peak years of East European immigration. Some 90,000 Jews still remained in the old East End and neighbouring districts. But many had begun to move out to the suburbs as increasing prosperity brought about greater mobility. Patterns of employment were also changing. The younger generation were moving out of the tailoring trades into shop-keeping and commercial travelling, although tailoring and furniture-making were still the dominant Jewish trades in London. Metal-working, printing, electrical contracting and office work were attracting increasing numbers of young Jewish men, whilst clerking and dress-making were expanding areas of employment for Jewish women.

Of course the early 1930s brought the economic slump. But London, with its greater prosperity and growing consumer industries, rode out the Depression much better than the provinces. Certainly the Jewish population of inner London suffered badly from the slump; the 1930s were 'hard times'.[1] Yet there are clear signs that the children of the East European immigrants were enjoying greater mobility and prosperity than their parents. There was an increase in the Jewish business community – albeit most concerns run by the first generation of British-born Jews were still small-scale before 1939. There was also an increase in the Jewish professional class.

After the Second World War there was 'a more rapid rush into the middle class'.[2] In 1961 it was estimated that 38 per cent of the Anglo-Jewish population could be classified as belonging to Social Class I or II, in comparison to the national average of 16 per cent. The proportion of Jewish and non-Jewish skilled workers was identical at 46 per cent. Among the younger geneation of Anglo-Jews, there was difficulty in finding any who could be classified as 'unskilled'.[3] None the less, although 'the romantic success story – from immigrant tailor to business tycoon in three generations' – may have much validity, Harold Pollins reminds us that 'diverse elements make up any community'.[4]

In 1982, some twenty years after Caribbean migration to England reached its peak, Britain was again in the grip of economic slump. Birmingham and the West Midlands bore the brunt of the recession. It ravaged the industrial heartlands of the West Midlands, decimating the traditional steel-making and metal-working industries, and severely affected car-manufacturing and component production.

According to official estimates, the male unemployment rate in the West Midlands reached 18 per cent in March 1982. The Third PSI Survey, however, suggested that this figure was an under-estimation. The PSI Survey also showed entrenched variations between white and black workers. In comparison to a rate of 19 per cent among white workers in the West Midlands, the unemployment rate among 'West Indian' workers had reached 34 per cent.[5] Average wage rates for all black male workers were at least 20 per cent below those of white colleagues.[6] Above all, the class profiles of West Indian and white workers diverged significantly, as the following table shows:[7]

Job level	White men (%)	West Indian men (%)	White women (%)	West Indian women (%)
Professional Employer Management	19	5	7	1
Semi-skilled manual	13	26	21	36
Unskilled manual	3	9	11	7

In 1982, 43 per cent of all West Indian households in Britain were concentrated in the inner-city areas of London, Birmingham and Manchester – compared to just 6 per cent of households in the white population and 23 per cent of the Asian population. None the less, in Birmingham, a gradual dispersal of the African-Caribbean population from the inner areas to the suburbs and to satellite towns such as Redditch and Bromsgrove was discernible, and a general improvement in housing conditions of the African-Caribbean population was apparent.

NOTES

1 *The New Survey of London Life and Labour* estimated that 13.7 per cent of east London Jews were living in poverty in 1929, in comparison to the local average of 12.1 per cent. See H. Llewellyn Smith (ed.) *The New Survey of London Life and Labour* (London, 1933), Vol. IV, pp. 285 ff.

2 Harold Pollins, *Economic History of the Jews in England* (London, 1982), p. 240.

3 See S.J. Prais and M. Schmool, 'The Social-Class Structure of Anglo-Jewry: 1961' in *The Jewish Journal of Sociology*, Vol. XVII, No. 1 (June 1975), pp. 7–11.

4 Pollins, op. cit., p. 240.

5 See Colin Brown, *Black and White: The Third PSI Survey* (London, 1984), p. 191.

6 ibid., p. 213.

7 ibid., p. 197–8.

Appendix II

MAPS

Map 1 Birmingham ward boundaries in early 1960s, showing Central Area and Middle and Outer Rings.
Source: Jerry White, *Rothschild Buildings* (London, 1980), p. 1.

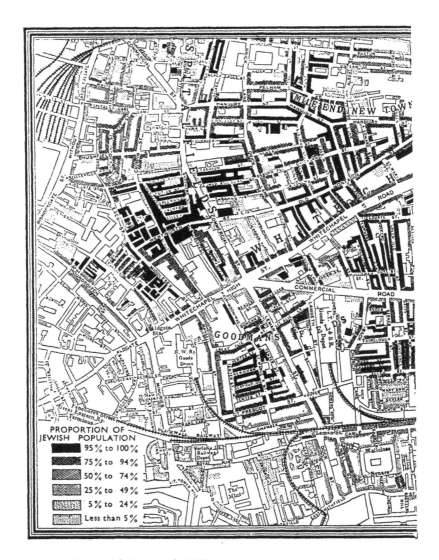

Map 2 The Jewish East End, 1900
Source: Anthony Sutcliffe and Roger Smith, *Birmingham, 1939–1970* (London, 1974), p. 183.

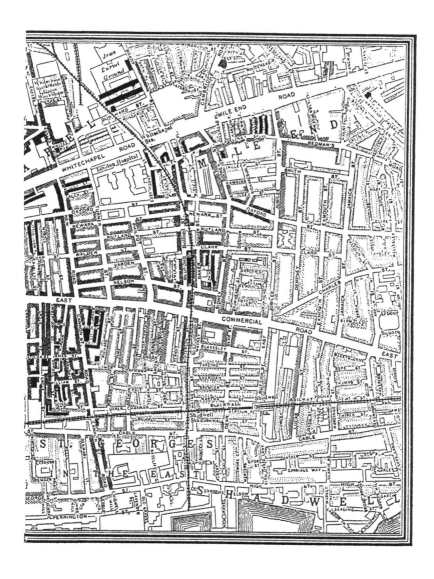

BIBLIOGRAPHY

ETHNOGRAPHIC MATERIAL

Sources marked 'Fircroft Survey' are taken from an extensive survey carried out in Birmingham in 1954 and 1955, by Fircroft College of Adult Education Race Relations Group, under the direction of the Principal, Leslie Stephens.

Leslie Stephens subsequently produced a paper, in 1956, based upon the Fircroft Survey, entitled *Employment of Coloured Workers in the Birmingham Area*. However, for the social historian, the raw material of the Fircroft Survey offers a great deal more than an insight into the practices of Birmingham industry in the mid 1950s. Indeed, the data in the survey throw detailed light on to a subject that is otherwise poorly documented – namely the early period of African-Caribbean migration to Birmingham.

In the course of the Fircroft Survey, extensive interviews were conducted with Birmingham employers, personnel managers, trade union officials and community leaders. In all, 35 places of employment were visited, which employed a total of 2,150 black workers out of their total workforce of 90,000. A number of locally based West Indian and Indian migrant workers were also interviewed on their experiences of seeking and finding work in Birmingham. Extensive interview notes were kept by the interviewers (some of whom were West Indian and African adult students), and these records, together with a large number of returned questionnaires, constitute the basis of much of the survey data and the information provided in Chapters 7 to 12 of this book.

Although the original survey records give the true names of individuals, employers, firms, trade unions. etc., I have, where indicated with an *, altered these details and provided fictitious names.

In cases marked with an #, I have 'reconstituted' the interview from the copious notes of the interviewers, in order to present the information in the form of an oral testimony. Dates given in the footnotes refer to the date of the interview, or the date on which the questionnaire was completed.

Sources dated in the 1980s are taken from taped interviews, carried out between June 1987 and September 1990. In all cases, names have been changed to protect the interviewee's identity, in line with assurances that were given at the time of the interviews.

NEWSPAPERS

East London Observer
Eastern Post
Graphic
Illustrated London News
Jewish Chronicle
The Nineteenth Century
The Times
Trades Union Congress, Report

Birmingham Gazette
Birmingham Journal (newspaper of Birmingham Trades Council)
Birmingham Post
Guardian
Sunday Mercury
Your Business

BOOKS AND ARTICLES

Anand, V.S. and Ridley, F., *The Emergence of Enoch Powell* (London, 1969).
Ball, W. and Solomos J., (eds) *Race and Local Politics* (Basingstoke, 1990).
Banton, M., *The Coloured Quarter* (London, 1955).
——— , *The Idea of Race* (London, 1977).
Barker, A., *The African Link: British Attitudes to the Negro in the Era of the Atlantic Slave Trade* (London, 1978).
Barker, M., *The New Racism: Conservatives and the Ideology of the Tribe* (London, 1981).
Ben-Tovim, G., Gabriel, J., Law, I. and Stredder, K., *The Local Politics of Race* (Basingstoke, 1986).
Bermant, C., *Point of Arrival* (London, 1975).

Bernstein, E., 'Einige Bemerkungen über die Jüdische Einwanderung in England' in A. Nossig (ed.) *Jüdische Statistik* (Berlin, 1903).

Besant, W., *East London* (New York, 1901).

Bolt, C., *Victorian Attitudes to Race* (London, 1971).

Booth, C., *Life and Labour of the People of London*, 10 volumes (London, 1902).

Booth, W., *In Darkest England and the Way Out* (London, 1890).

Bourne, H., 'Smethwick – A Warning and a Call to Action', in *Labour Monthly* (December 1964).

Briggs, A., *Victorian Cities* (London, 1963).

Bristow, E. J., *Prostitution and Prejudice* (Oxford, 1982).

Brown, C., *Black and White: The Third PSI Survey* (London, 1984).

Calley, M., *God's People: West Indian Pentecostal Sects in England* (London, 1965).

Cashmore, E. and Troyna, B., *Black Youth in Crisis* (London, 1982).

Castells M., *The Urban Question* (London, 1977).

Castles, S., Booth, H. and Wallace, T. *Here for Good: Western Europe's New Ethnic Minorities* (London, 1984).

Castles, S. and Kosack, G., *Immigrant Workers and Class Structure in Western Europe* 2nd edition (Oxford, 1985).

Centre For Contemporary Cultural Studies, *The Empire Strikes Back* (London, 1982).

Coard, B., *How the West Indian Child is Made Educationally Sub-normal in the British School System* (London, 1971).

Coates, K. and Topham, T., *The New Unionism* (London, 1972).

Cole G. D. H., *British Working-Class Politics, 1832–1914* (London, 1941).

Colls, R. and Dodd, P., *Englishness: Politics and Culture 1880–1920* (London, 1986).

Cowper, Katie, 'Some Experiences of Work in an East-End District' in *The Nineteenth Century*, Vol. XVIII (November 1885).

Cox, O. C., *Caste, Class and Race* (New York, 1948).

CRE and BBC (eds), *Five Views of Multi-Racial Britain* (London, 1978).

Cross, C., *The Fascists in Britain* (London, 1961).

Cunningham, W., *Alien Immigration to England* (London, 1897).

Curtin, P., *The Atlantic Slave Trade: A Census* (Madison, 1969).

Darragh, J., *Colour and Conscience* (London, 1957).

Davidoff, L., 'Class and Gender in Victorian England' in *Sex and Class in Women's History* (London, 1983).

Davie, M., *World Immigration* (New York, 1936).

Davies, T., 'The Forms of Collective Racial Violence' in *Political Studies*, No. 34.

Davison, R. B., *West Indian Migrants* (London, 1962).

——, *Black Mother: Africa and the Atlantic Slave Trade* (Harmondsworth, 1980).

Deakin, N., 'Labour Adopts a White Britain Policy' in *Venture* (April 1968).

Deakin, N., Cohen, B. and McNeal, J., *Colour, Citizenship and British Society* (London, 1970).

Drachler, J. (ed.) *Black Homeland: Black Diaspora* (London, 1975).

BIBLIOGRAPHY

Drage, G., 'Alien Immigration' in *Journal of the Royal Statistical Society* (March, 1895).

Dunraven, Fourth Earl of, 'The Invasion of Destitute Aliens' in *The Nineteenth Century*, No. 184 (June 1892).

Eggington, J., *They Seek a Living* (London, 1957).

Emechta, B., *Second Class Citizen* (London, 1974).

Evans-Gordon, W., *The Alien Immigrant* (London, 1903).

Fischer, P., *Das Ostende von London: Ein Soziales Nachtbild* (Berlin, 1895).

Fishman W., *East End Jewish Radicals, 1875–1914* (London, 1975).

———, W., *East End, 1888* (London, 1989).

Flett, H., Henderson, J. and Brown, B., 'The Practice of Racial Dispersal in Birmingham, 1969–1975' in *Journal of Social Policy*, No. 8, pp. 289–309.

Foot, P., *Immigration and Race in British Politics* (Harmondsworth, 1965).

Fryer, P., *Staying Power: The History of Black People in Britain* (London, 1984).

Gainer, B., *The Alien Invasion: the Origins of the Aliens Act of 1905* (London, 1972).

Garrard, J.A., *The English and Immigration, 1880–1910* (Oxford, 1971).

Gartner, L., *The Jewish Immigrant in England: 1870–1914* (London, 1960).

Giles, R., *The West Indian Experience in British Schools: Multi-Racial Education and Social Disadvantage in London* (London, 1977).

Gilroy, P., *There Ain't No Black in the Union Jack* (London, 1987).

Gish, O., 'Colour and Skill: British Immigration, 1955–1968' in *International Migration Review*, Vol. 3, No. 1 (1968).

Glass, R. and Pollins, H., *Newcomers* (London, 1960).

Glazier, W., 'A Workman's Reflections' in *The Nineteenth Century*, Vol. XIV (December 1883).

Godwin, G., *Town Swamps and Social Bridges* (London, 1859).

Griffith, J.A.G., *Coloured Immigrants in Britain* (London, 1966).

Griffiths, P., *A Question of Colour* (London, 1966).

Hadden, R.H., *An East End Chronicle* (London, 1880).

Hall, S., *Policing the Crisis* (London, 1978).

Henderson, J. and Karn, V., *Race, Class and State Housing: Inequality in the Allocation of Public Housing in Britain* (Aldershot, 1987).

Hill, O., *Homes of the London Poor* (London, 1875).

Hobsbawm, E.J., *Industry and Empire* (London, 1969).

Holloway, J.E., (ed.) *Africanisms in American Culture* (Bloomington, 1990).

Holmes, C., *Anti-Semitism in British Society, 1876–1939* (London, 1979).

———, *John Bull's Island: Immigration and British Society, 1871–1971* (Basingstoke, 1988).

Husbands, C., *Racial Exclusionism and the City: The Urban Support of the National Front* (London, 1983).

Hyndman, H.M., *The Record of an Adventurous Life* (London, 1911).

James, C.L.R., *Black Jacobins* (London, 1938).

Jones P.N., 'The Segregation of Immigrant Communities in the City of Birmingham'. University of Hull Occasional Papers in Geography No. 7, 1961.

Jordon, W., 'Modern Tensions and the Origins of American Slavery' in *Journal of Southern History*, Vol. XXVIII (February 1962).

Kaplan, S., 'The Anglicisation of the East European Jewish Immigrant as Seen by the London *Jewish Chronicle*, 1870–1897', in *YIVO Annual of Jewish Social Science*, Vol. X (1955).

Karn, V., 'The Impact of Housing Finance on Low Income Owner-Occupiers'. Working Paper 55, Centre for Urban and Regional Studies, University of Birmingham (1977).

Katznelson, I., *Black Men, White Cities* (London, 1973).

Kingsley, C. (Parson Lot), *Cheap Clothes and Nasty* (London, 1850).

Kirk, N., *The Growth of Working-Class Reformism in Mid Victorian England* (Beckenham, 1985).

Layton-Henry, Z., *The Politics of Race in Britain* (London, 1984).

Leon, A., *The Jewish Question* (New York, 1970).

Lipman, V.D., *Social History of the Jews in England 1850–1950* (London, 1954).

Little, K., *Negroes in Britain* (London, 1947).

Lorimer, D., *Colour, Class and the Victorians* (London, 1978).

Maccoby, S., *English Radicalism, 1886–1914* (London, 1953).

Mackenzie, J.M., *Imperialism and Popular Culture* (Manchester, 1986).

Mackey, H., 'The Complexion of the Accused: William Davidson, the Black Revolutionary in the Cato Street Conspiracy of 1820' in *Negro Educational Review*, Vol. XXIII (1972).

Marks, L., 'Jewish Women and Prostitution in the East End of London' in *The Jewish Quarterly*, Vol. 34, No. 2 (1987).

Maunder, W.F., 'The New Jamaican Emigration' in *Social and Economic Studies* (March 1955).

Mayhew, H., *London Labour and the London Poor* (London, 1861).

Miles, R., *Racism and Migrant Labour* (London, 1982).

Miles R. and Phizacklea, A., *Racism and Political Action in Britain* (London, 1979).

——, *Labour and Racism* (London, 1980).

Newman, A. (ed.) *The Jewish East End, 1840–1939* (London, 1981).

Newton, J., *Thoughts Upon the African Slave Trade* (London, 1788).

Newton, K., *Second City Politics: Democratic Processes and Decision-Making in Birmingham* (Oxford, 1976).

Nikolinakos, M., 'Notes Towards a General Theory of Migration in Late Capitalism' in *Race and Class*, Vol. 17, No. 1 (1975).

Oliver, J.L., 'In and Out of Curtain Road' in *Furniture Record* (18 December 1959).

Padmore, G., *Africa – Britain's Third Empire* (London, 1949).

Patterson, O., *The Sociology of Slavery: An Analysis of the Origin, Development and Structure of Negro Slave Society in Jamaica* (London, 1967).

Patterson, S., *Dark Strangers* (London, 1963).

Peach, C., *West Indian Migration to Britain: A Social Geography* (London, 1968).

Pelling, H., *A History of British Trade Unionism* (London, 1963).

Pipes, R., *Russia under the Old Regime* (Harmondsworth, 1977).

Pollins, H., *Economic History of the Jews in England* (London, 1982).

Potter, B., 'The Sweating System' in *The Charity Organisation Review*, Vol. IV, No. 37 (January 1888).

Prem, D. R., *The Parliamentary Leper: A History of Colour Prejudice in Britain* (Aligarth, India, 1966).

Prothero, I., *Artisans and Politics in Early Nineteenth-Century London* (London, 1979).

Radin, B., 'Coloured Workers and British Trade Unions' in *Race*, Vol. VIII, No. 2 (1966).

Ramdin, R., *The Making of the Black Working Class in Britain* (Aldershot, 1987).

Reeves, F., *British Racial Discourse* (Cambridge, 1983).

Reid, J., 'Employment of Negroes in Manchester' in *Sociological Review*, Vol. 4, No. 2 (December 1956).

Rex, J., *Race, Colonialism and the City* (London, 1973).

——, *The Ghetto and the Underclass: Essays on Race and Social Policy* (Aldershot, 1988).

Rex, J. and Moore, R., *Race, Community and Conflict* (London, 1967).

Rex, J. and Tomlinson, S., *Colonial Immigrants in a British City* (London, 1979).

Richmond, A. H., *Colour Prejudice in Britain* (London, 1954).

Roberts, G. W. and Mills, D. O., 'Study of External Migration Affecting Jamaica, 1953–55' in *Social and Economic Studies*, Vol. VII, No. 2 (1958).

Robinson, C., 'Coming to Terms: The Third World and the Dialectic of Imperialism' in *Race and Class*, Vol. XXII, No. 1 (1980).

Rose, E. J. B., Deakin, N., Abrams, M., Jackson, V., Peston, M., Vanags, A. H., Cohen, B., Gaitskell, J. and Ward, P., *Colour and Citizenship* (London, 1969).

Roth, C., *A History of the Jews in England* (Oxford, 1949).

Rowbotham, S., *Beyond the Fragments: Feminism and the Making of Socialism* (London, 1980).

Ruck, S. (ed.) *The West Indian Comes to England* (London, 1960).

Ruppin, A., *Soziologie der Juden*, 2 vols (Berlin, 1930).

Scholes, T. E. S., *Chamberlain and Chamberlainism: His Fiscal Proposals and Colonial Policy* (London, 1903).

Senior, C. and Manley, D., *A Report on Jamaican Migration to Great Britain* (Kingston, 1955).

Sheridan, R. B., *Sugar and Slavery: An Economic History of the British West Indies, 1623–1775* (Baltimore, 1973).

Sherwood, M., *Many Struggles: West Indian Workers and Service Personnel in Britain, 1939–1945* (London, 1985).

Sivanandan, A. V., 'Race, Class and the State: The Black Experience in Britain' in *Race and Class*, Vol. 17, No. 4 (1976).

Skidelsky, R., *Oswald Mosley* (London, 1981).

Sklare, M. (ed.) *The Jews: Social Patterns of an American Group* (Glencoe, 1960).

Smith, D. J., *Racial Disadvantage in Britain* (Harmondsworth 1977).

Smith, H. Llewellyn (ed.) *The New Survey of London Life and Labour*, 9 volumes (London, 1930–35).

211

Smith, S. *The Politics of Race and Residence* (Cambridge, 1989).

Smith S. and Mercer, J., *New Perspectives in Race and Housing in Britain* (Glasgow, 1987).

Smithies, B. and Fiddick, P., *Enoch Powell on Immigration* (London, 1969).

Stedman Jones, G., *Outcast London* (Oxford, 1971).

——, *Languages of Class* (Cambridge, 1983).

Sutcliffe A. and Smith R., *Birmingham, 1939–1970* (London, 1974).

Szajkowski, Z., 'The Attitude of American Jews to East European Jewish Immigration (1881–1893)' in *Publications of the American Jewish Historical Society* (March 1951).

Taylor, S., *The National Front in English Politics* (London, 1982).

Taylor, S., *Prelude to Genocide: Nazi Ideology and the Struggle for Power* (London, 1985).

Thompson, E. P., *The Making of the English Working Class* (London, 1963).

Thompson P., *Socialists, Liberals and Labour: The Struggle for London 1885–1914* (London, 1967).

Thompson T., (ed.) *Dear Girl: The Diaries and Letters of Two Working-Class Women* (London, 1987).

Tomlinson, S., 'West Indian Children and ESN Schooling' in *New Community*, Vol. VI, No.3 (1978).

Trollope, A., *The West Indies and the Spanish Main* (London, 1839).

Visram, R., *Ayahs, Lascars and Princes: Indians in Britain 1700–1947* (London, 1986).

Walvin, J., *The Black Presence: A Documentary History of the Negro in England, 1555–1860* (London, 1971).

Watson, A. R., *West Indian Workers in Great Britain* (London, 1942).

Webb, B., *My Apprenticeship* (London, 1926).

Webb, S. and B., *Industrial Democracy* (London, 1897).

White, A., 'The Invasion of Pauper Foreigners' in *The Nineteenth Century*, No. 133 (March 1888).

——, *The Modern Jew* (London, 1899).

—— (ed.) *The Destitute Alien in Great Britain* (London, 1905).

White, J., *Rothschild Buildings* (London, 1980).

Williams, E., *Capitalism and Slavery* (Chapel Hill, 1944).

——, *From Columbus to Castro: The History of the Caribbean 1492–1969* (London, 1970).

Wright, P. L., *The Coloured Worker in British Industry* (Oxford, 1968).

INDEX

Great Tailors' Strike 72
Green, Rev. A.L. 63
Griffiths, Peter 185, 187
Gunzburg, Baron Erzel 5

Hall, Stuart 188, 194
Handsworth 112, 114, 145, 190
Harris, Gershon 54
Hay, Claude 180
Hayes, Fisher W. 179
heder 62–3
Holloway, Joseph 167
Hollywood, Birmingham 146
Holmes, Colin 177
housing: in Birmingham
   140–6, 189–94; in East End
   52–5, 58

India 86, 97
Indian (and Pakistani)
   migrants in Birmingham
   97, 116, 120, 132, 134–6,
   142, 145
Illustrated London News 10, 11
Immigration Reform
   Association 177
Irish: in Birmingham 110, 124,
   130, 131–3, 160, 169, 189;
   in East End 19, 32, 55, 57,
   183
Isenberg, Abraham 46
Isaacs, George 90

Jacobs, Joseph 17
Jamaica 85–90, 93–5, 97, 100,
   106, 111
Jewish Board of Guardians 20,
   21, 43, 71
Jewish Chronicle 18, 20, 21, 63,
   72, 176
Jews Free School 63–5, 149

Katznelson, Ira 160
Keir Hardie, James 179
Kiev 11, 12
Kingsley, Charles 27
Kingston 93–4
King's Norton 120

Labour Exchange 118–9, 122,
   136
Labour Party 161, 188–94
labour shortage 100, 115–6
Londoners' League 179
Lopukhin, A.A. 6
Lieberman, Aron 72
Liverpool 6, 87, 99
Lloyd, Dr 138
Lozells 145

McCarran-Walter Act 91, 111
Maramaros, Sziget 10
Marx, Karl 17
Master Tailors' Protective and
   Improvement Association 72
Mayhew, Henry 26
medical staff in Birmingham
   106, 112
Midland Motor Company 97
Midlands Advisory Council 129
military service 4, 13, 14
Ministry of Labour 117, 121
Mocatta, F.D. 23
Mond, Ludwig 17
Montefiore, Claude G. 17, 23
Moses, Mark 72
Mosley, Oswald 177, 186–7
Mowlem Street Boys School 64
Mucklow, Albert 185
Mundy, Abraham 9, 23, 70

Narodnaya, Volya 6
National Front 150
National Union of General and
   Municipal Workers
   (NUGMW) 121, 127–8, 160
Newtown, Aston 144
Newton, John 103
Nicholas I, Czar 4, 5

Odessa 5, 6
Oglethorpe's settlement 20
Overseas Volunteers
   Programme 87, 97

Pale of Settlement 4, 69
Panama Canal 86

Parliamentary Alien
  Immigration Committee 177
Pennell, Joseph 10, 12
Perrins, Wesley 128
Personnel Officers 119, 124, 130
Piliso, Dr C. 109, 138
Pilgrim, Dr W. 138
Poland 3, 4, 48
Pollins, Harold 200
Poor Jews' Temporary Shelter
  9, 23, 24, 34, 70, 71
Post Office 137
Potter, Beatrix 28
Prem, Dr D.R. 131, 161
Pogroms 5, 6, 11, 12
prostitution 60–1

Queen Elizabeth Hospital 112,
  148

race: and colonialism 119–20,
  158–9; historical
  'renegotiation' 159–61; and
  housing policy 189–94
racism: in Caribbean 94;
  language of 97–8; racial
  discrimination in
  employment 116–30,
  157–61; racial 'hierarchy' in
  Birmingham firms 110,
  119–20; racism in schools
  149–51; see also
  anti-Semitism, housing,
  segregation
Reany, Rev. G.S. 175
Renton, David 165
Rex, J. and Moore, R. 169
Roberts, Alderman 141
Roberts, G. and Mills, D. 110
Rocker, Rudolph 72
Rothschild Buildings 34, 53, 55
Rothschild, Lord 17, 23
Rotton Park 145
Rowton House 105
Royal Air Force (RAF) 87, 90,
  96–7, 99, 106
Royal Electrical and
  Mechanical Engineers 94

Russia 4–7

St Kitts 92–3
St Lucia 92
St Thomas 91–2
Salisbury, Lord 175
Salvation Army 105, 142
Sanders, John 187
Sandwell 145
schooling: in Birmingham
  149–52; in Caribbean 92–3;
  in East End 62–6
Second World War 86, 96–9,
  104–5
segregation: in Birmingham
  105, 115, 141–5, 160;
  during Second World War
  98; see also housing, racism
Serlin, Morris 48–9
Shaw, William 176, 181
shop-keeping 44
Shurmer, Percy 105, 141
Silver, James 175–6
slave trade 102–3, 166–7
slave guns 102–3
Small Heath 142
Smethwick 119, 124, 130,
  186–8
Smith, Llewellyn 28, 53
Socialist movement in London
  72–3
Society for Suppression of
  Immigration of Destitute
  Aliens (SSIDA) 173–4
Soho, Birmingham 145
Sparkbrook 105, 145–6, 186,
  190
Stechford 121
Stedman, Jones G. 25
Stepney Borough Council 176
Stepney Housing Conference
  176
Stowaways 89, 100
'sweated trades' 27–9, 35–7
sugar production 86–7

tailoring 27
Tilbury 9, 69, 90